Diagnostic and Remedial Reading for Classroom and Clinic

third edition

Diagnostic and Remedial Reading for Classroom and Clinic

third edition

Robert M. Wilson
University of Maryland

CHARLES E. MERRILL PUBLISHING COMPANY
A Bell & Howell Company
Columbus, Ohio 43216

Published by
CHARLES E. MERRILL PUBLISHING COMPANY
A Bell & Howell Company
Columbus, Ohio 43216

International Standard Book Number: 0-675-08536-5
Library of Congress Catalog Card Number: 76-40398

2   3   4   5   6   7   8   9   10   —   78   77

Printed in the United States of America

Foreward

The mere fact that this is a third edition of a book that has received the accolades of those who have used it as a required text as well as those who have used it as a resource book, speaks eloquently of its timeliness, the scholarship of the author, and is mute testimony to the practicability of the tenants presented therein. Based upon the concept of *diagnostic-teaching,* the teacher will find suggestions that will enable her to judiciously adjust the reading/learning environment to allow for the different learning rates and learning problems manifested by the child.

Certain chapters of this book have been expanded to a degree. As with the first two editions, the types of diagnosis covered are: *informal-on-the-spot, classroom,* and *clinical.* The emphasis carried throughout these levels is continuous diagnosis so that a shift in classroom strategies and the employment of fresh new instructional materials can be effected, so the child will progress at an accelerated rate toward maturity in reading skills. Increased content has been provided for both the classroom teacher and the clinician. Thus, each will be able to extract better understanding, knowledge, and skills from this book, so that both a program of intervention and therapy can be provided for the child.

Chapters 4 and 5 have been expanded to a significant degree and contain not only a listing of evaluative instruments, but also an evaluation of some of them. The use of the cloze technique, criterion referenced tests, and informal diagnosis of comprehension skills are worthy of comment. By using a taxonomy of comprehension skills, that is, literal, interpretative, and problem solving, and applying to each the two processes of recalling and locating, a classroom teacher may obtain six types of comprehension scores. By utilizing suggestions of the author, a classroom teacher will be able to increase proficiency in *observation,* a technique that teachers must use to offset the limitations of standardized tests. The content of Chapter 5, Clinical Diagnosis, has been increased 25 percent, thereby giving clinicians the knowledge and understanding that will enable them to increase their skill as reading clinicians. Thus, by making a more detailed analysis of a child's responses, the clinician will obtain measures of the child's semantic and syntactic skills.

Chapter 9, Remedial Activities for Comprehension Skills, highlights a classroom strategy known as the Directed Reading Thinking Activity as suggested by Russell G. Stauffer. Also, questioning strategies are another new aspect presented in this chapter. Again, the author reiterates his posture on locating skills. To paraphrase, he claims that by stressing *locating* instead of recalling, the reader is encouraged to learn to use reading materials. Another feature of this chapter worthy of mention is *wait times.* Quoting research, he states that many teachers do not give students sufficient time to internalize or to mentally organize data relevant to the response. Thus, attention is directed to the recognition or recall of facts instead of the integration of data. It is interesting to note that wait time applies to the answering of questions, and sufficient time should elapse before posing the next question. Only minor revisions were made in the remaining chapters, yet it must be borne in mind that the content of the existing ones was excellent and that the changes have added to the intrinsic value of the book.

As has been stated explicitly or implied in this forword, the third revision of this text is an improvement over the second edition. It is testimony to the scholarship and integrity of the author. Scholars may disagree with some of the postulates, hypotheses, or conclusions as presented by the author, yet controversy leads to progress, else the *status quo* would become the dominant characteristic of our educational endeavors. If, through the reading of this book, the reader is stimulated to research further some of its contents, that reader has grown professionally, and such a search fulfills the *desideratum* the author has implied.

The book is informative and challenging, I invite your thoughtful and reflective reading of the scholarly manuscript with the hope that it will be as rewarding to you as it was for me.

Donald L. Cleland
June, 1976
Pittsburgh, PA

Preface

One makes certain assumptions in preparing a manuscript for general dissemination. The reader should be alerted to these assumptions so that the reading of the book can be facilitated.

First, this book is not a beginning text in reading. Rather, it is assumed that the reader will have had some experience with the teaching of reading; a basic course in reading; familiarity with the concepts behind such techniques as the directed reading activities, the language experience approach, and word attack skills; and some understanding of current learning theory.

Second, the book may best be seen as a beginning book in diagnostic teaching. It is not designed to answer all of the questions about problem readers nor is it meant to cover all aspects of teaching reading.

Thirdly, it is assumed that the reader has worked with students who are experiencing difficulty in reading while not knowing exactly what to do about it.

For the reader's information, the ideas in this revision come from experiences with thousands of students and hundreds of teachers, all of whom would like to see learning as a stimulating and pleasant experience. One tends to become leary of generalizations about problem readers, knowing full well that each case is indeed unique. At the same time, the general philosophy of this book has been tried and found to be effective with most of the students with whom we have worked.

Our clinic, at Maryland, is an exciting, stimulating environment for students. The staff members have been open to change and are thoughtfully critical of their techniques. This book, to a large extent, reflects the thinking and activities of that staff. Of course, their effectiveness with students who are experiencing extreme difficulty in learning to read goes far beyond technique—it also incorporates a sincere desire to help each reader in a special way to become a happy, successful learner.

And so, while the reader must beware, it is hoped that this book will reflect the practical experience of many persons and the best thinking which those persons can produce. The ultimate measure of the success of such a publication will be determined as you, the reader, initiate programs based upon these ideas. The successes which your students have as a result of these ideas will be the final test.

For the reader who may lack the necessary background for most effective understanding of this book, the author would like to suggest several books which may well serve as an overview of the reading process for you.

Coley, Joan D., and Gambrell, Linda B. *Programmed Sight Vocabulary for Teachers*. Columbus, Ohio: Charles E. Merrill Publishing Co., 1977.
> Provides a review of the various aspects of sight vocabulary needed for reading success.

Heilman, Arthur W. *Principles and Practices of Teaching Reading*, 4 th ed. Columbus, Ohio: Charles E. Merrill Publishing Co., 1977.
> Provides a thorough coverage of the basics of reading instruction.

Stauffer, Russell G. *Teaching Reading as a Thinking Process*. New York: Harper & Row, 1969.
> Provides an in-depth explanation of how to make reading meaningful for the reader.

Wilson, Robert M., and Gambrell, Linda B. *Programmed Comprehension for Teachers*. Columbus, Ohio: Charles E. Merrill Publishing Co., 1976.
> Provides a review of the various aspects of reading comprehension.

Wilson, Robert M., and Hall, MaryAnne. *Programmed Word Attack for Teachers*. Columbus, Ohio: Charles E. Merrill Publishing Co., 1976.
> Provides a review of the various aspects of word attack which teachers should know.

Wilson, Robert M., and Hall, MaryAnne. *Reading and the Elementary School Child*. New York: Van Nostrand Reinhold, 1972.
> Provides a thorough coverage of the basics of reading instruction.

Further readings are suggested at the end of each chapter. Those with limited experiences are encouraged to pursue these sources so that contrasting points of view can be considered.

Acknowledgments

The author wishes to acknowledge the many people who have encouraged and guided him toward the completion of this revision.

The inspiration and memory of my father C. B. Wilson has been a constant source of help. The generous encouragement and helpful criticism of my friend and former teacher Donald L. Cleland has always been appreciated.

University of Maryland clinic staff members, Bruce Brigham, Beth Davey, Martha Evans, and Dorothy Sullivan, have been stimulating, thought-provoking colleagues. Their ideas are reflected throughout this book.

My two research colleagues, Linda Gambrell and Walter Gantt, have been of great help in clarifying ideas.

Marcia Barnes, Marci Pollack, and Cheryl Wilhoyte each made important contributions and provided critical reactions during the development of the manuscript.

Susan Coles, a fine and speedy typist, is hereby acknowledged.

The input of Ward Ewalt, William Druckmiller, Donald McFeely, William

Powell, and Louise Waynant to the content of earlier editions of this book remains in the third revision.

And to the joys of my life—Rick, Jim, and Sharon—my children, who put up with me during the days of writing, my special thanks.

R.M.W.
College Park, Md.
August, 1976

Contents

1

Working with Problem Readers

Who knows better than the teachers of students with reading problems the importance of reading for school success? And who other than classroom teachers better realizes that the inability to read, coupled with the lack of desire to read, leads directly to school failure? Teachers know the type of problems presented by the students who cannot or will not read, for they face this reality daily. They must be armed with the diagnostic and remedial techniques necessary to instruct students as effectively as possible, since the atypical student is not included in the generalizations of most teachers' guides for instructional material.

A study of problem readers, then, must include the reality that classroom teachers not only are in the best position to help students, but also are professionally responsible to continue the education of the students as intelligently and efficiently as they can.

CHARACTERISTICS OF PROBLEM READERS

Although there is no single observable characteristic which isolates problem readers from their classmates, it is likely that they will demonstrate the characteristics of one or more of the three basic types of problem readers.

First, students may be problem readers because, for one reason or another, they do not read as well as their abilities indicate they should. They should not be judged by their reading skills in relation to their grade levels in school, but rather in relation to their potentials. Dull students reading below their grade levels in school may become problems, but this does not necessarily imply that they are retarded in the development of their reading skills. On the other hand, bright students, although reading well above their grade levels, may be considered problem readers when their reading levels fall short of their intellectual potentials. It becomes important to assess accurately the reading levels and abilities of students to arrive at a comparison determining whether or not they are operating below their potentials.

TABLE 1

Ability Compared to Reading

Student	Grade Level	Ability Level	Reading Level
Martha	4	3	3
Beth	4	6	3

NOTE: Martha is operating in comparison with her ability; Beth is not.

Secondly, students may be considered problem readers when, with the exception of a specific skill deficiency, all other measures of their reading are up to their levels of potential. They read satisfactorily in most situations, but they become problems because of a specific deficiency. Although their deficiencies are difficult to locate because most of these students' reading skills appear normal, once located, they are readily corrected due to the precise nature of the remediation necessary. The classroom teacher, being constantly alert to these deficiencies, is now less likely to label the students as either *lazy* or *careless*. For example, since many adults read slowly, they have a specific skill deficiency. They can perform on tests and seem to read very well, but their slow speeds make reading a bore and reduce their inclinations to read. Students, while appearing to read well, also may have specific skill deficiencies, such as speed, oral reading fluency, word attack, and study skills.

Thirdly, students also may be considered problem readers when, in spite of reading skills in good relationship to their potential, they lack the desire to read. Strang points clearly to this problem when she says, "If the book is interesting they read it eagerly and with enjoyment . . . . Students confronted with dull, drab, uninteresting reading material show the opposite pattern. They read reluctantly, they skip and skim so that they can get it over with more quickly.''[1] These factors mentioned by Strang discourage students from using available skills and tend to dampen their desire to read. It is important that a lack of desire to read be considered a reading problem because often no other reading problem may be apparent. Clinic reports for such students show that they are frequently subject to ridicule and disciplinary action, since it is often assumed that there is no excuse for their poor reading habits. An understanding of the students' real problems, however, will indicate the need for adjustment in the school situation to develop a better attitude toward reading.

Perhaps the most common characteristic of problem readers is that, in the past, they have experienced a year or more of work with a teacher who did not know how to meet their needs. Often problem readers seem to cluster in certain classrooms with certain teachers. Perhaps they are criticized, blamed for what they cannot do, and subjected to penalties which range from subtle to direct. In other words, the problem teacher creates problems for students whose learning development is not concomitant with that of other students. A year or more of such treatment causes the reader's educational lag to become compounded by a poor self-concept, emotional stress, and a tendency to give up. From this point of view, any student who is in an unprofitable learning situation can be considered to be having a reading problem.

As problem readers are studied on the following pages, it must be kept in mind that a student can have these characteristics in any combination and with varying degrees of severity.

Specific Traits of Problem Teachers and Readers   *Problem Teachers*

In order to look specifically at the traits of the problem reader, one also must look at the traits of problem teachers. Problem teachers are difficult to identify prior to entering the classroom. They are frustrated by their inability to help the readers who are not progressing ''normally.'' Their frustration stems from inadequate teacher education programs, outside pressure, senses of inadequacies, lack of dedication to the task of teaching, or pure inability. They seek ways out of their frustration through ability grouping, labeling students *(careless, dyslexic,* or *deprived),* excessively requesting special services (reading teacher, psychologist, or medicaide), and eventually by simply not working with the student. Adequate teachers also may possess one or more of these traits, but they continue to work with the student as a developmental human being who they believe can and will learn.

How convenient it would be if problem readers could be described through easily identifiable traits, but such is not the case. They cannot be

---

[1]Ruth Strang, *Diagnostic Teaching of Reading* (New York: McGraw-Hill Book Co., 1969), p. 106.

identified by sight, for their appearance does not reveal them. The problem reader—usually a boy—can be seen in almost any classroom. A study of these types of students generally reveals individuals who recognize that the majority of their scholastic activities are unsatisfactory experiences. It is likely that they see little possibility of school's being anything but a series of frustrations and failures. As a result, they may react in one of the following ways: withdraw and shyly avoid the reading process whenever possible; show resentment and become belligerent toward the reading situation; cover their deficiencies by showing a lack of concern, acting as if their problems do not make any difference; and, finally, try to escape the reality of their problems by drifting and spending abnormally long periods of time with television and comic books or by diverting the teacher's attention with unacceptable behavior. These and other responses to failure in reading provide us with insights into the difficulties of problem readers.

A closer look at problem readers reveals that their problems have been recognized for some time, usually since first grade. Early identification often results in program adjustments which allow differing rates of growth, thus diminishing the problem. In other cases, such identification results in the types of frustrations already discussed.

Occasionally, such readers are successful in the early grades in which required reading skills are fewer and less complicated. However, their problems become more pronounced when they are introduced to the content areas and are expected to learn from a textbook. Here they can no longer rely upon memory for word recognition; therefore, they react poorly to new reading situations. As their scores in all verbal areas fall below the norm, arithmetic computation scores probably will remain relatively high. The teacher finds it difficult to separate students' reactions to failure from the failure itself. As a result, they are often misunderstood, coaxed, bribed, threatened, and punished until they no longer have any confidence that school will ever be a successful situation. Thus, problem readers, face many frustrations beyond their failure to read.

How serious is the problem? It all depends upon what criteria one chooses to use. Some frustration in reading is likely to be experienced by 1 student in 4.[2] Serious reading problems probably occur in 3 to 5 out of every 100 students.

RAMIFICATIONS OF THE READING PROBLEM

Problem readers are not only a problem to themselves but eventually cause problems in school and at home.

---

[2]J. E. Allen, "The Right to Read—Target for the 70's" (Address given to the National Association of State Boards of Education, Sept. 23, 1969).

In School

In school, where students often are pressured to achieve a certain grade level of performance, problem readers are a source of never-ending disappointments. Whether the pressure is subtle or direct, both the readers and the teachers sense failure. Teachers may react by giving up on them or by feeling that they are indifferent, lazy, or troublesome. These reactions may be followed by punishment that usually fosters a hostile attitude between the teacher and students who are ill-equipped to accept hostility. Frustrated by the rejection and the labels which they have received, problem readers either cannot or will not work independently. As more and more frustrating materials are heaped upon them, they are likely to busy themselves with noneducational activities and finally decide that an education is just not worth the effort. As they fall behind in their classroom work, they may be forced to repeat a grade, with the threat of further repetition constantly being called to their attention. Excessive absenteeism and complete rejection of the school program are inevitable as they proceed through school being promoted on the basis of age alone. A brief look at the reading level of high school dropouts tells the remainder of the story. Penty says, "More than three times as many poor readers as good readers dropped out of school before graduation."[3]

Not all problem readers become school dropouts; however, the strained school-pupil relationship increases dropout possibilities. An additional possibility exists for there are also those who drop out emotionally although they continue to attend class. Psychological dropouts are in every school; they generally create problems for both the teacher and students who are there to work. In either case, the situation is critical.

With Peers

Although peers often treat them kindly, it is not uncommon for problem readers to be teased and taunted. They are not with the "in" group and are often found alone at play as well as in the classroom. Other children are not likely to seek their efforts for committee work since their contributions are limited. Rejection encourages them to seek companionship with others in the "out" group. A further complication is problem readers' repetition of a grade, which places them one year behind their peers. They clearly recognize that they do not "belong" either in the group with which they are placed or with their peers. If they continue to meet peer group disapproval, they become highly susceptible to undesirable influences; the consequences of which are

[3]Ruth C. Penty, "Reading Ability and High School Dropouts," *Journal of the National Association of Women Deans and Counselors,* National Education Association, October, 1959, p. 14.

seen in the reports of police authorities who handle juvenile delinquents. Summarizing a study from the Children's Court in New York, Harris reports, "Among those tested . . . 76 percent were found to be two or more years retarded in reading, and more than half of those were disabled five or more years."[4] Again, it should not be concluded that all problem readers turn to delinquent behavior, but merely that continued rejection from peers makes these students more susceptible to undesirable influences.

With Parents

Parents become anxious when their children are not succeeding in school. They may try to solve the problem by urging or forcing the children to make greater efforts. This often means piling on more of the same type of frustrating work which makes them reject school. When such children balk, it is not unusual for them to be compared openly to siblings or playmates. Seemingly ashamed of their children's behaviors, parents often will look for someone to blame. Students are not blind to this shame and rejection, and they too will look for someone to blame. Even more important, they are likely to look elsewhere for that acceptance which all children need from their parents.

By observing problem readers, it can be concluded that the ramifications of their problems are felt not only by themselves but also by the school, peers, and family. Their inability to solve their own problem causes the future to look dark indeed.

Not all problem readers follow the patterns mentioned above. Indeed, some are capable of reasonable adjustment, usually with the help of an understanding, intelligent teacher. The problem facing the teacher, then, is what can be accomplished in a regular classroom of twenty-five to thirty-five students when a student with a reading problem is among them? A classroom without at least one such student is rare. The following pages will provide several possible solutions to this problem.

REACTIONS TO SYMPTOMS—REACTIONS TO CAUSES

When a student with a reading problem is found in the school situation, what diagnostic procedures should be used? Should the *symptoms* of the problem be considered valid enough for a diagnosis, or is it more desirable to conduct a thorough diagnosis designed to establish *causation?* An examination of the following situation will help to place each of these approaches in proper perspective.

---

[4]Albert J. Harris, *How To Increase Reading Ability* (New York: David McKay Co., 1970), p. 3.

Tony is not alone. He is one of many students across the country who, day after day, sits in an elementary school classroom in which he encounters reading situations well above his level. Tony, however, may be ranked among the fortunate, for his teacher, Mr. Coley, realizes that Tony cannot read well enough to do fifth-grade work. He quickly discovered that Tony could read accurately at the third-grade level and that he could read only with frustration at the fourth-grade level. He noticed that Tony refuses to attack unknown words, and, on the rare occasions when he does try, his pronunciation is inaccurate.

He also noticed that Tony's reading is characterized by word pronunciation without fluency, that he is uncomfortable in the reading situation, and that he seems hindered by what the teacher calls "word reading." A quick check of the school records indicates that Tony is average in ability but that each year he seems less responsive to the reading instruction.

Therefore, after carefully considering the information available to him, combined with his analysis of Tony's reading performance in the classroom, Mr. Coley set into motion a two-pronged program to supplement Tony's regular reading. First, he encouraged Tony to read more fluently by providing highly interesting reading material at a lower level of difficulty; second, he taught essential phonic skills from the sight words that Tony knew. Realizing that Tony's problem might be more deeply rooted, he asked for an evaluation by a reading specialist. This approach to the situation reflects an interested, informed classroom teacher analyzing a student's problem and attempting to correct it, while waiting for the services of the reading specialist.

When the reading specialist, Mrs. Smith, saw Tony, she knew that, to arrive at the cause of Tony's problem, a careful diagnosis would be essential. She realized that, among other things, she needed to have complete information concerning Tony's ability, his knowledge of phonics, his auditory skill, and his emotional stability. Therefore, the specialist set into motion a thorough diagnosis in an attempt to establish the cause of the problem; without such diagnosis she doubted that she could properly recommend a program of correction.

This example clearly illustrates two different reactions to Tony's symptoms. The classroom teacher used a pattern of symptoms to set into motion a program of correction. The specialist realized that the problem could best be understood by a more careful study of the student. Both the classroom teacher and the reading specialist reacted properly! The teacher instituted a program of correction as quickly as possible after carefully considering the symptoms, his basic concern being the continuation of Tony's educational program. The specialist initiated a program of diagnosis attempting to determine, as accurately as possible, the cause of Tony's difficulty, her concern being the recommendation of the most appropriate program of remediation.

To further clarify the difference between symptoms and causes of reading disability, *symptoms* are defined as those observable characteristics of a case that lead to an educated guess about a reader's problems. Teachers must look for reliable patterns of symptoms so that an intelligent program of correction can be initiated with minimal delay to the student's educational progress. Harris states, "many of the simpler difficulties in reading can be corrected by direct teaching of the missing skills, without an intensive search for reasons why the skills were not learned before."[5] One must consider that average classroom teachers have neither the time, the training, nor the materials necessary to conduct thorough diagnoses. They must use a reliable pattern of symptoms. Their procedure is to:

1. examine observable symptoms, combined with available school data.
2. form a hypothesis.
3. begin work.

With the possible necessity for referral in mind, they must formulate and conduct the most effective corrective programs possible within the limitations of the regular classroom situation. It then becomes obvious that the reliability of a pattern of symptoms has a direct influence on the effectiveness of their instruction with problem readers. Reference may be made to Chapter 2 for patterns of symptoms applicable to the classroom diagnosis of problem readers.

Causation may be defined as that factor or those factors which, as a result of careful diagnosis, might be accurately identified as being responsible for the reading problem. Robinson presents data to support the multiple nature of causation in reading problems.[6] The reading specialist is acutely aware that, since there is rarely one cause for a given problem, a careful examination for causation is necessary. Poor home environment, poor physical health, inadequate instruction, lack of instructional materials, personality disorders, and many other factors have been established as interfering to some degree with the development of reading skills.

The reading specialist realizes that if causes can be determined programs of prevention are made possible; for as Robinson states, "preventive measures can be planned intelligently only if causes of difficulty are understood."[7] The cause, in Tony's case, may have been a lack of auditory discrimination skills needed to learn phonics or, perhaps, an overemphasis on isolated word drill in earlier grades. The reading specialist, after a diagnosis designed to determine

---

[5]Harris, *How To Increase Reading Ability*, p. 201.
[6]Helen M. Robinson, *Why Pupils Fail in Reading* (Chicago: The University of Chicago Press, 1946), p. 219.
[7]Robinson, *Why Pupils Fail in Reading*, p. 219.

causes, sets the groundwork for a program of correction. In Tony's case, this might involve a revision of portions of the reading curriculum from grade one on or, perhaps, the establishment of a more thorough readiness program in the early grades. Thus, a careful diagnosis is the first step toward the implementation of a preventive program.

The reading specialist may also be interested in causation to lead more accurately to the most effective program of correction, especially with the more seriously retarded reader. Strang states, however, that diagnosis is complex and that causes are difficult to uncover.[8] If Tony's classroom teacher's program of correction is not effective, it is obvious that a more thorough diagnosis will be essential. This, then, is the other function of the reading specialist. Based upon her diagnosis, she will be able to assist the classroom teacher with recommendations to implement the most effective corrective program.

That specialists look for causation and classroom teachers for patterns of symptoms in no way excuses classroom teachers from being aware of possible implications and complications concerning the causes of reading problems. Nor does it excuse them from gathering as much diagnostic information as possible. Certainly, the more informed they become concerning causation, the more effective they will become in analyzing a pattern of symptoms intelligently. And, as Harris states, they should be "able to carry out the simpler parts of a diagnostic study."[9] At the same time, teachers' major job is to better instruct all students in their care, and, as stated above, this obligation generally precludes thorough diagnosis in any one case. It is also possible that after a most careful diagnosis the reading specialist will not yet be able to accurately identify the causes of the student's reading problem. Causative factors may be elusive, but the elusiveness of the problem does not free the reading specialist from attempting to identify those causes as accurately as possible.

To better understand these concepts, the following examples illustrate the effectiveness of both procedures when applied to the four major areas of reading problems: the physical, intellectual, emotional, and educational. For a more complete pattern of symptoms and a more thorough discussion of causation, see Chapters 3 and 4.

Physical Problems

"Bill, how many times have I told you not to hold your book so close to your face?" Despite repeated efforts to have him hold his book at the proper distance, his teacher, Ms. Barnes, noticed that Bill insisted on this type of visual adjustment. Knowing this to be a symptom of a visual disorder, she

---

[8]Strang, *Diagnostic Teaching of Reading,* p. 26.
[9]Harris, *How To Increase Reading Ability,* p. 201.

began to observe Bill more closely. She noticed unusual watering of the eyes and an unusual amount of blinking, especially after longer sessions involving seat work. Her response was to adjust the classroom situation to allow Bill the maximum amount of visual comfort (i.e., regulating visual activities to shorter time periods and assuring Bill the most favorable lighting conditions). Realizing that he might have a serious problem, the teacher referred him to a vision specialist.

The teacher's job, then, was to recognize the symptoms and react: first, to continue to teach Bill by adjusting the physical setting to enable him to perform as comfortably as possible and, second, to refer him to a specialist for whatever visual correction was necessary.

The reading specialist's, Mr. Murdock's, reaction to Bill was a little different. He saw the symptoms of the difficulty, and he too realized that referral was a possibility. However, in this case, a visual screening test involving near-point vision[10] was first administered in an attempt to determine whether Bill's problem was one of visual disability or one of bad habit.

In all physical problems, referral to the proper specialist is the appropriate action for personnel in education; therefore, both the reading specialist and the classroom teacher considered the referral of Bill for visual analysis. The difference in their approach is important. Ms. Barnes observed a pattern of symptoms which told her that there was a good possibility that vision was interfering with his educational progress. Since Bill's education is her first responsibility, the teacher's proper reaction was to adjust the educational climate so that Bill could operate as effectively as possible. She also was obligated to make a referral for the proper visual analysis. The reading specialist, however, was not immediately confronted with Bill's day-to-day instruction; rather, he was obligated to determine as accurately as possible whether vision was the factor interfering with Bill's education. He was justified in his attempt to screen thoroughly before making recommendations for visual referral or for adjustment to educational climate.

Intellectual Problems

Jim scored poorly on the group intelligence test given at the beginning of fifth grade. His teacher, Mr. Geyer, noticed that his mental age and his reading achievement age were about the same; however, Mr. Geyer realized that Jim's oral vocabulary seemed much above average and that he seemed to be much better in arithmetic than in other content areas. Jim was also more attentive than average. He concluded that Jim might have more ability than his mental age indicated and that perhaps his intelligence test score was a result of the

---

[10]Distance of eyes from print—twelve to fifteen inches.

reading performance necessary in this type of test. His assumption, then, was that Jim had more ability than his records indicated. Therefore, the teacher urged him to perform at a higher academic level. To assure himself of the most accurate information, he referred Jim for an individual intelligence test. While waiting for the results of this test, he motivated Jim to achievement beyond his present levels. He was obligated to rely upon a pattern of symptoms for his analysis of Jim. That pattern involved arithmetic ability, oral vocabulary development, and attentiveness in school.

The reading specialist's, Mrs. Kravse's, reaction was to administer, or to have someone else administer, an individual intelligence test to determine, as closely as possible, Jim's actual potential. Without accurate knowledge in this area, it would be difficult to make precise recommendations for his educational program. Again, we notice that the reactions of the classroom teacher and of the reading specialist were proper, for both realized the necessity for the administration of an individual intelligence test due to the limitations of group tests with children who do not read well. The teacher, however, while waiting for the results of this examination, relied upon a pattern of symptoms which indicated that Jim might well have more potential than the school records indicated. The specialist again used diagnostic procedures. Her first task was to determine as accurately as possible the degree of the student's actual potential. In the area of intellectual problems, the classroom teacher is seriously limited by training, time, and the availability of testing materials. He has no recourse but to rely upon a pattern of symptoms of scholastic aptitude, such as group intelligence tests, oral vocabulary, and arithmetic skills. It should also be noticed that the reading specialist, who has the training, the time, and the appropriate materials, is in an excellent position to conduct an examination for a more precise measure of scholastic aptitude. It is also important to notice that in both cases here the personnel involved were aware that they should not rely upon *one* measure of ability and that each searched for the most effective technique available.

Emotional Problems

"Sally, haven't you finished your library book yet?" Sally continually resisted Mrs. Wilhoyte's efforts to encourage her reading. She lagged behind in all personal reading assignments. Concerned about Sally's attitude, Mrs. Wilhoyte also noticed that she seemed extremely anxious for praise, but, at the same time, frequently drifted off into a private world of daydreams.

A check of the development of Sally's reading skills through the school records assured Mrs. Wilhoyte that her primary task was not going to be one of instruction in the basic reading skills. Correspondingly, it became obvious that Sally's reading situation was in need of adjustment to assure more successful, pleasant experiences which would merit her teacher's praise. In an effort to alleviate Sally's rejection of her personal reading, the teacher lowered the level of difficulty in reading assignments. At the same time, she continued to observe any reaction for possible emotional complications. If such occurred, she would make a referral for a thorough psychological evaluation.

When the reading specialist, Dr. Wiley, saw Sally, his first reaction was to administer certain personality evaluations and to study her life at home, with her peers, and in the classroom to determine the degree of deviations as they might apply to her reading problem. If such deviations appeared to be significant, the specialist would refer Sally's case to a psychologist, a psychiatrist, or a social worker.

While recognizing the potential of Sally's emotional problems, the classroom teacher realized that, though she could not give up on the child, she did not have the training, the time, nor the materials to make a thorough diagnosis. Again we see both the classroom teacher and the reading specialist willing to refer the child elsewhere. The teacher's willingness was based upon the recognition of a pattern of symptoms. Since her primary concern was for immediate educational progress, she attempted to make adjustments in the learning climate to facilitate Sally's progress.

The specialist, being alert to the possible complications in this case, again used diagnostic procedures. Although he realized that he was not a psychiatrist, he knew that a thorough evaluation through tests and case analysis would put him in a better position to, first, refer the child to the proper person and, second, make recommendations for the adjustment of the educational situation. So, again, we see that both reactions were proper although different. The specialist does not feel inclined to start corrective programs with students who, in his opinion, have basic emotional problems. The classroom teacher does not have that choice; so, with an intelligent reaction to a pattern of symptoms, she proceeds with Sally's education program, ever alert to problems which may arise!

Educational Problems

As you may recall, Tony was weak in his ability to use word attack skills and was considered by Mr. Coley to be a word-by-word reader. He clearly saw that Tony's reading problem was educational in nature (i.e., Tony had either missed some instruction, his teachers had skipped instruction, or he had received poor instruction). Although he was concerned about the cause of Tony's problem, Mr. Coley could not stop to trace the problem to its source; rather, he attempted to improve Tony's learning situation through individualization of the classroom procedure. Bond and Tinker hold the view that remedial reading instruction is the same as good classroom instruction which is individualized.[11] Quite properly, the teacher arranged for this individualized instruction and proceeded with Tony's education. The reading specialist began a thorough diagnosis. She was aware of Betts' warning: "Poor teaching in a large sense is the chief cause of retardation in reading.[12] She realized further that, at best, the teacher had closed the gap for Tony, but that, unless a preventive program were instituted, Tony's problem would appear again and again in other children. The specialist finds support again in Betts who says that "each community will find the need for a careful analysis of its peculiar problems."[13] It is obvious that the reading specialist is more capable of making this "careful analysis" and that it cannot be the responsibility of the classroom teacher. By analysis of groups of students, often in different grades, the reading specialist may well find the flaw in the educational program and prevent future problems from occurring. Herein lies a major responsibility for the reading specialist to alleviate the problem through preventive educational programs.

School Screening Committees

Many schools have organized all resource personnel into screening committees. These people meet regularly with the building principal to make decisions regarding teacher referrals. The screening committee might consist of the reading specialist, the special education specialist, the specific language disability (SLD) teacher, the speech therapist, and others. When a teacher makes a referral, that teacher meets with the screening committee. Sometimes the student or the parents attend the meeting. All available information concerning the student is considered, and it is decided which specialist is best suited to work with the teacher to help the student. Periodic reports of progress are then given to the screening committee.

Several advantages to this approach have been noticed:

1. The principal is informed concerning what the specialists in the school are doing.
2. Records are maintained by the principal so that parents can also be informed.
3. Specialists, working together, find less conflict of interests.
4. Overlapping of responsibilities diminishes.

---

[11]Guy L. Bond and Miles A. Tinker, *Reading Difficulties: Their Diagnosis and Correction* (New York: Appleton-Century-Crofts, 1967), p. 15.

[12]Emmett A. Betts, *Foundations of Reading Instruction* (New York: American Book Co., 1946), p. 52.

[13]Betts, *Foundations of Reading Instruction,* p. 54.

5. All attention is given to bring the full resources of the school to assist students to be successful learners.

In each case described on the preceding pages, screening committee action would have been appropriate had screening committees existed.

ACCEPT AND CHALLENGE

Through working with students who are having difficulty reading, we at the University of Maryland reading center have adopted the following motto: accept and challenge. We must *accept* problem readers, for they are but products of their experiences. If we reject and criticize those experiences, we are, in fact, rejecting and criticizing the student. Instead, we must accept those experiences and must genuinely accept the total students, their language, their habits, their attitudes, and their skills. By accepting, we gain the students' confidence and encourage them to continue to try. Several examples of specific "accepting" activities might be used as illustrations:

1. Provide large portions of instruction in the area of students' strengths. Problem readers need to demonstrate their strengths to their teachers, their peers, but most of all to themselves. They must see themselves as having reading skills.

2. Teach from diagnostic information. Make certain that the problem readers are working with materials with which they can cope.

3. Provide alternatives at every opportunity. Let students make choices. They almost always pick activities which they can do best. By accepting their choices, teachers can demonstrate trust and respect for the student.

All teachers illustrate in numerous ways that they are accepting students. They should utilize these methods in their early work with every student and should continue to utilize them because accepted students learn, while rejected students do not.

Each student should also be *challenged*. Learning situations should be planned so that they require effort from the students and result in success. Students who are having difficulty learning often find that their efforts result in failure and frustration. Challenge also involves teaching strategies which are highly interesting. Several examples may help:

1. Contract with students to complete a certain amount of work in a certain amount of time. Individual contracts allow students to realize success for their efforts.

2. Teach and reinforce skills through games. Win or lose, games challenge many students, and they'll work to do their best.

3. Utilize instructional materials from the everyday world of the students. Magazines, newspapers, various types of manuals, and package labels are interesting and relevant. Students are challenged when reading activities are related to their real-life reading needs.

All teachers have used many other challenging activities with students. While all students need to be challenged, those who have trouble with learning need acceptance and challenge desperately. As we consider the Accept and Challenge motto, the following selected authorities add insight into its value:

Waetjen stresses, "if a person is accepted and valued and esteemed, he becomes an inquiring person and he actualizes himself."[14]

Raths claims, "if our meanings gained from our experiences are frowned upon, are devalued—it constitutes a rejection of our life, and that is intolerable to everyone of us so treated. . . ."[15]

Bowers and Soar say, "the more supportive the climate, the more the student is willing to share, the more learning will take place. . . ."[16]

Cohen says, "tolerance for failure is best taught through providing a background of success that compensates for experienced failure. . . ."[17]

Prescott puts it, "the unloved child who fails is in double jeopardy . . . to his insecurity is added the feeling of inadequacy, and he becomes more and more reluctant to try again with each failure."[18]

While planning work for students experiencing reading difficulty, some time should be spent developing techniques which will help them develop a desire to learn. Perhaps the most crucial factor in successful program adjustment lies in the area of teacher attitude toward students.

If the motto accept and challenge can be followed, school can be a happy, fun-filled environment for all learners. As Margaret Mead put it, "If learning to read were seen as a path to individual triumphant success . . . each child's

[14]Walter B. Waetjen, "Facts about Learning," *Readings in Curriculum,* ed. Glen Hass and Kimball Wiles (Boston: Allyn and Bacon, 1965), p. 243.

[15]Louis E. Raths, "How Children Build Meaning," *Childhood Education* 31 (December 1954): 159-60.

[16]Norman D. Bowers and Robert S. Soar, "Studies in Human Relations in the Teaching-Learning Process," *Evaluation of Laboratory Human Relations Training for Classroom Teachers* (Chapel Hill, N.C.: University of North Carolina Press, 1961), p. 111.

[17]S. Alan Cohen, *Teach Them All To Read* (New York: Random House, 1969), p. 231.

[18]Daniel A. Prescott, *The Child in the Educative Process* (New York: McGraw-Hill Book Co., 1957), p. 359.

mastery of reading could, in its own way, be celebrated,"[19] just like walking and talking are. As you read on, keep the motto in mind and notice the activities, both diagnostic and remedial, suggested which will fit into it. Use them. Try some that you are not too certain of. Discard those that do not allow for accepting and those that do not challenge.

THE CULTURALLY DIFFERENT CHILD

Much has been written about students who come from culturally different environments. Some claim these students come to school with a cultural disadvantage and, therefore, label them *disadvantaged*. Others attribute their difficulty in school to their cultural background, implying not only differences but undesirable influence as well. Labels such as *disadvantaged* and *undesirable* hold no value for diagnosis, while they do create many assumptions which hurt these students. That numerous children from poor families, particularly from minority groups, have difficulty in school is a fact. Students from restricted urban environments and isolated rural environments are often far below their peers in reading skills.

However, it is not true that the environment alone has caused the reading problem. Indeed, evidence also points to a lack of equal educational opportunity.[20] Yet culturally different children come to school with a fully developed language and with wide backgrounds of experiences. Teachers who work with these students should be alert to their strengths, not to their degree of difference. Teachers must recognize culturally different students as having distinct and good cultures. They can be taught if their strengths are evaluated and their programs adjusted so that they feel accepted and challenged. For example, if they can talk, they can be taught through the language-experience approach. Therefore, variations in technique are recommended on the basis of diagnosis rather than on the basis of generalizations about culturally different children. Alan Cohen claims, "Learning disability patterns as measured on clinic tests of disadvantaged retarded readers do not differ markedly from the learning disability patterns of middle-class children who are retarded readers."[21]

In our work with low-income black students in inner-city schools, Gantt, Wilson, and Dayton found that almost all students produced larger portions of standard English than divergent English.[22] We were impressed by the sophis-

[19]Margaret Mead, *Reading Teacher* 28 (October 1974): editorial inside front cover.

[20]James S. Coleman *et al., Equality of Educational Opportunity* (Washington, D.C.: U.S. Department of Health, Education and Welfare, 1966).

[21]S. Alan Cohen, "Cause vs. Treatment in Reading Achievement," *Journal of Learning Disabilities,* March 1970, p. 43.

[22]Walter N. Gantt, Robert M. Wilson, and C. Mitchell Dayton, "An Initial Investigation of the Relationship Between Syntactical Divergency and the Listening Comprehension of Black Children," *Reading Research Quarterly* 10, no. 2 (1974-75): pp. 193-208.

tication of these elementary grade students in terms of their ability to use standard syntatical structures. We now feel strongly that one or two divergent usages may cause teacher attention even when the student uses as many as twenty standard usages. Concentration on these divergent uses may cause students to feel inadequate. We also found very low correlations between divergent usage and ability to listen to standard English. Apparently the world of the user of divergent English is filled with opportunities to learn to listen to standard English and comprehend it.

In this book, the emphasis will be on doing away with unneeded labels and the inferences which go with them. Instead, diagnose for strengths and adjust programs so that all students can profit from reading instruction. With culturally different students, accept and challenge may be a most useful philosophy.

SUMMARY

It should be remembered that the teachers' first responsibility is to educate all of the students in their classrooms as effectively as possible, reading problems notwithstanding. They most effectively fulfill this responsibility by examining observable symptoms, evaluating the students' difficulties through this pattern of symptoms, adjusting the educational climate, and considering the possibility of referral. In contrast, reading specialists' first responsibility is to upgrade the effectiveness of the reading instruction of all students through diagnosis of reading problems within and among the various classrooms. Furthermore, reading specialists are responsible for the accurate diagnosis of seriously retarded readers.

SUGGESTED READINGS

Bond, Guy L., and Tinker, Miles A. *Reading Difficulties: Their Diagnosis and Correction*. 3d ed. New York: Appleton-Century-Crofts, 1973. The reader will find Chapter 4, ''General Nature of Reading Disability,'' of particular benefit under this topic; it is quite thorough.

Strang, Ruth. *Diagnostic Teaching of Reading*. New York: McGraw-Hill Book Co., 1969. Chapter 2, ''The Role of the Teacher in Diagnosis,'' is an excellent discussion of diagnosis in the classroom. The student will find this a handy reference for both this and the following chapter.

Waetjen, Walter R., and Leeper, Robert R., eds. *Learning and Mental Health in the School*. Washington, D.C.: Association for Supervision and Curriculum Development, 1966. Several chapters by different authors illustrate the necessity for consideration of a theory behind your instructional strategies. Of particular value to the Accept and Challenge motto are the writings of Syngg.

Gambrell, Linda B., and Wilson, Robert M. *Focusing On the Strengths of Children.* Belmont Calif.: Fearon Publishers, 1973. Rationale for focusing on strengths and numerous specific examples are included. The first three chapters provide the basic arguments in support of focusing on strengths.

2

Introduction to Diagnosis

Regardless of the educator's professional position (e.g., classroom teacher or reading specialist), diagnosis is essential to good teaching. Diagnosis implies that the educator will actively search for clues to assist in evaluating the present state of the reader's skill development and the developmental history of the reader's attitudes and habits toward reading and learning.

Strang has developed a model to use in explaining the reading process.[1] This model helps to clarify the role of diagnosis in instructional situations:

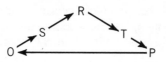

O = Organism, the reader

S = Situation, the situations in which learning takes place

---

[1]Ruth Strang, *Invitational Addresses—1965* (Newark, Del.: International Reading Association, 1965).

R = Response, the responses readers make to the learning situations

T = Traces, the traces or impressions from the responses which are left with the nervous system of the reader

P = Perceptions, each reader assimilates new traces with past traces in a highly individualized manner. These assimilated traces become perceptions which the reader brings to the next learning situation.

Strang admitted when she presented the model that it was an oversimplification of a complex process. However, it is useful when considering the various aspects of diagnosis. Obviously all readers respond differently to a given learning situation because they enter that learning situation with different perceptions. It is also obvious that all readers respond and assimilate in a highly individualized manner. New learning situations must be viewed in terms of what readers obtained from past learning situations. Learning, then, is not an occurrence, but a never-ending cycle. Learners and learners' perceptions cannot be separated. While learners' perceptions can never be fully understood, diagnosis helps us to be aware of some of the differences in their strengths as well as needs.

Applied directly to diagnosis, one can understand that diagnosis can take place prior to the learning situation in an attempt to understand what the students are bringing to the learning situation, or it can take place after the learning situation to evaluate what the students obtained from the learning situation. Effective diagnosticians will also evaluate the students' progress during the learning situations.

Apparently almost all teachers use diagnostic strategies. The day is long gone when diagnosis was surrounded by an aura of mystery. However, several myths relating to diagnosis continue to prevent some teachers from utilizing diagnostic information which is available to them. Some of these myths include:

1. Diagnosis requires the use of specially designed tests. (Teacher observation of students during various learning situations and informal evaluations of their performances provide highly useful and valid diagnostic information.)

2. Diagnosis requires a highly specialized, well-trained person. (Of course there are levels of competency, and some diagnosticians are highly competent and well trained. However, every teacher can use diagnostic teaching procedures. These procedures are not reserved for specialists; most teachers use them regularly.)

3. Diagnosis calls for a case study write-up. (College reading training programs traditionally have included case development in their programs.

While case development is an extremely useful educational experience, diagnosis does not always call for such an approach. Notes from diagnostic observation should be maintained, but they are often of the simplest form.)

As teachers realize that diagnostic teaching is not reserved for those with specialized training and materials, their diagnostic teaching should increase, thus benefiting more students. Realistically, the reading specialist will be unable to handle the number of referred students unless the classroom teacher assumes major responsibilities in diagnosis. The type of diagnosis used will be dependent, however, upon the educator's ability to use various diagnostic tools. The three types of diagnoses to be discussed in this chapter are informal on-the-spot, classroom, and clinical.

INFORMAL ON-THE-SPOT DIAGNOSIS

Diagnosis is taking place constantly in the modern classroom where the teacher recognizes symptoms of educational lag through informal procedures. As a result of such diagnosis, teachers can make immediate adjustments to provide maximum learning efficiency. Informal on-the-spot diagnosis involves evaluations of students' reactions to such classroom situations as questions asked by the teacher, informal teacher-made tests, reading exercises, and the use of library facilities. Alert to the first signs of student frustration, teachers will prevent serious reading problems from developing by using informal diagnosis, followed by immediate instructional adjustment. Informal on-the-spot diagnosis takes place both during and after instruction (O-S-R). Through evaluation of the responses of students, plans are made for the next learning situation. Teachers try to determine through evaluation of a reader's performance if that student is ready for the next step in learning. They will continuously assess learning performances, repeating or adapting instruction as necessary. Some of these diagnoses may be conducted with groups of students and some may be individualized, but the process is an ongoing, vital part of the total learning situation in the classroom. How well teachers can conduct informal on-the-spot diagnosis will relate directly to their understanding of the students and the skills which they need.

The following examples illustrate the types of situations which can be used to diagnose students' responses to instruction:

1. Oral reading: By having several pairs of students read orally at the same time, a teacher can move from pair to pair, listening to the oral reading. The teacher, after noting various students' strengths and weaknesses on index cards, can make instructional adjustments. This technique permits the students to practice oral reading in an environment which does not call for a

"performance," before the entire group; it also allows them to read long portions of material, for as the teacher listens to one pair, the others are practicing.

2. Question asking for comprehension checks: Attending to successes and failures in answering questions is diagnostic. If a teacher uses a modification of Durrell's every-pupil-response technique,** all students can respond to every question. For example, yes and no cards can be used to check the literal understanding of the story. If, in answer to specific questions, the teacher notices that certain students are in error or are responding sluggishly or not at all, the learning situation should be adjusted immediately. Perhaps, those who respond well can read independently while the teacher alters the learning situation so that the other students can be successful.

3. Book selection: When students are free to choose books for independent reading, teachers can make observations which may indicate the students' interests. Alert teachers often can note strengths which, when included in instructional periods, assure students of successes.

4. Spelling: By analysis of successful and unsuccessful spelling attempts, teachers often notice patterns which can lead to instructional needs. For example, if a student always spells the first consonant and vowel correctly but misses endings, instruction can stress attention to word endings.

Other examples could be cited; opportunities occur daily for informal on-the-spot diagnosis. Attention to such opportunities can result in classroom adjustments which lead to success rather than failure.

CLASSROOM DIAGNOSIS

If a problem persists even after informal adjustments have been made, the teacher initiates a classroom diagnosis which involves a more formal and directed effort without removing the student from the classroom environment. In this type of diagnosis, the teacher utilizes the diagnostic material available to formulate a pattern of symptoms, which will assist in understanding more clearly a particular student's reading skills. This understanding necessitates the direct observation of the student in the reading act, the use of school records, the direct testing of skills, the assessment of intellectual potential, and a compilation of relevant data. In this type of diagnosis, the teacher gathers information, evaluates its appropriateness, and relates the findings to the instructional situation. During instruction, the teacher observes the student's

---

**See Appendix B. Double asterisks throughout the text refer the reader to Appendix B; a single asterisk, to Appendix A; and a triple asterisk to, Appendix C.

responses to the adjusted situation. Classroom diagnosis calls for formal diagnosis at the O level and informal diagnosis at the R level (Q-S-R).

Teachers might use classroom diagnosis in situations such as the following:

1. After several adjustments of instruction following informal diagnosis, the student remains unable to respond successfully. The teacher then attempts to obtain more information through direct observation or testing.
2. Following a unit of work, the teacher administers a group test to determine how well the students have mastered the skills. Two students scored very poorly. An individual test for these two students might reveal the source of the difficulty they had with the group test.
3. During reading lessons a student avoids opportunities to respond. The teacher cannot determine whether this student is unable to respond or unwilling. An individual lesson can provide the answer.

Classroom diagnosis requires individual study of the student. Both testing and observation can be used. Teachers with skills in testing and observation can make important decisions concerning the instructional plans for students who are having difficulty.

CLINICAL DIAGNOSIS

As the term implies, this type of diagnosis is reserved for the more complex type of reading difficulty. Conducted by the reading specialist, often with the assistance of other specialists, it usually requires the removal of the student from the classroom so that individual examinations may be administered in surroundings that are conducive to full performance. Characteristic of this type of diagnosis are more precise measures of intellectual potential, word attack and comprehension skills, visual screening, and the like. These measures will be evaluated to diagnose as accurately as possible the precise nature of the student's reading problem. Clinical diagnosis involves more detailed planning, more careful analysis, and more precise instruments for testing than does classroom diagnosis. It is recommended that diagnostic teaching lessons follow clinical diagnosis. If visual discrimination exercises are called for from the diagnostic data, the reading specialist should construct several activities to test the accuracy of the diagnosis. If the student's performance in the diagnostic lessons are in conflict with the diagnostic findings, further analysis is required. Clinical diagnosis emphasizes the O prior to instruction, with checks on the diagnosis at the R, through diagnostic lessons (Q-S-R). Clinical diagnosis usually results in reporting in the form of a case analysis.

While clinical diagnosis has the advantage of highly individualized study and the use of precise instruments for evaluation by a carefully trained person, it is not without limitations. One limitation concerns the behavior observed in a one-to-one situation and how that behavior relates to a student's behavior in the classroom when that student is working with others. A second limitation is the manner in which a student reacts to two different people, the teacher and the reading specialist. A third is that while the specialist may check diagnosis with the diagnostic teaching lessons, the teacher, on the other hand, may be unable (for one of many reasons) to make necessary instructional adjustments. For these reasons, the results of the diagnosis should be discussed with the teacher as well as providing a written report. In order to illustrate the techniques being recommended in the report, the reading specialist should offer to work with the student in the classroom for a lesson or two.

SEQUENCE OF DIAGNOSIS

The following sequence will provide a better understanding of the relationships among the types of diagnosis.

The classroom teacher makes an informal on-the-spot diagnosis and adjusts instruction accordingly. If this fails, the teacher conducts a classroom diagnosis and again individualizes instruction. Should this step by unsuccessful, the teacher refers the student to a reading specialist for a more thorough analysis via clinical diagnosis. Instruction is adjusted according to the recommendations of the specialist. If the entire sequence cannot produce the desired results, the necessity for other referrals is likely. It is unlikely that a single failure will result in the teacher's moving immediately to the next type of diagnosis; rather, the teacher will utilize each diagnostic step thoroughly and repeatedly, if necessary, before moving to the next. It should be noticed that at each step in this sequence the possibility of referral is present (see Figure 2).

Since all effective learning relies upon informal on-the-spot diagnosis and its subsequent follow-up, it is assumed that this type of diagnosis is normal to good teaching situations. It is also obvious that the types of diagnosis are not clearly separated. Neither are specific techniques reserved for the reading specialist; classroom teachers might use clinical diagnostic tools when appropriate. All types of diagnosis rely upon observation of the student once instruction is adjusted. In most instances, the burden of making diagnosis work falls directly upon the classroom teacher. Therefore, diagnosis which is not helpful to assist the teacher is of little value.

DIAGNOSTIC PROCEDURES

Diagnostic procedures vary with the purpose and scope of the diagnosis. While similarities exist, there are noticeable differences among informal on-the-spot, classroom, and clinical diagnostic procedures.

Sequence of Diagnosis

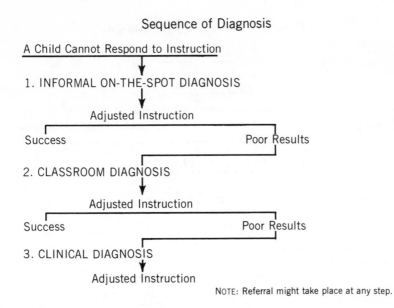

A Child Cannot Respond to Instruction

1. INFORMAL ON-THE-SPOT DIAGNOSIS

Adjusted Instruction

Success   Poor Results

2. CLASSROOM DIAGNOSIS

Adjusted Instruction

Success   Poor Results

3. CLINICAL DIAGNOSIS

Adjusted Instruction

NOTE: Referral might take place at any step.

Informal On-the-Spot Diagnosis

Informal on-the-spot diagnosis implies that teachers are concerned about the ability of students to respond to instruction, that they can observe symptoms of frustration, and that they have alternate strategies for immediate implementation. Therefore, in this type of diagnosis, students are identified by their inability to respond to instruction. Teachers will note such inabilities, consider the student's skill strengths and needs, and immediately attempt to adjust the instructional situation so that the student can be successful. The teacher also will record appropriate notes for use in future planning of instruction in that particular area.

Classroom Diagnosis

Classroom procedures must be designed around the idea that individual study is required. The following procedures may be studied in chart form in Figure 3.

1. Identification: The classroom teacher, unlike the reading specialist, is in the best position to first notice potential problem areas. In this way, the classroom diagnosis is actually underway by the time the student has been identified; informal on-the-spot diagnosis has previously established certain diagnostic information which the teacher will use in classroom diagnosis.

   Hopefully, the tendency for educators to wait until a problem is well developed can be avoided by increased attention to classroom diagnosis at

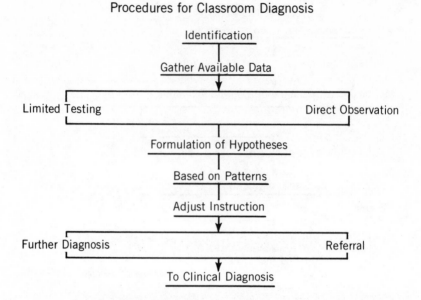

Procedures for Classroom Diagnosis

all age levels, including first grade. It is through immediate attention to first symptoms of the reading problems that the number of seriously handicapped readers can be reduced.

2. Gathering available data: The classroom teacher then makes an intensive search for available information about the student and organizes it for further consideration during the diagnosis. Using school records, interviews with past teachers, health reports, and other such sources, considerable data may be available concerning past development, successes, and failures of this student. Obviously, notes made during informal on-the-spot diagnosis will be extremely useful, particularly if the teacher doing the classroom diagnosis did not conduct the previous one.

3. Limited testing: When necessary, classroom teachers may administer and interpret appropriate tests designed to provide information in the area of the difficulty. Testing, of course, is limited in terms of the time that teachers have for individual testing as well as their skill in using these instruments.

4. Direct observations: Based upon the information available at this stage of classroom diagnosis, classroom teachers will find it advantageous to observe students in various reading situations with particular emphasis on the verification of other diagnostic information. Again, the link to informal on-the-spot diagnosis is clear. When observations and other data complement previous findings, the next step can be taken. When they do not support each other, there is a need for a reevaluation, more observation, possible testing, and new conclusions.

5. Formulation of hypotheses: Based on the patterns observed, the teacher will then form hypotheses about adjustment of instruction, for the group or the individual, and about the possibility of referral.

Once instructional hypotheses have been formed, teachers then adjust instruction and test each hypothesis. For example, if the diagnostic hypothesis was "Jack will read more fluently if I reduce the level of difficulty by one grade level," then the teacher finds materials at the level indicated and places Jack in a learning situation. If, in fact, Jack can read fluently in these new materials, then the hypothesis is accepted. If he cannot, then it is back to the diagnostic procedures to develop another hypothesis.

That classroom diagnosis is time-consuming is a given fact. However, teachers can do several things to minimize the amount of time needed. They can utilize existing records; they can conduct the diagnosis during times when other students are otherwise occupied; and they can collect diagnostic data over a period of time, for example, ten minutes each day for three days instead of thirty minutes on one day. As teachers gain proficiency with diagnostic procedures, they will find them to be rewarding and less time-consuming.

Clinical Diagnosis

Clinical procedures may be implemented through individual study of the student outside of the classroom. These procedures are listed in Figure 4 and described below:

FIGURE 4

Procedures for Clinical Diagnosis

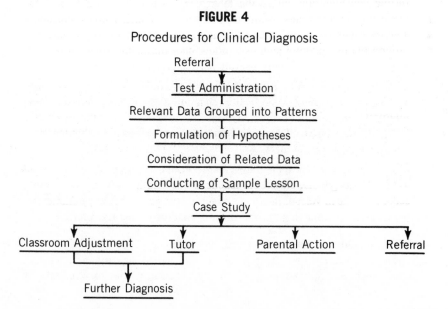

1. Referral: The specialist has the advantage of starting to work with a student previously identified as a possible reading problem. The classroom teacher either has attempted classroom diagnosis or identified the student as one in need of clinical diagnosis. All available information about the student should be forwarded to the reading specialist at the time of referral. It is not uncommon for parents to identify the problem readers; however, it is the specialist's responsibility in these cases to consult with the classroom teacher to obtain as much information as possible.

2. Administration of a battery of tests: Based upon a tentative evaluation of a student and that student's needs, the reading specialist proceeds with the administration and analysis of a battery of tests necessary to gathering objective data concerning the student's reading skills.

3. Observation of patterns: The reading specialist then makes careful observations of behavior patterns during the testing. When combined with test scores and an inner analysis of the reading responses on tests administered, these observations will facilitate the grouping of relevant data into more meaningful patterns.

4. Formulation of hypotheses: From the observable patterns, the reading specialist then forms tentative hypotheses concerning the causes of the problem.

5. Consideration of related data: Once the hypotheses have been formed, the specialist weighs related data with parent and teacher conferences, school records, previous diagnostic results, and so on. The specialist finds that the hypotheses are supported by related data; hence, the diagnosis gains validity. At other times, conflicting information forces reconsideration of the original hypotheses. In many cases, further testing or reexamination of the results of previous tests are needed to gain clearer insights into the problem.

6. Conducting of sample lessons: The lessons conducted during a clinical diagnosis are brief and specifically related to diagnostic hypotheses. Parts of the lessons should be directed to the student's strengths and parts to the student's weaknesses. Diagnosis is thus further verified through short-term instructional sessions.

7. Formulation of recommendations and referrals: After consideration of all relevant data, the reading specialist develops a case study which includes recommendations for adjustments of school programs, remedial treatment, possible parental action, further testing, and/or necessary referral.

The amount of time needed for effective clinical diagnosis will vary with the age of the student, the effectiveness of classroom diagnosis, and practical matters such as clinician load. Normally, a clinical diagnosis should be conducted in an hour or two. However, in some cases, much more time will be needed.

But reading specialists' job does not end here, for they are often involved directly in remediation, in assisting the classroom teacher, or in the initiation of preventive programs, each of which may call for further diagnosis. Morris includes the following thoughts in his discussion of diagnosis, "the challenge is to get to grips more directly with the problem and by working with the individual pupil try to understand what is leading him astray."[2] It is sufficient to say that diagnosis often may reach its ultimate conclusion during instruction.

SOURCES OF DATA

The reading specialist and the classroom teacher have many sources of diagnostic data available to them. Much, but by no means all, of the data available in a reading diagnosis is in the form of tests. Harris views the diagnostic use of tests as follows:

> the heart of diagnosis is not testing; it is, rather, the intelligent interpretation of the facts by a person who has the theoretical knowledge and the practical experience to know what questions to ask; to select procedures, including tests, which can supply the needed facts; to interpret the meaning of the findings correctly; and to comprehend the interrelationships of these facts and meaning.[3]

Therefore, it should be remembered that it is the person conducting the diagnosis and his ability to interpret the data, not the data itself, which leads to effective diagnosis. It should also be remembered that the student who is the object of the diagnosis is more important than an accumulation of test scores.

In general, data for classroom diagnosis are less formal than those for clinical diagnosis. School records, observations of the teacher, evaluation reports from past teachers, interviews with students and parents, home visits, and available test scores form the major sources of data for a classroom diagnosis.

Data for clinical diagnosis normally take the form of tests of intellectual performance, tests and evaluations of personal adjustment, physical screening tests, tests of reading performance, interviews and questionnaires, observations during lessons, and professional reports. Data are supplemented by

---

[2]Ronald Morris, *Success and Failure in Learning to Read* (London: Oldbourne, 1963), p. 159.

[3]Albert J. Harris, *How to Increase Reading Ability* (New York: David McKay Co., 1970), p. 201.

observing the reader during testing and are normally compiled in the form of a case study which illustrates the importance and interrelationships of the data collected.

GUIDELINES FOR DIAGNOSIS

Several guidelines should be understood as one enters into diagnostic activities. While it may be difficult to apply these guidelines in every instance, failure to do so can drastically interfere with student performances.

1. To establish rapport: For students to perform at their best, a situation must be established where tensions are relaxed and the students are encouraged into a cooperative attitude. The reading specialist confronted with conducting diagnosis outside normal classroom situations must be more alert to the necessity for establishing rapport than must the classroom teacher who, through daily contact with the student, is more likely to have established rapport.

2. To provide for individual study: Since many group testing situations tend to produce unreliable results, individual study is essential. Individual sessions with students tend to reduce those competitive activities which are frustrating to problem readers.

3. To provide for group study: Evaluation of students as they interact can offer useful diagnostic insights. Diagnostic results which come from data collected during individual study only are often difficult for teachers to apply. How students react when working in a group situation may be quite different from their performances during individual study. Obviously, both types of data are needed for a thorough diagnosis.

4. To test, not teach: By resisting the urge to help students when they experience difficulty during testing, more accurate data will be available. Comments such as "That was almost correct—try again," can serve to encourage some students and discourage others. This guideline applies most directly to clinical diagnosis and during testing. Of course, diagnostic teaching activities involve normal student-teacher interactions.

5. To maintain efficiency: In terms of efficiency, a diagnosis includes only those tests and observations which are likely to help the examiner arrive at pertinent results. There is a tendency to rely upon a systematic diagnostic procedure regardless of the needs of the student, creating pointless testing situations which, at best, are often frustrating experiences. An efficient diagnosis, then, is one which includes those measures needed by the educator to arrive at a solution to the problem; it eliminates those which have questionable value in relation to the objectives of the diagnosis.

6. To evaluate diagnostic data in terms of patterns: The examiner must look for patterns in data and refuse to rely upon a single measure as being meaningful or significant. Therefore, diagnosis must include several inter-related measures of the child's reading abilities. For example, it would be best to compare one's results on a word recognition test with the results on an oral reading test. When similar student performance occurs, a pattern of performance is established.

DIAGNOSIS FOR STRENGTHS

While a student's weaknesses naturally might be the concern of the teacher, diagnosis for strengths is equally important. Since instructional adjustment should start with areas of strengths, deliberate diagnosis to determine those strengths is necessary. However, as we observe diagnostic reports of students with reading problems, we frequently find no mention of their strengths. *All students have strengths.* Each student should be made aware of them, and the teachers should note them during diagnosis. In fact, given a choice, I favor diagnosis for strengths. What students know is important. What they do not know can be assumed from what they do know. As we moved toward strengths diagnosis at the University of Maryland clinic, we noticed that educators receiving the report felt better about the reports and the students. Parents also appreciated them for most of them had only negative reports concerning their child's scholastic performances. Most important was our ability to discuss diagnostic results with the students in terms of their skill strengths. Such conferences with students left them feeling worthwhile.

We have established in previous chapters that reading disabilities are caused by a variety of factors. The areas indicated by Bond and Tinker (intellectual, physical, emotional, and educational) are inclusive enough to explain this variety of causes.[4] Intellectual, physical, and emotional diagnosis will be discussed in Chapter 3. Chapter 4 will contain a discussion of educational causes. It is important for the reader to remember that it is the specific responsibility of educators to diagnose and correct reading problems in this fourth area, educational.

SUMMARY

Through an understanding of the similarities and differences in the diagnostic procedures, data and principles as they apply to the classroom and clinical

---

[4]Guy L. Bond and Miles A. Tinker, *Reading Difficulties: Their Diagnosis and Correction* (New York: Appleton-Century-Crofts, 1973), Chapters 5 and 6.

settings establish clear limitations. There are advantages and limitations to all types of diagnosis, and, therefore, each can be used effectively. Consideration of the importance of students, their strengths and weaknesses, their feelings, and their self-concepts must be of utmost importance to the diagnostic teacher. Without diagnosis, instruction can be effective only by chance.

SUGGESTED READINGS

Bond, Guy L., and Tinker, Miles A. *Reading Difficulties: Their Diagnosis and Correction.* 3d ed. New York: Appleton-Century-Crofts, 1973. Chapter 7 contains a careful introduction to the broad principles of diagnosis. The reader who desires more specific information on this general topic will find this chapter rewarding.

Harris, Albert. *How to Increase Reading Ability,* Chapter 1. New York: David McKay Co., 1970. Harris' discussion of reading and reading disabilities will provide another view of the role of diagnosis.

Strang, Ruth. *Diagnostic Teaching of Reading.* New York: McGraw-Hill, 1969. As an introduction to this book on diagnosis, Chapter 1 provides carefully organized discussion of the principles, approaches, and other concepts related to the diagnosing of reading disabilities.

Strang, Ruth. *Invitational Addresses—1965.* Newark, Del.: International Reading Association, 1965. The address sets the background for the reading model presented in this chapter. The reader may want to refer to the original source for more detail.

3

Intellectual, Physical, Emotional Diagnosis

This chapter will assist the educator in identifying potential problems, referring effectively, and recognizing the difficulties involved with diagnosis in
each of the areas—intellectual, physical, and emotional.

Diagnosis discussed in this chapter requires specialized training outside
the field of reading. However, teachers and reading specialists should be
informed about this diagnosis even if they are unqualified to conduct it.

INTELLECTUAL DIAGNOSIS

Estimates of intellectual potential are useful in diagnosing reading problems.
An estimate of the student's potential can assist the teacher in setting realistic
instructional goals. Such goals should be flexible, however, for the best
measures of intelligence are subject to error. Therefore, recognition of the
advantages and limitations of measures of intelligence is essential for interpretation of such data in a reading diagnosis.

As a cause of reading disabilities, intelligence is suspect. In fact, intelligence is related to *causes* of reading problems only in relation to the ability of

the school to adjust the educational program to the abilities of various types of students. It is important to realize that it is not intelligence—or lack of it—that prohibits students from reading up to their potential; rather, it is the fact that school programs, which are often geared to the majority of average students, do not give ample consideration to those at the extremes (the bright and dull students). The inability or the impossibility of a given situation to provide these necessary adjustments often causes bright or dull students to become reading problems. Although accurate measures of intellectual performance are essential to the diagnosis of reading problems, the intelligence of a given student per se is not the cause of his problem.

Complications of Intellectual Testing

Complicating the use of intelligence tests is the educator's tendency to misuse test scores by grasping at high or low scores as the most easily observable division between the problem and the normal reader. How many students have thus been labeled can only be guessed at, but that many have been mislabeled is fact. A brief review of the limitations of measures of potential will indicate the difficulties encountered when such data are used in diagnosis.

Reliability. Has the test measured accurately? Has the test measured by chance? If students were to retake the test, would they obtain the same score? All tests are subject to error; therefore, most test constructors provide information about the test error in the teacher's guide. Error information is of two types, reliability coefficient and standard error of measurement. *Reliability coefficients* are usually reported in decimals (e.g., .90). Made into a percentage, the test may be said to measure the true score 90 percent of the time and error 10 percent of the time. Reliability coefficients below the .90 level cause concern about the reliability of the test.

The *standard error of measurement* usually is reported in terms of the raw score or mental age score on the test (e.g., four months). The standard error, in theory, is explained as follows: If students were to take the test repeatedly, their scores would fall within a range of plus or minus four months of the score obtained with the current administration. Therefore, if a student obtained a mental age score of 9.5 months and the test had a standard error of four months, that student's score would be interpreted as falling somewhere between 9.1 and 9.9 months about two-thirds of the time. For students who score in the extremes, very high or very low, errors of measurement are greater than those scoring in the middle or average ranges of the test. The necessity for awareness of reliability and standard error scores becomes clear. Without this information, one cannot interpret a given score.

Validity. Does a test measure what it purports to measure? Validity involves the problem of what intelligence is. Of the many dimensions which intelligence must surely have, most tests measure only a few; some measure only one. Presumably, the most prominent aspects of intelligence have been included in the best constructed tests. While a test which measures listening comprehension is measuring a significant aspect of intelligence, the resulting score —called a mental age—implies more than can be covered by such a narrow measure. Another complication is encountered when a given test also requires specifically learned skills, such as reading. The test's validity is then in interference with the reading achievement of the person taking the test.

Most test constructors attempt to prove the validity of their measure by comparing the results of their test with another test, usually one of established reputation. These figures usually appear as decimals (e.g., .70). For interpretation purposes, the decimal must be squared (.49) to find the percent (49 percent) of the variance measured, in common, by each test. Other test constructors are content to logically defend the test's content as an obvious factor or factors of intelligence.

When two tests of intelligence are administered, a student probably will obtain two scores which, at times, are quite different. Then the problem is to determine which score is most valid. However, an obvious concern arises. Would the student have scored even better on another measure?

To complicate validity further, many tests contain problems which are dependent upon cultural experiences. Students from cultures other than those on which the test was normed may score significantly poorer than will students from cultures similar to the ones on which the test is based. In such cases, is the test a fair measure of intelligence? Obviously not.

Test Administration, Scoring, and Interpretation. Despite the efforts of the American Psychological Association, persons other than qualified psychologists administer intelligence tests. Many of these people do so without training and without directed supervision; they often make serious errors in test administration, scoring, and interpretation. Tests administered by unknown personnel must be held suspect and should not be considered useful information in a reading diagnosis.

Group Intelligence Tests. For several reasons, group tests of intelligence are inappropriate for students suspected of having a reading difficulty. First, many of the group tests require that students read in order to take the test. Obviously, if they cannot read well, their scores will reflect their poor reading as well as intelligence, and the two will be hopelessly confused. Second, rapport is difficult to establish in group testing. For students who have been subjected to considerable failure, any group test may threaten them further and result in a poor performance. Third, the reliability of many of the group tests is very poor, making score interpretation nearly impossible. MacDonald comments on the difficulty with group intelligence tests.

Because both group type intelligence tests and reading achievement tests involve reading, the common element present in both kinds of tests represents two measures of the same categories of skill. Poor readers are doubly penalized with significant underestimation of probable mental ability.[1]

Awareness of the limitations inherent in measures of intellectual performance will lessen the possibility of intelligence test scores being used or interpreted improperly. For the best assessment of intellectual performance, at least one of the measures of intelligence must be individual and nonreading in nature. Major discrepancies between test scores are justifiable reasons for referral for psychological examination. An accurate I.Q. is *not* found by averaging conflicting scores.

Considering the limitations of intelligence testing and particularly of group testing, it seems inconceivable that school reading personnel would use such scores to control admission to a program to aid those having reading difficulty. However, many schools limit admission to reading programs to those with group intelligence test scores above a certain score. Such a practice seems indefensible and should be changed since a student who needs help probably will be denied it. Furthermore, that same student might score much higher on an individual measure. Discriminations of this type are not based on a knowledge of the instruments being used.

Instead of relying on such scores, other options are available. What is the nature of a student's problem in reading? How long has the problem existed? How does the teacher feel about it? How did last year's teacher feel about it? Are there any evidences of school success outside the language areas? Eventually the school will have to deal with such a case, for every student has the right to the best programs possible.

Measures of Potential Reading Ability
Suitable for Clinical Diagnosis*

Revised Stanford-Binet Intelligence Scale. * Considered by many to be the most accurate single test for measuring intelligence, the Binet test may be administered and scored only by personnel with formal course work and laboratory experience. The test ranges from preschool to adulthood, yielding a mental age and an intelligence quotient. The test measures several aspects of intelligence, is heavily verbal, takes about one hour to administer, is individual in nature, and requires precise administration and interpretation for reliable results.

Wechsler Intelligence Scale for Children (WISC). * Another popular, accurate test of intellectual performance, the WISC requires individual administration

---

[1]Arthur S. MacDonald, "Research for the Classroom," *The Journal of Reading* 8 (November 1964): 115-18.

and should be administered by personnel who have had formal course work and laboratory experience. Measuring several aspects of intelligence, the WISC yields a performance and a verbal score, with the verbal score normally considered the most valid predictor of performance in reading. With problem readers, however, the performance score probably provides the best measure of reading potential. The students' verbal scores may be limited by the same factors that limit their performance in reading. When WISC scores show a higher performance than verbal rating, there is just cause to encourage students with their development in reading. Deal summarized fourteen studies of WISC subscores and found that the researchers were far from unanimous in their findings concerning interpretation of subscores.[2] Farr, summarizing sixteen studies, found several fairly consistent subscore patterns on the WISC for retarded readers.[3] No cause-and-effect relationship was determined, however. The teacher is cautioned about the use and interpretation of such subscores for reading diagnosis and subsequent adjustment of instruction. Since WISC scores are best interpreted by psychological personnel, most reading personnel should await their analysis. The *Wechsler Adult Intelligence Scale* (WAIS), also available, may be used with older children and adults. Both the WISC and the WAIS take approximately one hour to administer.

The Peabody Picture Vocabulary Test (PPVT). * Designed to test one's ability to associate one of four pictures with the word pronounced by the examiner, the PPVT is a test of listening vocabulary taking approximately fifteen minutes for individual administration and requiring little special preparation by the teacher. Neville found no significant difference between the performance scores of fifty-four children on the PPVT and on the WISC, although they are limited to one aspect of intelligence (i.e., auding).[4] Strang contends, "Ability to comprehend by listening (sometimes called auding) is another indication of potential reading ability."[5] It is valuable to refer to the M.A. score on the PPVT as the child's *auding age* and to the I.Q. as the *auding quotient.* These terms imply potential for reading but avoid the implication of overall intelligence. For a quick indication of potential, the PPVT is considered to be practical and useful when Binet or WISC scores are not available. The *Slossen Intelligence Test,* * the Ammons *Full Range Picture Vocabulary Test,* * and the verbal opposites section of the *Detroit Tests of Learning Aptitudes* are also useful instruments for quick, limited indications of intellectual performance.

---

[2]Margaret Deal, "A Summary of Research Concerning Patterns of WISC Subtest Scores of Retarded Readers," *The Journal of the Reading Specialist* 4 (May 1965): 101-11.

[3]Roger Farr, *Reading: What Can Be Measured?* (Newark, Del.: International Reading Association, 1969), pp. 93-94.

[4]Donald Neville, "The Relationship Between Reading Skills and Intelligence Test Scores," *The Reading Teacher* 18 (January 1965): 257-61.

[5]Ruth Strang, *Diagnostic Teaching of Reading* (New York: McGraw-Hill Book Co., 1969), p. 15.

*Durrell Listening-Reading Series.** As another measure of auding ability, these tests require students to associate words and paragraphs which have been read to them with pictures. The auding scores then are compared to reading vocabulary and reading paragraph scores. Testing time requires approximately eighty minutes and requires little formal preparation for either administration or scoring.

Arithmetic Computation. For students who have attended school for two or more years, a test of arithmetic computation, not involving verbal problems, is useful in estimating academic potential. Included as a factor on several intelligence scales, arithmetic computation scores show how well students succeed in school in nonverbal tasks, thus indicating their levels of potential. Arithmetic computation scores verify suspicions of potential that have gone undetected when they vary noticeably from reading achievement. In some types of more seriously handicapped readers, arithmetic computations scores do not indicate potential. This is especially true when students react against the total learning environment with emotional rejection. Arithmetic computation, however, remains a valuable tool as one of the first indicators of intellectual potential.

Other measures of intellectual performance also are available for clinical diagnosis; however, most of them require special preparation and laboratory experience, as do the Binet and the WISC.

Measures of Potential Reading Ability Suitable for Classroom Diagnosis

*The Binet and the WISC.** These are not normally administered by the classroom teacher, but their scores are often found in the school records of the problem readers. The other tests mentioned under clinical diagnosis can be administered by a classroom teacher as a part of normal school procedures or as a part of classroom diagnosis.

Group Intelligence Tests. Although group intelligence tests are inherently unsatisfactory in reading diagnosis, several of them do separate reading and nonreading factors. The *California Test of Mental Maturity,** for example, provides an M.A. and I.Q. for both language and nonlanguage performance. The teacher who uses this type of test and finds a major discrepancy between the two scores (nonlanguage I.Q.—140, language I.Q.—100) should be encouraged to look for other signs of intellectual performance, for the student may be capable but hindered in the language section by lack of reading ability. Other measures of reading potential, such as those mentioned under clinical diagnosis, should then be checked, or the student should be referred for an individual intelligence examination. However, unless group intelligence tests have nonlanguage features, they are not useful in estimating the reading potential of students with reading problems. Even then, their usefulness is highly questionable.

Teacher Observation. The experienced teacher often is able to note characteristics of reading potential through direct observation of the student's response to various school activities. Roswell and Natchez state that a teacher "can form some idea of the child's intellectual ability from his general responsiveness in class."[6] Specifically, noticeable characteristics are:

1. ability to participate effectively in class discussions, both listening and speaking
2. ability to achieve more successfully in arithmetic than in subjects requiring reading
3. ability to participate effectively in peer group activities
4. ability to demonstrate alert attitudes to the world
5. ability to perform satisfactorily on spelling tests

Admittedly, such observations are not highly liable indications of reading potential. Teacher observation is limited by the possibilities of teacher bias; they may well see just what they are looking for. For example, a teacher's observation may be controlled somewhat by previous test performances and prior impressions of the student. However, ability in the above areas is often the first symptom to be noticed. By such observations, students who have been intellectually misjudged may be referred for more accurate evaluations.

Remember that a student's score on a given test is only a reflection of total ability. The student is always greater as a person than any test score can show. Therefore, teachers are encouraged to look for the best in all students.

Reading Potential and Degree of Retardation

Measures of intellectual performance greatly aid in determining the degree of reading retardation. A comparison of the best estimates of reading potential with the best estimates of reading achievement will result in an arithmetical difference. When potential exceeds achievement, one is concerned that the student is not working up to capacity. The larger the difference, the more serious the degree of retardation.

---

[6]Florence Roswell and Gladys Natchez, *Reading Disability* (New York: Basic Books, 1964), p. 27.

Perhaps the most common technique for estimating the seriousness of retardation is a simple comparison of mental age grade equivalent [I.Q. divided by 100, multiplied by chronological age (C.A.)−5] to reading achievement.[7] This technique is particularly limiting with very young children of high ability, for it assumes a considerable development of reading skills prior to school attendance. A six-year-old child with an I.Q. of 140 entering first grade may be considered to have a mental age of 8.4 (140/100 × 6.0 = 1.4 × 6.0 = 8.4 − 5 = 3.4) but should not normally be expected to be reading at the third-grade level because of a lack of social, emotional, and educational experiences for that degree of achievement. Even with older, bright students, this technique tends to place reading potential scores unrealistically high. On the other hand, acknowledging these limitations, one can estimate the seriousness of retardation by this technique. Harris recommends a formula which places priority on mental age: (Reading Expectancy = 2MA + CA/3) as another alternative.[8]

Bond and Tinker circumvent the limitations mentioned above by using the formula (I.Q./100 multiplied by years in school + 1.0) as compared to reading achievement.[9] The child discussed above would have a reading potential of 1.0 upon entrance to the first grade:

$$(\frac{140}{100} \times 0) + 1.0 = 1.0$$

As children advance through school, this approach expects them to make accelerated progress so that upon entrance to third grade these same children are expected to be reading at the 3.8 grade level:

$$(\frac{140}{100} \times 2.0) + 1.0 = 3.8$$

Bond and Tinker's research shows that this formula is much more realistic than formulas using mental age, such as that mentioned above.[10] In using this formula, consideration must be given to three factors. First, it must be understood that the term *years in school* does not mean the student's grade placement, but rather, the actual number of years of school completed. Therefore, for a student who has a grade placement of 4.8 and who has not accelerated or repeated a grade, the appropriate entry would be 3.8 for years in school. (For this formula, kindergarten does not count as a year in school.) Second, the teacher must have accurate data concerning the grades repeated or accelerated. Third, the addition of 1.0 years in the formula is to compensate for

[7]Albert Harris, *How to Increase Reading Ability* (New York: David McKay Co., 1970), p. 211.

[8]Harris, *How to Increase Reading Ability*, p. 212.

[9]Guy L. Bond and Miles A. Tinker, *Reading Difficulties: Their Diagnosis and Correction* (New York: Appleton-Century-Crofts, 1973), p. 92.

[10]Bond and Tinker, *Reading Difficulties*, p. 94.

the manner in which grade norms are assigned to tests, 1.0 being the zero month of first grade. Despite its obvious advantages, most teachers, lacking complete understanding of it, refrain from using this formula.

Cleland prefers to average four factors, giving equal weight to each, in arriving at a reading potential score which is compared to reading achievement.[11] In this formula, he computes the grade equivalents of chronological age, mental age, arithmetic computation, and the *Durrell-Sullivan Reading Capacity Test:*

$$
\begin{array}{ll}
\text{C.A.} - 5 = 6 - 5 & = 1.0 \\
\text{M.A.} - 5 = 8.4 - 5 & = 3.4 \\
\text{Arith. C.} & = 1.5 \\
\text{D/S Cap.} & = \underline{2.5} \\
& 8.4 \div 4 = 2.1
\end{array}
$$

This formula has several advantages: first, although mental age is used without the compensation that Bond and Tinker give, it is equalized somewhat by the use of chronological age; second, the use of reading capacity adds auding as a factor (any auding test can be substituted for a capacity score); and, third, the use of arithmetic computation provides measures of the student's ability to do nonverbal school work. It is important to note that grade equivalents of M.A. and C.A. are obtained by subtracting five for the five years the child did not attend school. (Harris recommends subtracting 5.2.) This formula, or variations of it, is commonly used in clinical diagnosis. We find it compares much more favorably to the Bond and Tinker formula than to the mental age formulas.

To compare the child's score on a test of auding with achievement test performance is another relatively easy way of determining the degree of retardation. In this case, the auding score is an estimate of reading potential and may be obtained from tests such as the *Peabody Picture Vocabulary Test* and the *Botel Listening Test.* On the Peabody, the auding age equivalent may be converted to grade equivalent by subtracting five years.

How large the difference between reading potential and achievement must be to be considered serious will vary with the grade placement of the student. There may be many students who fall slightly short of full reading potential, yet would not be considered problem readers. Older students can manage a larger variance between potential and achievement without the severe ramifications that occur with younger students.

The scale in Table 2 may be useful in selecting a cutoff point between a tolerable difference and one that is sufficient to interfere with the child's progress in reading and other subjects. Tolerable differences are presented in

---

[11]Donald L. Cleland, "Clinical Materials for Appraising Disabilities in Reading," *The Reading Teacher* 17 (March 1964): 428.

this table by individual grade level in Column 1 and by groupings for primary, intermediate, and junior and senior high school levels in Column 2. Although this scale should not be adhered to rigidly, it does provide reasonably useful limits. However, since diagnosis includes considerably more analysis than the estimation of potential and achievement, it would be folly indeed for the educator to evaluate progress in reading by this technique alone.

TABLE 2

Degree of Tolerable Difference between
Potential and Achievement

End of:	1	2
1st grade	.3	
2nd grade	.5	.5 of a year
3rd grade	.7	
4th grade	.8	
5th grade	1.0	1 year
6th grade	1.2	
7th grade	1.3	
8th grade	1.5	1.5 years
9th grade	1.7	
10th grade	1.8	
11th grade	2.0	2 years
12th grade	2.2	

NOTE: Tolerable difference ranges must be used as judgment points, not as absolutes.

When selecting the method for computing the degree of reading retardation, the following factors should be considered:

1. The number and type of students selected as retarded in reading will vary with the method employed.
2. Each method is only as good as the instruments used to obtain the scores for its computation.
3. A student with a specific skill deficiency may not be discovered by these types of formulas.

It is useful to include the standard error of measurement when reporting reading potential scores. In Figure 5, the student's chronological age, auding age, oral reading accuracy score, and silent reading comprehension score have been plotted. The two heavy lines reflect the standard error plus and minus the actual potential score.

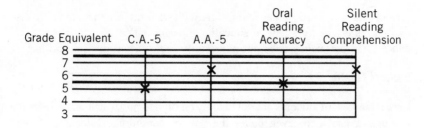

Grade Equivalent	C.A.-5	A.A.-5	Oral Reading Accuracy	Silent Reading Comprehension

Although neither reading score is as high as the auding age, both of them fall within the standard error of the auding age. This treatment of auding scores expresses to all who receive the report that the score should not be taken as a precise measure.

Some Additional Cautions

Many students could fail to receive the help they need if potential formulas are used as the only indicators of need. Students with specific skill deficiencies or attitudinal problems might well be missed. Students with low potential scores might need a language development program prior to starting a reading program.[12] On a given day, a student might well score differently on the reading tests. These and many other problems call for examiners to evaluate the total reader not just the test scores. Attention to the reader's responses during testing may be more important than the resulting score. How the use of potential fits into classroom and clinical diagnosis is discussed in the following two chapters.

PHYSICAL DIAGNOSIS

A physical limitation is considered a cause of a reading problem when it interferes with a student's potential and performance. If Sara cannot see a printed page adequately, she cannot be expected to read it as well as her potential indicates she should. Whose job is it to assess the severity of physical disability? Although physical limitations are recognized first in a classroom or clinical diagnosis, medical personnel or other specialists are responsible for specific identification, corrective measures, and recommendations. Both the reading specialist and the classroom teacher can refer students either on the basis of reliable patterns of symptoms or as a result of certain screening devices available to educators.

Specifically, the areas of physical diagnosis of reading problems are general health, visual, auditory, and neurological. Limitations which are

---

[12]John J. Pikulski, "Assessing Information about Intelligence and Reading," *The Reading Teacher* 29 (November 1975): 162.

serious enough in these areas to interfere with performance in reading are also likely to interfere with general educational performance. However, a general educational deficiency does not necessarily indicate physical disabilities.

General Health

Large numbers of students are not healthy enough to profit efficiently from the instruction provided, even under the best of conditions. Educators should know those aspects of general health which interfere with school progress and which should be evaluated in the diagnosis of reading problems.

Malnutrition. Malnutrition causes the student to lose weight or to lag behind in physical and mental vitality. Malnutrition does not necessarily show itself in loss of weight, however. Many suffering from diet imbalance are quite chubby (e.g., those suffering from imbalance of starches). The sluggish behavior which results interferes with school performance.

Glandular Defects. These have also been diagnosed as causing educational problems. When the glands which maintain important balances in the body fail, more than physical discomfort may result.

Mental or Physical Fatigue. Caused by lack of sleep, poor sleeping habits, lack of exercise, or overexertion, mental or physical fatigue can cause students to be inattentive and easily distracted in a learning situation.

Poor General Physical Condition. Often characterized by frequent illness, poor general physical condition causes a lack of stamina with resulting gaps in the educational instruction. Factors such as overweight, underweight, poor teeth, hay fever, etc., can result in difficulty with school tasks.

Alertness to signs of poor health is essential in a reading diagnosis. Many such cases are first identified by individual attention to a student's performance during diagnosis.

The classroom teacher combines information from school records, reports from the school nurse and the family doctor, information from the parents, and observable symptoms which are characteristic of students with general physical deficiencies. Sluggishness, inattentiveness, failure to complete assignments, apparent lack of interest, sleeping in school, and general lack of vitality often are symptoms which cause a student to be labeled *lazy* or *indifferent*. Classroom teachers should observe these symptoms, contact the home to report the problem, and make medical referrals when appropriate. At the same time, they should adjust the instruction to make the learning environment as comfortable as possible for the student. This adjustment may take the form of relaxing the tension caused by the student's apparent indifference, allowing the fatigued student a program of varied activities and necessary rest periods, and, if possible, following the recommendations of medical personnel. It does not take a medical report to make us aware that all students, not just those with reading problems, need good health for optimum school performance. Necessities, such as adequate rest, a balanced diet (particularly a good breakfast), annual physical checkups, and large doses of play activity after school are vital requirements for good school performance.

One of the reading specialist's responsibilities in diagnosis is to evaluate reports received from medical personnel in terms of the total case picture of the student involved and to recommend the appropriate classroom adjustment and/or remedial program.

Visual Diagnosis

The classroom teacher is aware that deficiencies in visual ability and ocular comfort may well impede a student's growth in reading. Reports relate that from 15 to 40 percent of students need professional visual attention. The relationship of vision to reading problems is complicated since many students with visual problems are not problem readers. The more careful research reports show a relationship between certain types of visual deficiencies and failure in reading and have found that certain visual disabilities and ocular discomfort greatly interfere with students' reaching their reading potentials.[13] In general, functional problems, such as awkward eye movements and poor fusion, more often cause reading difficulty than do organic difficulties, such as nearsightedness, farsightedness, or astigmatism. A review of some of the aspects of vision and ocular comfort pinpoints the relationship.

Acuity. Acuity, the clearness of vision, is normally measured at far-point targets (a Snellen Chart twenty feet away from the student).[14] Such screening tests of acuity provide us with information concerning the student's acuity at the far point (e.g., ability to see the chalkboard). The results of this type of visual screening are expressed in terms of what the average person can see at twenty feet. The term *20/20* means that a person can see at twenty feet the same target that a person with normal vision can see at twenty feet. This test, when used alone, however, cannot detect all visual deficiencies. In the first place, we do not normally read targets which are twenty feet from the eyes; neither do we read with one eye at a time. The eyes must efficiently move from one target to another rather than merely fixing on and identifying a target. Kelley claims, "The misconception that the Snellen Chart will do an efficient job of screening out students who need visual care is a major block in the road of those trying to establish good school visual screening programs."[15]

---

[13]Charles A. Kelley, *Visual Screening and Child Development* (Raleigh, N.C.: North Carolina State College, 1957), chapter 2, p. 11.

[14]"The Snellen Chart" (Southbridge, Mass.: American Optical Co.).

[15]Kelley, *Visual Screening and Child Development,* p. 11.

Screening devices to measure near-point acuity are essential in the diagnosis of a problem reader, although they generally take more time and training to administer properly. One who passes the Snellen Chart may still have a visual deficiency which is causing problems in reading. The farsighted reader, seeing far-point targets better than near-point targets, may pass the Snellen Chart yet not see well enough or efficiently enough to read with comfort at the near point. The nearsighted reader, who sees near-point targets better than far-point targets, is likely to fail the Snellen Chart, but, while obviously limited by a visual defect, may read effectively in most cases. Therefore, proper visual screening must measure both far- and near-point acuity. This need has been partially met by the development of a type of chart for use at a distance of fourteen inches. Additional techniques, described below, are generally more desirable for accurate near point screening.

Fusion. Fusion involves the ability of the brain to blend or fuse the image from each eye into an adequate image. A student who looks with one eye and psychologically blinds the other gets a clear image but does not have good fusion. Those with sluggish fusion seldom see a clear target adequately; thus, they experience ocular discomfort and inefficiency that should be identified in a near- and far-point visual screening.

Color Recognition. It is important for the young child to recognize colors accurately. Simple far-point color blindness tests generally are adequate for screening, with the precise measurement of color limitation left to the vision specialist. The reading teacher, with a knowledge of the child's color confusion problems, does not expect the child to perform in tasks requiring color discrimination.

Ocular Motility. The efficient operation of the eye in motion is a requisite for effective reading. In particular, ocular motility refers to good left-to-right motion (pursuit), saccadic movement, fixations, and focusing power. Screening devices are available for evaluation in these areas and should be considered in a diagnosis of reading problems.

1. Left-to-right motion: In the reading act, the eyes must fix on a target, move to the right, fix on another target, move to the right, fix on another target, then sweep back and take hold of the next line in a manner which is not natural at birth, but learned. Students who are grossly inefficient at this task of left-to-right eye movements or accurate fixations will likely experience difficulty in the reading act.

2. Pursuit eye movement: Eyes should be able to follow a moving target smoothly, not stopping and starting, but following with an effortless, fluid movement. The ability to do so allows students the efficient eye motion between fixations without which they are likely to have trouble following a line of print.

3. Saccadic eye movement: Accurate change of fixations from one word to another or from the end of a line of print to the beginning of the next line is an important ocular-motor skill related to reading. When deficient in this skill, students lose their places, skip words, and read more slowly than is necessary.

4. Focusing power: Prolonged reading demands the power to maintain focus on a target for a long time. The student with deficient focusing power is likely to become fatigued much sooner than others.

5. Binocular vision: During the reading act, some students tend to suppress the vision of one eye and do all the reading with the other. The continuation of this type of reading can lead to serious visual complications which can only be evaluated by the visual specialist.

The areas of ocular motility are seldom investigated in usual school screening; however, when diagnosing a reading problem, the teacher or reading specialist should make every effort to evaluate them:

1. A test using a telebinocular* provides near- and far-point screening of acuity, stereopsis, and fusion, as well as a test of color vision. The proper administration and analysis of this test requires supervised experience to assure reliable results. It should be noted that the telebinocular screens the visual skills related to the ability of the eyes to fix only on a stationary target.

2. The reading specialist must also be concerned about the eyes as they operate in reading situations. The *Spache-Binocular Reading Tests** provide an analysis of binocular vision during the reading act. In these tests, the student looks at a card that has been placed in the telebinocular and reads a story containing some words that only the right eye can see and some that only the left eye can see. By marking the student's responses, the examiner can determine the degree to which each eye operates in the reading act. Referral is based on certain characteristics which are identified in the accompanying manual.

3. For screening pursuit, saccadic eye movements, and focusing power, a pocket flashlight is used in the following way: holding the light upright in front of the student, approximately eighteen inches from the eyes, the examiner asks the student to look at the light. The examiner then moves the light in a place eighteen inches from the eye in straight vertical, horizontal, and diagonal lines twelve to eighteen inches in length, and, then, in a circle with a radius of about twelve inches clockwise and counterclockwise. Referral should be considered if (1) students cannot follow the light without moving their heads, even after being told to hold still; (2) the reflection of the light cannot be seen in both a student's pupils at all times; or (3) the eye movements are saccadic (i.e., they follow the light jerkily instead of

smoothly). To test converging power, the light is again held eighteen inches from the eye, moved slowly to a position one inch directly between the eyes and held for one second. Since some students do not understand what they are to do the first time, there is justification for referral only if they cannot hold this fixation after three attempts.

Not having any of this screening equipment available, classroom teachers must rely upon a pattern of symptoms observable in the reading act or in other school situations. The check list prepared by the American Optometric Association (Table 3) includes a list of these symptoms.[16] Copies of this check list may be secured from the American Optometric Association, 4030 Chouteau Avenue, St. Louis, Missouri. Note that this check list recommends that *all* students who are not performing well in terms of their capacity should be referred for visual examinations.

Students with these symptoms normally will be referred to the school nurse; however, if screening equipment is limited to the Snellen Chart, the classroom teacher is obligated to present the information to the parents, with the suggestion of a complete visual examination by a specialist. Until the student receives treatment, the teacher should make every effort to provide a most comfortable and efficient visual environment. This may be accomplished by placing the student in a position of maximum lighting, by eliminating glare, by adjusting seating to ease board work, or by reducing the reading load.

TABLE 3

Teacher's Guide to Vision Problems
with Check List

To aid teachers in detecting the *children* who should be referred for complete visual analysis, the American Optometric Association Committee on Visual Problems in Schools has compiled a list of symptoms —a guide to vision problems. The committee recommends:

1. that all *children* in the lower third of the class, particularly those with ability to achieve above their percentile rating, be referred for complete visual analysis.
2. that every *child* in the class who, even though achieving, is not working within reasonable limits of his own capacity be referred for a complete visual analysis.

Following are other symptoms which may indicate a visual problem, regardless of result in any screening test.

[16]*Teacher's Guide To Vision Problems* (St. Louis: American Optometric Association, 1953).

Observed in Reading:

Dislike for reading and reading subjects.

Skipping or re-reading lines.

††Losing place while reading.

Slow reading or word calling.

Poor perceptual ability, such as confusing *o* and *a, n* and *m,* etc.

Other Manifestations:

Restlessness, nervousness, irritability or other unaccountable behavior.

Desire to use finger or marker as pointer while reading.

††Avoiding close work.

††Poor sitting posture and position while reading.

Fatigue or listlessness after close work.

Inattentiveness, temper tantrums, or frequent crying.

Complaint of blur when looking up from close work.

Seeing objects double.

Headaches, dizziness, or nausea associated with the use of eyes.

††Body rigidity while looking at distant objects.

Undue sensitivity to light.

Crossed eyes—turning in or out.

Red-rimmed, crusted or swollen lids.

Vocalizing during silent reading, noticed by watching lips or throat.

Reversals persisting in grade 2 or beyond.

Inability to remember what has been read.

Complaint of letters and lines "running together" or of words "jumping."

††Holding reading closer than normal.

††Frowning, excessive blinking, scowling, squinting, or other facial distortions while reading.

††Excessive head movements while reading.

Writing with face too close to work.

Frequent sties.

Watering or bloodshot eyes.

Burning or itching of eyes or eyelids.

††Tilting head to one side.

††Tending to rub eyes.

Closing or covering one eye.

Frequent tripping or stumbling.

Poor hand and eye coordination as manifested in poor baseball playing, catching and batting, or similar activities.

††Thrusting head forward.

††Tension during close work.

Only a complete case study will determine whether inadequate vision is a significant factor in nonachievement.

---

††Found to be particularly significant in a recent study.

Visual Referral Problems. Referral in vision is complicated by the reluctance of educators to overrefer (i.e., referring a student who may not be in need of help). Kelley views the problem as follows:

> The cardinal purpose of school visual screening procedures is to refer children who may need visual care. It generally is considered more serious for a screening program to *fail to refer* a child in real need of care than for it to *refer* a child not actually in need of care.[17]

Shaw says:

> My opinion is that a child's first opthalmological examination should be given at about age three. . . . The persistance of abnormal symptoms would suggest the need for eye examination regardless of the results of a screening test.[18]

Ewalt sees the problem in overreferral as follows:

> You have heard screening programs seriously criticized because they refer too many youngsters for visual examination. Nonsense! Most of the agencies of this country, dealing with vision, whether they represent the opthalmologists as the National Association for the Prevention of Blindness, or the optometrists as the American Optometric Association agree that every school child should have an annual examination. If all school children need an annual examination, we need not be too concerned with an occasional overreferral.[19]

The schools, through their notorious reluctance to refer, have permitted many students to operate daily with eye strain which leads to more complicated, permanent problems. I believe that all students should have periodic visual examinations by a specialist. Until the schools assume this responsibility, it remains a parental obligation. The teacher, then, should not hesitate to refer any student who demonstrates the symptoms indicated in Table 3. This in no way implies that an indiscriminate attitude toward referral should be adopted; however, this procedure is the best way by which many students can receive necessary visual attention.

The necessity for visual referral is complicated further by changes in the eyes following visual adjustment. The nature of school, requiring hours of close work, may make it necessary for lenses to be changed periodically.

---

[17]Kelly, *Visual Screening,* chapter 2, p. 11.

[18]Jules H. Shaw, "Vision and Seeing Skills of Preschool Children," *The Reading Teacher* 18 (October 1964): 36.

[19]Ward H. Ewalt, Jr., "Visual Problems of Children and Their Relationship to Reading Achievement," *The Optometric Weekly,* October 22, 1959.

Therefore, the teacher should not hesitate to refer students who have symptoms of visual discomfort, even if they are wearing glasses.

A third complication of referral is the strongly motivated student who, regardless of visual strain and discomfort, completes school work and shows no signs of academic deficiency. Again this student, showing symptoms listed in Table 3, should be referred without hesitation before the possibility of consequential harm.

Finally, one must choose to whom the referral should be made. The term *vision specialist* has been used to avoid complication. By vision specialist is meant either an optometrist, an opthalmologist, or an oculist. A competent specialist in any of these fields should be considered satisfactory for referral. Opthalmologists and oculists are medical doctors who have specialized in vision. The optometrist has a doctor's degree in optometry. Each is qualified to prescribe lenses and visual training. In the case of eye disease, an optometrist will refer the patient to the ophthalmologist or oculist. Regardless of the degree held by the vision specialist, educators should make an effort to seek out those who have a special interest in the visual development of students and in the problems of functional vision that relate to reading achievement.

A form, such as Figure 6, will aid the vision specialists to understand the reasons for referral and will provide them with basic educational information.

FIGURE 6
Visual Referral Form

_____(name)_____ was screened visually and did not perform satisfactorily in the following area(s):

_____

_____

His/her present reading level is _____ ,
but his/her reading potential is about _____ .
Will you please inform us if, after your examination, a visual deficiency may have been causing this student some problems in reading.

_____
Signed

The educator's tone when making a referral is especially important. If the educator's tone is authoritative, conflict with visual specialists and parents might occur. It is best to state the referral in terms similar to these; "Since Tom appears to be having serious difficulties in reading and since he has not had his eyes checked recently, we would like you to take him to a specialist for an examination. As we start to work with Tom, it will be best to correct any visual disorder first. If he has none, then we will not need to be concerned about visual discomfort.''

In summary, both the reading specialist and the classroom teacher should consider students who have reading problems as potential visual problems. Therefore, they should use screening devices and observe symptoms to refer possible problem cases. Under no circumstances should the teacher or the reading specialist consider a battery of screening devices, no matter how highly refined, as a substitution for a thorough eye examination and visual analysis. Screening tests, at best, are limited to their designed function: the identification of those in need of visual attention.

Auditory Problems

Obviously, students who cannot hear adequately face problems in school. Many students with auditory limitations are placed in special schools or special classes for the deaf and hard of hearing so that they can receive specialized educational opportunities. Many others with hearing losses, however, remain in the normal school situations. For the most part, school nurses have been able to identify these students early and to refer them to specialists.

Auditory problems affect reading in several ways. In the first place, students with a significant hearing loss are likely to find phonic instruction beyond their grasp because of a distortion of sounds or the inability to hear sounds at all. Most auditory deficiencies concern high frequency sounds; therefore, due to the high frequency of many of the consonant sounds, the most common limitation that a hearing deficiency places upon a reader is in the area of consonant recognition and usage. Students with hearing difficulties are hindered as well by their inability to follow directions since they may not hear them clearly. They are, therefore, likely to lose their places in oral reading activities when listening to others, fail to complete homework assignments, and appear inattentive and careless.

It is important to recognize the difference between the student who is unable to hear a word and the one who is unable to discriminate between sounds. In the first case, the student has a hearing loss which is a physical problem, and, in the latter, the student has an auditory discrimination problem which has educational implications. Auditory discrimination will be discussed under educational diagnosis in Chapter 4.

Ideally, auditory screening should include a test of pitch (frequency) ranging from low to high and one to measure varying loudness (decibels). This screening can be adequately conducted using an audiometer,* an instrument adaptable for either group or individual auditory testing. Although opinions vary concerning a satisfactory audiometer score, it is safe to conclude that a screening score which reports a loss of twenty-five decibels at 500, 1,000, 2,000 and 6,000 frequencies and thirty decibels at 4,000 indicates possible interference with reading instruction and that such a student should be referred.[20]

The Classroom Teacher. Again, it is unlikely that the classroom teacher has the time, experience, or equipment to conduct the type of screening mentioned above. Classroom teachers have been advised that a watchtick test or a whisper test is possible in the classroom. However, classroom teachers do not use these tests, perhaps because they have not had enough supervised experience with them and the possibilities of overreferral are too great. Therefore, the classroom teacher should rely upon a pattern of symptoms which, when occurring in a student who has failed in reading, is justifiable cause for referral. These symptoms are:

Physical Symptoms:

1. Speech difficulties (particularly with consonant sounds)
2. Tilting of the head when being spoken to
3. Cupping of the ear with the hand in order to follow instructions
4. Strained posture
5. Persistent earaches
6. Inflammation or drainage of the ear
7. Reports of persistent buzzing or ringing in the head

Behavioral Symptoms:

1. Inability to profit from phonic instruction
2. Inability to follow directions
3. General inattentiveness
4. Excessive volume needed for comfortable radio and phonograph listening.

Normally, the student is referred to the school nurse for audiometric screening. Then in an effort to encourage as much success as possible in the classroom for a student with a suspected hearing loss, the classroom teacher should move the student's seat so that it is: in the center of a discussion area; close to the teacher; and away from outside distractions, such as radiators, fans, cars, and traffic noises. A teacher must also be willing to repeat assignments for this student to insure that they have been properly understood.

---

[20]Darrell E. Rose et al., *Audiological Assessment* (Englewood Cliffs, N.J.: Prentice-Hall, 1971), p. 150.

Referral outside the school normally would be made to a general practitioner or to an otologist, a medical doctor who specializes in hearing problems. Again, the medical referral is to be made in terms of the observed symptoms of auditory difficulty, with a request for results of the audiometric examination.

The Reading Specialist. Required information may be obtained from a recent report of a medical examination or from a screening conducted through the use of an audiometer. Although the reading specialist may not plan to conduct an audiometric examination with every student, such an examination is called for when the student shows signs of problems in speech and/or phonics instruction. The reading specialist must also attempt to establish the period of time during which the hearing loss first noticeably interfered with school work and then relate this information to the entire case study. For example, students affected by a hearing loss after the primary years, in which oral instruction and basic phonic sounds are presented, had the opportunity to learn their basic skills while they had normal hearing. Although such students may be handicapped, remedial techniques will vary in terms of the type of instruction they received prior to the hearing loss.

Neurological Disorders

Neurological disorders include direct damage to the brain and defective neurological systems resulting in either malfunction or disorganization. There is little evidence that neurological disorders are a major cause of reading problems. Bond and Tinker state, "Evidence indicates that brain damage is a relatively rare cause of reading disability.[21] Nevertheless, some believe that many problem readers show symptoms of abnormal neurological patterns. Robinson named neurological disorders as one of the casual factors in 18 percent of the cases in her classic study.[22] Approximately 8 percent of the students tested in the University of Maryland clinic have enough symptoms of neurological disorders to be referred for neurological examination. It should be noted that our population in the clinic is drawn from students having serious difficulties in school and is by no means a normal population. Initially, the problem for the educator in this complex area is to identify the student who may be neurologically handicapped. However, precise identification ultimately is the job of medical specialists who themselves have some concerns about the accuracy of diagnosis in this area. Let us say simply that most problem readers are adequate enough neurologically to preclude this area as a cause of reading disability; at the same time, let us admit that there remains a small percentage of problem readers who, in fact, do have these symptoms and need medical referral.

---

[21]Bond and Tinker, *Reading Difficulties,* p. 118.
[22]Helen M. Robinson, *Why Pupils Fail in Reading* (Chicago: University of Chicago Press, 1946), p. 218.

The classroom teacher and the reading specialist are likely to find themselves relying heavily upon a pattern of symptoms for initial identification. Because individual symptoms used for neurological referral are, when viewed in isolation, not peculiar to the neurologically disturbed, it becomes necessary to seek a highly reliable pattern. Without this pattern, the educator may interpret educational indifference as neurological disorders. If the identification is made in the initial diagnosis, it is necessary to have a pattern of several symptoms (three to four) to properly refer a student for neurological examination. However, if a student fails to respond after the best diagnosis and remedial instruction, one or more of these symptoms or any history of the following causes of neurological disorders should be considered when deliberating a neurological referral. These causes include:

1. Difficulties at birth—birth complicated by prematurity, use of instruments, or by anoxia or hypoxia
2. Head injuries—blows or accidents in which the head is severely bruised
3. Diseases—those resulting in inflammation and/or pressure in the area of the brain (i.e., rheumatic fever, encephalitis, continuously high temperature, and the like)

Symptoms for neurological problems fall into two categories—physical and educational. Physical symptoms include:

1. Physical incoordination—grossly awkward walking, running, writing, etc., in relation to overall physical development
2. Overactivity—inability to concentrate which causes the child to complete his assignments rarely, to annoy others, and to appear disinterested
3. Headaches—history of persistent headaches
4. Speech impediments—persistent blockage of speech or articulation difficulties which are peculiar for his age level
5. Visual incoordination—saccadic eye movements, inability of the eyes to focus or to visually hold a line of print

Educational symptoms of neurological problems include:

1. Average or better than average intelligence—general educational development deficient in terms of valid measures of intelligence
2. Phonic blending deficiency—knowledge of sounds but inability to blend them into words
3. Poor contextual reader—knowledge of the sight vocabulary but inability to use known words in sentences
4. Slow reading speed—poor reading rate, even with easy, familiar material

5. Poor auditory discrimination—inability to discriminate between sounds of letters, without evidence of a hearing acuity deficiency

6. Distractability—inattentiveness to designated tasks

7. Abnormal behavior—overreaction to stimuli (i.e., laughing long after others have ceased)

8. Poor ability to remember sequences—although apparently normally intelligent, difficulty in remembering sequences, verbal and nonverbal

Obviously, these symptoms in isolation do not necessarily indicate neurological disorder. It is imperative to gather a pattern of symptoms which includes four or more of the above. Students with this number of symptoms, whether identified in classroom or in clinical diagnosis, should be considered legitimate referrals for neurological examinations. It does not follow, however, that a strong pattern of symptoms leads the educator to a neurological diagnosis, just to a referral.

Clements summarizes the ten most frequently cited characteristics of minimal brain dysfunction from over 100 publications:[23]

1. Hyperactivity

2. Perceptual-motor impairments

3. Emotional lability

4. General coordination defects

5. Disorders of attentions

6. Impulsivity

7. Disorders of memory and thinking

8. Specific learning disabilities in reading, arithmetic, writing, spelling

9. Disorders of speech and hearing

10. Equivocal neurological signs and electroencephalographic irregularities

Many educators seem reluctant to make neurological referrals, for they are overly concerned about either the psychological effects of such a referral or the great possibility of overreferral. An understanding of the procedure generally followed in a neurological examination may reduce the educator's hesitancy to refer. Neurological referral normally will include an office appointment during which a detailed neurological examination and case history will be obtained. If, at that time, the medical specialist finds symptoms of abnormal tendencies, another appointment will be made for a more involved

[23]Sam D. Clements, Minimal Brain Dysfunction in Children, (Washington, D.C.: U.S. Department of Health, Education, and Welfare, 1966), p. 13.

neurological examination, often requiring hospitalization. For those interested, Clements discusses diagnostic evaluation in more detail.[24]

Since educators are professionals justified in the use of patterns of symptoms, they should not be reluctant to refer. If, in fact, they should overrefer, they should be relieved to find that the student's problem is *not* neurological in nature, and they can proceed with an educational diagnosis.

The reading specialist, upon receipt of the neurological report, relates the findings to other information gathered for the case study. Again the relationship of neurological problems to the entire case history must be considered in the recommendations for educational adjustment.

The classroom teacher, while waiting for the neurological report, should relieve the student from unnecessary frustration by relaxing tension and providing reading experiences in the area of the student's strengths. If the report indicates that the student does not have a neurological problem, the teacher will continue with a classroom diagnosis in an effort to find the area where correction should start. However, if the report does reveal a neurological problem, the classroom teacher should refer the student to a reading specialist who will conduct a careful case evaluation, noting all educational aspects and precise recommendations concerning remedial techniques.

Medical personnel should be encouraged to write reports so that educators can understand them. A neurological report stating the findings in technical terms is difficult to interpret and of little value to most educators. Reports written for educators, however, are of value. For example, a recent report stated in relatively simple terms that the student had a receptive problem in the tactile areas, although auditory and visual receptive areas were normal. Such a report leads to effective educational adjustment, which, in this case would not include the tracing or VAKT technique (to be discussed in Chapters 7 and 8).

The final analysis of all physical difficulties is the responsibility of medical personnel; however, since physical problems frequently interfere with reading efficiency, the educator often identifies a physical problem first. The educator is obligated to refer to the medical specialist and, while awaiting that diagnosis, to make practical classroom adjustments. The educator then considers medical recommendations carefully in terms of the student's total diagnosis.

EMOTIONAL DIAGNOSIS

Emotional difficulties, when considered as causes of reading problems, create cause-and-effect confusion. Sometimes emotional disturbances cause reading

---

[24]Clements, Minimal Brain Dysfunction, pp. 14-15.

problems; however, many emotional problems are not the cause but the result of a failure in reading. Unfortunately, there is often no clear line of distinction. When emotional disturbances cause reading problems, performance in all learning areas suffer. Often, it is in the diagnosis of a problem reader that this area of difficulty is first uncovered; however, assessing the severity of that difficulty is properly the task of psychological personnel. Conversely, although emotional reactions may complicate a reading problem, they are often not the cause but rather an effect of the reading failure itself. Most students referred to as problem readers exhibit some symptoms of emotional conflict, and these symptoms often diminish or disappear with effective instruction after the diagnosis. In summarizing the research, Bond and Tinker conclude, "Examination of all the evidence, however, does make it pretty clear that the emotional maladjustment is much more frequently the effect than the cause of reading disability."[25] An effective diagnosis may result in relieving the student of some home and school pressures by exposing the fact that the student's difficulty is not due to a poor attitude or a low level of intellectual potential, but rather to a skill deficiency which, when corrected, will permit the student to perform as expected. When these diagnostic conclusions are explained satisfactorily to cooperative parents, a more favorable learning atmosphere can be established.

The classroom teacher and the reading specialist must be aware that most students with reading problems react emotionally to their failure through such behavior patterns as refusing to read, not enjoying school, disliking their teachers, or causing problems at home. Furthermore, emotional reactions to specific situations may be opposite within a given student at a given moment, and they may be opposite between two disturbed students. For example, when frustrated, an emotionally disturbed student may withdraw and be quiet or lash out in defiance. In comparing emotional diagnosis to intellectual diagnosis, Carroll states: "Personality traits are more complex and less consistent than intelligence and so more difficult to measure objectively."[26] The more thorough an understanding the teacher has of the intrafamilial, peer, and school relationships, the more likelihood of an effective diagnosis. The examiner must anticipate certain types of emotional reactions, note them, include them in the diagnosis, and consider them in the recommendations; however, it is with caution that these reactions should be labeled as causative, for their presence does not necessarily make the student a candidate for referral.

Realistically recognizing their limitations as detectors of emotional difficulties and at the same time recognizing the emotional entanglement of these

---

[25]Bond and Tinker, *Reading Difficulties*, p. 129.
[26]Herbert A. Carroll, *Mental Hygiene* (New York: Prentice-Hall, 1947), p. 246.

types of students, the reading specialist and the classroom teacher follow similar diagnostic procedures. Through the cooperation of all the educators in contact with the student, information may be gleaned concerning the student, the home, the school situation, and the student's reactions in peer group situations.

Information Concerning the Student

Due to their daily contact with the student, the classroom teachers are in a unique position to obtain valuable information about the student's reactions to many situations. The reading specialist is obligated to rely upon the information supplied by the teacher and parents or to obtain it from a personal interview. Desirable information should include:

1. The student's attitude toward family, school, teacher, and friends
2. The student's awareness of the problem and the student's suggestions for its solution
3. The student's attitude and reaction to reading
4. The student's development of worthwhile personal goals

Gathered informally by the classroom teacher or formally by the reading specialist, all information in questionable areas must be checked for reliability. One can do this easily by comparing reliable sources. A student may have said that he makes B's and C's in school. The educator will rely more readily on the student's other statements about school if, when checking the school records, she finds that the student does indeed make B's and C's.

Personality testing of a formal nature is available. *The California Test of Personality,* * one of the more popular instruments for classroom use, provides standardized evaluations of the student's reactions to questions concerning personal and social adjustment. This test may be administered individually or in classroom-sized groups. Since adequate performance requires the student to possess reading skills close to the grade level of the test, the seriously retarded reader will be unable to read the questions. In evaluating the *The California Test of Personality,* one is cautioned against the tendency to place undue emphasis on any low set of scores; however, such scores may be considered indicative of areas of potential personality problems. Scores indicating the necessity for referral are described in the test manual. Final verification will not come from this type of testing, but rather from teacher observation and referral to psychological personnel.

Personality testing through the use of incomplete sentences is an informal way of obtaining valuable information. The student is expected to respond to several incomplete sentences, some examples of which might be the follow-

ing: "I like books, but . . . ." "My home is . . . ." "I like my brother and
. . . ." Strang provides an example of responses in informal inventories
including some advice on the techniques of interpretation.[27] The most reliable
use of this type of information is to note patterns of responses and to verify
them by direct observation of the student in situations where these responses
may be reflected in the student's behavior. Again, the examiner is cautioned
against excessive analysis of any slightly deviate responses and urged to leave
for psychological personnel final assessment of the emotional stability.

Personality tests of the paper-and-pencil variety are considered inherently
weak since students often anticipate what they consider to be acceptable
responses. These tests tend to record "of-the-moment" responses. Those who
have had bad days may score poorly on such tests; however, twenty-four hours
later, they may score many points higher. When this occurs, it is obvious that
the scores obtained, besides not validly indicating personality traits, have
severely limited use in diagnosing emotional problems.

A technique for noting personality characteristics in a more natural
situation is to observe the students at play. An investigation of play behavior
may be based on the following type of questions: Do they play with others their
own age? Does it appear that they are accepted by their peers? Do they play
fairly? Do they play enthusiastically? Answers to such questions provide
further analysis of the total behavior pattern without the limitations of paper-
and-pencil tests. Shafer and Shoben feel that the analysis of free play has
definite advantages in emotional diagnosis. "Many diagnostic suggestions
may be drawn from watching a child in free play. . . . The communications of
very young children tend to be symbolized only in the activities of play. . . ."[28]
Forest also feels that such observation of play is desirable. "Emotional release
through play activities due to a sense of competency and mastery may be
observed in normal groups of children."[29] Note that both of these authorities
suggest that play analysis has particular value with younger children.

A Study of the Home

Although the home usually is not visited as a result of a reading diagnosis,
under certain circumstances, such a visit is profitable. When it appears that
situations at home are impeding the student's language and/or emotional
development, the educator who hopes to improve these conditions must make
a home visit. In cases where a home visit would be of little value, one may
gather information concerning home conditions through parental interviews or

---

[27]Strang, *Diagnostic Teaching of Reading,* pp. 262-63.
[28]Laurance F. Shafer and Edward J. Shoben, Jr., *The Psychology of Adjustment,* 2d ed.
(Boston: Houghton Mifflin Co., 1956), p. 508.
[29]Isle Forest, *Child Development* (New York: McGraw-Hill Book Co., 1954), p. 64.

questionnaires. These are constructed to obtain the following types of information: socioeconomic status of the home, availability of books, intrafamilial relations, parental efforts to assist the child, general family activities, and overall acceptance of the child in the home.

Abnormal home conditions should be brought to the attention of appropriate personnel (school officials, home-school visitors, social workers, and psychologists). Neither the classroom teacher nor the reading specialist is justified in offering unsolicited advice to parents about home conditions unrelated to the student's educational progress. There are times when parents will turn to an educator and ask for consultation. Although it depends upon the individual situation, it is my opinion that an educator is normally acting out of the proper professional role in offering advice in such cases. Offering advice concerning domestic affairs implies that one has training or information about "best" solutions.

The educator will want to contact the social worker when home problems appear to be a basic source of difficulty for the student. These professional persons are skilled in working with parents and investigating home situations. Many schools have found it worthwhile to have social workers on their professional staffs.

A Study of the School

The classroom teacher gathers relevant data for a classroom diagnosis and submits it to the reading specialist for case analysis. From the school it is necessary to obtain information relating to attendance, behavior, ability to work and play with others, and reactions to various types of failure. School records do not always contain this type of information, although teachers are often encouraged to write comments concerning outstanding characteristics of students. When such notations are available, they should be included in the diagnosis; when not accessible, the information should be gathered through interviews or questionnaire responses from the teacher.

While students are reading, teachers should note peculiar reactions which reflect anxiety, frustration, and emotional disturbance. Roebuck found that the emotionally disturbed tend to read orally with tense voices, to react more definitely to the material being read, and to read compulsively.[30] In compulsive reading, the students never stop or hesitate; rather, they read on whether they know the words or not, skipping and/or mispronouncing unknown words. Other noticeable symptoms are refusal to read aloud, profuse sweating of the hands during oral reading, and unusual book selections for free reading.

---

[30]Mildred Roebuck, "The Oral Reading Characteristics of Emotionally Disturbed Children," *International Reading Association Proceedings* 7 (1962): 133-38.

If the educator is to be effective in obtaining such information, students and parents must be assured that it will be handled confidentially and will not find its way into the hands of irresponsible people. A cooperative attitude on the part of both parents and educators is necessary for reliable data collection.

One justifiable reason for an educator to consider emotional difficulties, other than for possible referral, is to discourage improper labeling. It is easy to decide that problem readers are lazy, troublesome, or delinquent before considering their emotional difficulties. These symptoms are displayed quite often by students with emotional problems; the unwarranted label complicates the difficulty of accurate diagnosis and remediation.

After psychological referral has been made, the classroom teacher adjusts instruction to avoid further complicating potential emotional difficulties while awaiting referral recommendations. Adjustments include avoiding placement of the student in failing situations which cause unnecessary embarrassment, avoiding implications that the student is lazy or stupid, and providing a sensible program of discipline by which the student can gain a degree of composure and self-reliance. Carroll points out some of the difficulties involved with discipline for students with these symptoms:

> The causes of misconduct insofar as classroom conditions are concerned are not hard to identify. Every child needs to succeed. If the academic tasks set for him are too difficult, he feels frustrated. Frustration is uncomfortable, and he feels driven to do something about it. . . . Denied the opportunity to satisfy his need for scholastic achievement, he strikes out against environment.[31]

He also says that they must have their successes recognized by the group and by the teacher, whether the successes are large or small. Furthermore, he states, "She (the teacher) will be more lavish with praise than criticism. She will help every child to maintain his self-respect."[32] In discussing the control of the group when this student is disruptive, Carroll points out that the teacher will have to take disciplinary measures but adds, "She should never use fear as a technique of control."[33]

The classroom teacher must consider this student to be one who needs and deserves special considerations; negative reactions can only drive the student to further reject the learning processes and the environment. At the same time, the teacher has an obligation to the other students in the room to provide an environment conducive to learning. When the student with symptoms of emotional problems disrupts this environment to the detriment of the entire group, the teacher must meet the needs of the group.

---

[31]Carroll, *Mental Hygiene*, p. 210.
[32]Carroll, *Mental Hygiene*, p. 210.
[33]Carroll, *Mental Hygiene*, p. 211.

Prevention of complex emotional disorders is also in the hands of class-room teachers. Their reactions, for example, to the initial signs of frustration and failure within a given student may cause the student's acceptance of their temporary situation or a reaction against it. Although students must be challenged in school, not all will meet these challenges with the same degree of success. Teachers may relax tensions and feelings of failure by their attitudes toward the efforts of the less successful. All students must succeed in school. The successes of all, but particularly the less successful, should be high-lighted. Beware, however, of false praise—everyone resents it. Instead of false praise, one should structure situations in which, with a little effort, a student can legitimately succeed and be praised. More of these types of techniques are discussed under remediation in Chapters 6 and 10.

All information and notations concerning the student's emotional be-havior should be included and evaluated in the case analysis. The reading specialist should apply the recommendations for the necessary educational adjustment. If the classroom teacher, after the institution of these recommen-dations, finds further complications, the student should be referred to the reading specialist.

A note of caution concerning emotional referral may be helpful. Teachers are prone to interpret obscure symptoms as signs of emotional problems within students that are suspect, for example: if they are only children, if they do not talk much, if parents are divorced, or if a parent is under psychiatric care. While such observations should be noted, they do not constitute a legitimate referral; the student's behavior must call for it. Nor should emotional diagnosis be made on the basis of test performance alone. Abnormal scores *do not* call for psychological evaluation unless observed performance confirms the test score. Referring on too little evidence clogs the referral system with those who are not in need. Many times this causes parents needless anguish and expense.

SUMMARY

As we understand the educators' role in these complex areas of diagnosis we see that they must be aware, informed, and skilled in making observations of various types of behavior. Generally, they attempt to make immediate adjust-ments of the learning environment and refer the students to appropriate specialists. Team effort which brings all of the resources of the school to assist those students who are experiencing difficulty is the recommended procedure.

SUGGESTED READINGS

Cleland, Donald L. "Clinical Materials for Appraising Disabilities In Reading." *The Reading Teacher* 17 (March 1964): 428. This interesting, easy-to-read article presents summaries of the various appraisal materials available for clinical diagnosis. Of particular interest is the discussion of reading capacity and appropriate techniques for determining it.

Clements, Sam D. *Minimal Brain Dysfunction in Children.* Washington, D.C.: U.S. Department of Health, Education, and Welfare, 1966. In fifteen pages, Clements summarizes terminology to clarify several issues and to offer a blue print for action on minimal brain dysfunction. The information contained in this monograph will be useful to those who have not read widely in this area.

Harris, Albert J. *How To increase Reading Ability.* New York: David McKay, 1970, pp. 216-21. Harris discusses several techniques for the use of mental age in determining reading expectancy scores. For a review of alternate methods, the reader is encouraged to refer to these pages.

Kelley, Charles R. *Visual Screening and Child Development.* The North Carolina Study. Raleigh, N.C.: North Carolina State College, 1957. This book reports a little-known, but carefully organized study concerning the scope and sequence of vision and scholastic effectiveness. The reader who is interested in a more detailed study will find it worthwhile.

Money, John. *The Disabled Reader.* Baltimore, Md.: The Johns Hopkins Press, 1966. A book of readings collected by Money under the topic of dyslexia. Attention provided to medical and psychological opinion as well as to educational opinion. Essential reading for those working with the seriously handicapped.

Reeds, James C.; Rabe, Edward F.; and Maniken, Margaret. "Teaching Reading to Brain-Injured Children." *Reading Research Quarterly,* Summer 1970, p. 379. An excellent review for those interested in brain-injured children. Claiming a lack of evidence for specific program adjustments for brain-damaged children, the authors review several of the most high respected sources.

Robinson, Helen M. *Why Pupils Fail in Reading.* Chicago: University of Chicago Press, 1946. Robinson presents a discussion of the multiple causation theory in terms of the most prominent authorities and also in terms of her research in this area. Of particular importance are the conclusions which she reaches through her technique to determine causation.

Strauss, Alfred A., and Lehtinen, Laura E. *Psychopathology and Education of the Brain-Injured Child.* New York: Grane & Stratton, 1947. This book provides the rationale for the syndromes of distractability and perseveration. It is a basic book for those who are interested in more thoroughly understanding the aspects of minimal brain injury. Explanations are given in terms designed for educators.

Stuart, Marion. *Neurophysiological Insights Into Teaching.* New York: Pacific Books, 1963. This book provides relatively elementary explanations of diagnosis and treatment of readers with neurological limitations.

4

Classroom Diagnosis

An analysis of the student's reading skills, attitudes, and interests is the major function of educational diagnosis. Educational diagnosis rests basically with the classroom teacher and the reading specialist.

A classroom teacher, who has a relatively long acquaintance with a student, relies heavily upon observation and informal testing procedures for educational diagnosis. A reading specialist, who is permitted only short-term pupil acquaintance, finds a more formal testing and evaluation program effective. Before careful examination of the two approaches to educational diagnosis, one should consider briefly the causes of problems in this area. Educational difficulties can be said to cause a reading problem when the problem can be corrected or prevented from recurring by the adjustment of the learning climate. However, educational adjustment alone might not correct a problem which has been ignored for a long period of time and to which there is a severe emotional reaction.

EDUCATIONAL CAUSES

Educational causes can be grouped into the following seven categories: lock-stepping, outside pressure, instructional techniques, reading methods, absence, classroom size, and materials for instruction.

65

Lockstepping

Perhaps the most serious educational problem is the system of lockstepping students through school. This refers to such practices as having all students in a group read the same book at the same time, having all in a group learn the same skills at the same time, and labeling those who do not learn in the specified time as failures. An example of this is labeling students who have not finished book one by the end of first grade as *failures*.

Fortunately, lockstepping is decreasing. Many school systems and thousands of teachers now recognize that students need to be involved in decisions involving pacing of material for learning to take place. Emphasis on mastery of material is replacing "covering" the book in a year. However, the problem continues to exist, and many students are falling farther and farther behind within a group which is moving on.

Pressure from Outside

Teachers are increasingly feeling pressure from sources outside of the classroom. Accountability legislation, test scores published in newspapers, teaching objectives formulated at state and central office levels, and increased interest and awareness by parents are examples of pressures being felt by teachers. While some manage to tolerate these pressures, others react negatively. It is not uncommon, following the publication of reading test scores in newspapers, for curricula to be revised, textbooks to be changed, and teachers to be reassigned; or perhaps for additional emphasis to be placed on phonics and spelling. While none of these changes are inherently bad for students, each of them can be. Educational decisions made without teacher involvement can lead to poor quality instruction.

Instructional Techniques

In the primary grades, a child normally has one teacher each year. If that teacher is incompetent, indifferent, poorly educated, or insensitive toward students, one year of exposure can do serious harm. While most students survive a year of poor teaching without permanently harmful results, others fall far enough behind in their reading skills to be considered problem readers. The solution to the reading problems caused by this type of teacher is twofold: first, the handicapped student must receive the appropriate instruction at a later date; second, incompetent teachers must be helped to improve their instructional techniques. The former solution relates to a student's next teacher; the latter becomes the problem of the reading specialist in cooperation with the school administration. Many consider poor instruction the major cause of reading problems. With this assessment, I must agree but hasten to add that other interferences usually complicate the problem.

Reading Methods

While instruction focuses on what the teacher does regardless of the method, method focuses upon the basic approaches and materials used to teach reading. While students need varied instruction due to unique learning styles, it is not uncommon to find all students in a given class assigned to the same teaching method and the same materials. If, for example, the methods and materials stress a sight-word approach and the student is a strong auditory learner, then the method is working against the strengths of this student. Early identification of the learning style strengths of students is important if methods are to be adjusted to those strengths.

Absence

When students experience long periods of continuous absence, the sequential development of their skills may suffer. Yet they may be pushed along to more advanced skills without the background upon which to develop them successfully. It is often difficult for a teacher to provide the instruction necessary to counterbalance excessive absence. Therefore, reading disability can occur if students are not taught the skills they have missed. Unless their programs are modified, they may fail in future assignments. Teachers are finding many useful techniques for overcoming the problem of excessive absence which include: using peer instruction, teacher aides, volunteer parents, telephone instruction, and programmed instruction. As teachers consider the many means available to assist students whose absences are excessive, the problem will lessen.

Classroom Size

In overcrowded classrooms, a teacher may have difficulty following the sequential development of each student's reading skills. Here some may falter, undetected, until they fall too far behind to catch up without special instruction. Although particularly damaging in the primary grades where the development of reading skills follows a closer sequence than in the later elementary years, the failure to provide basic skill development may cause difficulty during any period of the student's schooling.

To alleviate overcrowded classrooms, some schools have hired teacher assistants. By assuming many of the less important routine tasks, the assistant frees the teacher to provide the needed instruction. As in the case of excessive absence, the use of peer instruction, volunteer parents, and special programs can assist students in overcrowded classrooms. Individualization of instruction through diagnostic teaching and the use of learning centers permits the teacher to work with small groups or individual students even in large classrooms. Pairing is also useful (that is, students work cooperatively with each other on a given assignment). Such pairing can be changed frequently and eliminated whenever desirable; but through its use learning becomes more effective, and problems can be identified more quickly. Teachers in over-crowded classrooms will find it necessary to alternate between group instruction and individualized instruction and between large and small group work.[1]

Materials for Instruction

Economy-minded school administrators frequently fail to provide adequate materials to enable the classroom teacher to adjust instruction. Therefore, unless a teacher can devise materials and techniques to instruct students with minor skill deficiencies, the possibility of their becoming problem readers increases. With adequate materials and knowledge of their use, most teachers can prevent serious skill deficiencies.

Many larger school districts have established curriculum libraries in which a wide variety of materials is available for individual teachers and teacher committees to examine and consider. In this manner, it is possible to maintain reasonable economy and, at the same time, to permit careful analysis and wise selection of materials. Other schools have designated small groups of teachers as "materials selection committees" for the various areas. They are the persons to contact concerning the value of particular materials. Teachers also are sharing the instructional techniques they use with new materials. For example, if a given material has been selected for use, three teachers might try it. Each of the three would observe the other, refine their procedures, and then present their collective ideas to the staff.

TYPES OF CLASSROOM DIAGNOSIS

Classroom diagnosis can take place either before, during, or after instruction as discussed in Chapter 2 (Q–S–R). While all three times can result in effective diagnosis, each uses different techniques, and each had advantages and limitations.

Diagnosis before Instruction

Many teachers attempt to determine the strengths and weaknesses of their students by testing them prior to instruction. These teachers use the test results for planning future instruction and for grouping. Five types of testing instruments are available for classroom diagnosis: standardized tests, prepared informal inventories, teacher-made informal inventories, cloze tests, and criterion-referenced tests.

[1]Robert M. Wilson and Jerilyn K. Ribovich, "Ability Grouping? Stop and Reconsider!" *Reading World* 13 (December 1973): 84-91.

The selection of the testing instrument must be in terms of the information needed for the diagnosis. Some instruments are designed to measure the progress of groups of students. Others are designed to provide information on individual students. Some help teachers obtain information concerning the reading levels of students. Others provide information on skill development. By first determining what type of information is needed, teachers can make intelligent choices of instruments. The following descriptions provide an overview of the various types of instruments available for classroom diagnosis.

Standardized Tests. Most schools test regularly with one of the major standardized tests *(Iowa Test of Basic Skills, California Reading Test, Stanford Reading Test, Metropolitan Reading Test,* or the *Gates MacGinitie Reading Test).* Each of these tests is in common use, and many teachers have the scores available to them. The tests usually yield total reading, vocabulary, and comprehension scores. Students usually take these tests in class-size groups, and their performance is to be completed within reasonable time limits; most of these tests can be administered within a half-hour to an hour. Some of the tests have subscores relating to various types of reading vocabulary and comprehension skills. Standardized test scores are norm based, i.e., the scores obtained are compared to the score distribution obtained from the population upon which the test was normed. This procedure necessitates that approximately equal numbers of students will score above and below the test's normed mean.

Standardized test scores are nearly useless for classroom diagnosis.[2] The tests' limitations have been discussed by many authorities in reading. First, that they are administered to groups necessitates multiple-choice answers and encourages guessing. Second, the standardizing procedures are subject to error, a fact which causes considerable concern about their reliability. Third, their ability to match the student with a given reading level is constantly under question. Finally, the use of subtests has been discouraged due to the extreme lack of reliability of these measures.

However, since schools administer tests to determine how well students are doing generally, two diagnostic uses of standardized test scores are recommended.

1. While the earned scores do not reflect accurate reading grade levels, extremely low scores usually indicate reading difficulty. Therefore, prior to instruction, teachers can gain an idea of which students might experience difficulties; they might identify those students most in need of informal

---

²Roger Farr, *Reading: What Can Be Measured?* (Newark, Del.: IRA, 1969), pp. 97, 212-18.

diagnosis. If the scores, in Table 4, were obtained at the beginning of fourth grade, Jack and Portia logically would be selected as those most in need of informal diagnosis due to their extremely low performance.

TABLE 4

Example:	Student	Word Meaning	Paragraph Meaning
	Jack	1.3	2.1
	Portia	2.4	2.4
	Larry	3.4	3.5
	Marcia	2.7	3.7
	Cheryl	3.5	3.8
	Judy	3.6	3.7
	Pat	3.7	3.9
	Don	4.1	4.0
	Robin	4.2	3.9
	Dolores	4.1	4.1

2. While subtest scores do not meet reliability standards, extreme differences in subtest scores can serve as indicators of "possible" skill difficulties. For example, in Table 4, Jack and Marcia exhibit extreme differences between word meaning and paragraph meaning scores. The teacher should not accept these scores at face value. Instead, the scores should suggest that something *might* be wrong. The teacher should continue the diagnosis, usually through the use of informal techniques.

These two uses of standardized test scores are suggested only if scores are available. Tests should not be administered solely for the purpose of obtaining such scores, however, since they are more reliably obtained from other sources.

Prepared Informal Inventories. Several publishing companies and many school districts have prepared informal testing instruments which are useful for classroom diagnosis. Informal inventories are usually developed by teachers from the actual materials the students will be expected to use during instruction. Inventories already prepared for teachers generally use a sampling technique, i.e., words are selected from a sampling of commonly used reading materials. Other inventories include paragraphs for oral and silent reading. Teachers using these instruments can obtain measures of the student's oral reading accuracy and silent reading comprehension as well as skill development. The paragraphs are usually evaluated through the use of readability formulas or taken from materials that have been graded previously.

One informal instrument is the *Botel Reading Inventory*. Three sections of this inventory are useful for reading diagnosis: word recognition—the student reads graded lists of twenty words aloud to the teacher, word opposites (reading)—the student identifies antonyms from graded lists of ten words, and phonics—the student identifies graphemes as the teacher pronounces words. Both the word opposites and the phonics sections are group tests. The two group measures can be administered in about thirty minutes. Using prepared informal inventories can result in a teacher's obtaining results which assist in the identification of students' skill strengths and weaknesses and which yield estimates of reading levels.

TABLE 5
Botel Reading Inventory

Student	Word Recognition	Word Opposites	Phonics*% Correct		
			Consonants	Blends	Vowels
Betty	2-1	2-2	90	80	80
Jim	2-1	2-2	50	40	20
Janet	2-1	2-2	75	60	40
Les	2-2	2-2	80	60	70
Mae	3-1	2-2	90	80	50
Linda	3-1	3-1	90	90	70
Joe	3-1	3-1	100	100	90
Jane	3-2	4-1	90	60	90
Joan	3-2	4-1	60	50	40
Bill	4-1	4-1	90	90	80

*The Botel phonics section has many more categories.

Results, such as those in Table 5, can be useful in matching students to books and in making decisions about skills which they have or need. The word recognition column indicates how well students can decode certain levels of words. The word opposites column reveals how well the students can get at word meanings. The phonics columns show how well they have mastered the various phonics skills. Although in columns one and two, Betty and Jim appear to be operating on the same levels, their phonic skills development is entirely different. And, while Joan appears to be reading better than most of the others, her phonic skills are deficient.

The usefulness of the data from the *Botel Reading Inventory* is obviously greater than the data on Table 4, because it relates more closely to instruction. When teachers add data concerning oral reading and comprehension, it can be even more useful.

Early in the school year teachers can administer these types of inventories to help make instructional adjustments. Group type tests can be administered first to survey students' strengths and needs. Oral reading testing is, of course, done individually. Using the score from the group test, teachers can obtain supplemental data by asking students to read aloud from material at those levels. Silent reading comprehension can also be tested from materials available for instruction.

Teacher-made Informal Reading Inventories (IRI). Obviously, teachers can develop informal tests having the same features as those prepared commercially. Using the material from which they intend to teach the students, teachers can assess children's abilities to recognize words, to read orally, and to read silently for comprehension. Many school systems develop IRIs for use by their teachers. The construction of such instruments can be time-consuming and requires considerable knowledge of both the reading process and test construction. Interpretation can be even more difficult. Powell raises serious questions concerning traditional norms used on informal inventories.[3] Others also have found the subject of norms for informal inventories rather perplexing.[4] Betts is acknowledged as creator of the IRI as a functional measurement instrument.[5] Since then, Powell has conducted numerous studies attempting to establish criteria that teachers can utilize when interpreting informal inventories.[6] He cites differences in criteria depending upon whether or not the student has read silently before reading orally. Since silent reading is recommended before oral reading it seems logical that an informal inventory should be administered in that manner. He also found that the criteria of oral reading accuracy changed as the difficulty of the material changed. His findings are presented in Table 6:

TABLE 6

Word Recognition Accuracy in Oral Reading after Silent Reading

	PP-2	3-5	6+
Independent	1/17 (94%)	1/27 (96%)	1/36 (97%)
Instructional	1/12–1/16	1/20–1/26	1/25–1/36
Frustration	1/11 (90%)	1/19 (95%)	1/26 (96%)

[3]William R. Powell, "The Validity of the Instructional Reading Level," *Diagnostic Viewpoints in Reading,* 1971, pp. 121-33.

[4]William K. Durr, ed., *Reading Difficulties* (Newark, Del.: IRA, 1970), pp. 67-132.

[5]Emmett A. Betts, *Foundations of Reading Instruction* (New York: American Book Co., 1946).

[6]William R. Powell, "Revised Criteria for the Informal Reading Inventory," speech presented at International Reading Association, May 3, 1974, New Orleans, La.

A student reading a second-grade book would be considered reading at an independent level when making one word recognition error per seventeen running words. A student reading from a fourth-grade book would be considered reading at the frustration level when making one or more word recognition errors for every nineteen running words. Powell checked this criteria against a dependent criteria that the student should be able to score 70 percent on a test of comprehension at each level cited above. Test results can be used in much the same manner as that suggested for commercially prepared informal inventories. A major advantage of teacher-made inventories centers around the convenience of having to make the test cover a wider range of reading materials than do many commercially prepared tests. The larger sampling tends to produce more reliable results. However, two serious problems occur with their construction: Can the teacher select materials and ask questions which are accurate measures of the student's development, and are the materials accurately graded?

The answer to the first question is yes. With some training, teachers can select materials and ask questions which are accurate measures of the student's development. Also, they are more capable of interpreting the results when they have developed the instrument. However, without training and without a thorough knowledge of the skills of reading, many sloppy, inaccurate, relatively useless instruments have been developed.

The answer to the second question is probably not. Publishers tend to pay little attention to the readability level of materials even if they place grade level numbers on the books.[7] Even then the readability level is generally an average of the readability levels of the individual pages. Through readability checks on several basals, teachers become aware that any "fifth grade" basal can range in readability from third- to seventh-grade level. If the teacher uses these materials for an informal inventory and happens to select pages that are at the extremes of the ranges (third- and seventh-grade levels in the above example), the assessment of a student's reading ability will be inaccurate.

The *Autobiography of Malcolm X* was rated as having a readability level of fifth grade, eighth grade, and tenth grade.[8] In this study, the examiner used three different readability formulas. The question raised is, What factors are considered when one discusses "readability level"?

A problem exists with matching performance prior to instruction with any given material. In fact, mismatching probably occurs all too frequently. That a student's reading ability tends to change with the material's content contributes to the mismatching. Books tend to be inaccurately marked, particularly

---

[7]Robert E. Mills and Jean R. Richardson, "What Do Publishers Mean By Grade Level?" *Reading Teacher,* March 1963, pp. 359-62.

[8]Mae C. Johnson, "Comparison of Readability Formulas" (Ph.D. diss., University of Maryland Reading Center, 1971).

in the content areas. Informal inventories, even when considering their limitations, provide more useful information than do standardized tests. With teacher-made inventories, mismatching is held to a minimum since the student is being tested from samples of the same material in which instruction will take place.

Cloze Tests. One approach, closure testing, may help circumvent the problem of mismatching and labeling. Closure tests constructed from the types of materials students are expected to use can provide relatively useful information concerning the students' abilities to work with various types of printed materials. The procedures for closure testing are as follows:

1. Select several passages of at least 100 words from the various books to be used.
2. Retype the selection, deleting every fifth word.
   Mary had a little _____. Its fleece was white _____ snow.
   Everywhere that Mary _____ the lamb was sure _____ go.
3. Have the student read the selection, supplying the printed word. Older students can write the words in; younger students can read the passage to you.
4. Determine a score by counting as correct responses the number of words actually used by the author.

A score of 40 percent or better indicates that the book should be one that the reader can handle.[9] A score below that level indicates that the book is probably too difficult. The student will need more help reading it or should be permitted to use easier material. The use of closure eliminates the necessity of matching a grade-level score with a book, for the test derives from the various types of material which the student will be expected to read. Closure tests are easily constructed, scored, and interpreted. While they are not without flaw, they may be the most useful type of testing instrument for use prior to instruction that is available to the classroom teacher. A word of caution is necessary. Considerable research is being conducted with closure testing materials. Adjusted norms will be reported indicating possible differences from the 40 percent criterion mentioned above. As one works with students of different ages and materials from different content areas, adjusted norms can be expected. The reader should watch for reports of such changes for the most useful application of closure in reading diagnosis.

Criterion-referenced Tests (CRT). "CRTs are designed to measure specified behaviors performed by an individual toward mastery of a specific skill."[10]

---

[9]Earl F. Rankin and Joseph W. Culhane, "Comparable Cloze and Multiple Choice Comprehension Test Scores," *Journal of Reading,* December 1969, p. 194.

[10]William H. Rupley, "Criterion Referenced Tests," *The Reading Teacher* 28 (1975): 426.

Unlike standardized norm-referenced tests which compare students with one another, CRTs get at how much of a specific skill a student can demonstrate. The effectiveness of CRTs for use in reading diagnosis is limited to whether or not the objective of the test is important and whether or not the test can measure the objective.

Numerous CRTs are finding their way into classrooms. Some CRTs are reported to measure hundreds of objectives with a few test items per objective. The tests are often justified as a management system for teachers; however, unless used with cautious interpretation, they can lead to mismanagement, calling for the teaching of unimportant subskills and locking all students into the identical path to reading. It is up to the teacher to utilize only those parts of such tests that relate to what they think is important. In the area of phonics subskills, in particular, this is true.

How well a test, any test, measures an objective is important. In CRTs the testing objective and the teaching objective are the same. In fact, unlike norm-based tests, teachers are encouraged to teach directly to the CRT. The question these tests answer is, How well did the student learn what was taught?

One advantage of CRTs, when teacher constructed, is that the teacher has the opportunity to develop large numbers of items to sample the students' behavior. Large sampling tends to increase the reliability of tests. When few items are included to measure a given behavior, CRTs have the same reliability problems as do standardized tests.

Diagnosis during and after Instruction

The advantages and disadvantages of diagnosis before instruction make an obvious case for diagnosis during and after instruction. In classroom diagnosis, observation of the student's ability to respond to instruction is of prime importance. Through the direct observation of the student's responses, the teacher can avoid some of the time-consuming, costly, and sometimes questionable testing commonly linked to diagnosis. Teachers can conduct diagnosis in each of the following four skill areas:

1. *Readiness skills* involve the ability to approach the page with effective mechanical skills (orientation), to operate effectively with the language, and to display effective auditory and visual discrimination skills.

2. *Sight vocabulary* involves the recognition and meaning of a word instantly and consistently.

3. *Word attack* involves the ability to decode words not recognized by sight.

4. *Comprehension* involves the ability to bring meaning and understanding to words and groups of words and their interrelationships.

The reader should note that each of these skill areas affects the total reading process; that is, each influences the manner in which a reader decodes the printed message and associates the decoded message with past experiences. These areas, then, include the skills necessary for effective decoding and association (i.e., reading). For each of these skill areas, the classroom teacher must obtain the answers to the following three questions:

1. What is the instructional level? It must be determined at which level this student can respond most effectively to instruction; normally, it is a point at which the student makes errors but does not fail completely. Teachers have numerous opportunities to observe students reading different types of materials. They realize that students do not have one instructional level, but several. In social studies materials, a given student might read at levels considerably above materials read in other areas. As a student encounters materials which are obviously too hard, instructional adjustments are necessary in either increased assistance through word introduction and concept development prior to reading or reduction of the difficulty of the material by selecting different books.

2. Specifically, what types of skills do the readers possess? (What are their reading strengths?) Diagnostically, the teacher looks for those skills which the students have apparently mastered. For example, if a student always attacks the initial portion of the word accurately, initial consonants may be listed as mastered. The teacher also notes observed patterns of errors. Thus, both strengths and needs are credited.

3. What classroom adjustment can be used to teach to the students' strengths? What adjustments can be made to assist students in areas of needs? By starting with adjustments which will permit students to demonstrate strengths, success experiences can be developed. Awareness of adjustments which will help students in the areas of need will help teachers plan for continued student development.

To answer each of the above questions, teachers directly observe students in three reading situations: word recognition and word meaning exercises, oral reading, and silent reading. Reading situations differ from skill areas in that each situation requires the use of one or more of the skills for acceptable performance. Improvement in the skill areas results in improvement in reading situations when the diagnosis has been effective in establishing the instructional strengths and needs of students. Word recognition exercises provide teachers with information concerning the ability of a student to handle words in isolation. Since almost all reading activities call for dealing with words in context, word recognition diagnosis is of little value. However, it does give the teacher some insight as to the word knowledge of a student. Word meaning exercises focus on the various meanings of words. Again, in isolation most word meanings are vague. What does *bank, ball, run, happy,* or *awkward* mean without a sentence of support? And service words such as *if, and, on,* and *when* carry meaning only as they relate to other words. Observation of students in oral reading provides teachers with the best insight into their overt reading behavior. It provides teachers with their only observation of the overt reading behavior of students when reading in context. That oral and silent reading require somewhat different behaviors is a given fact. Probably oral and silent reading are more similar for beginning readers and become less similar as readers gain maturity. Silent reading provides teachers with the best situation to determine the comprehension performance of students. Observations in each situation provide information which is important for the complete picture of students' reading performances. Teachers add these observations to any testing information which they might have and formulate diagnostic hypotheses which they will attempt to interpret into instructional adjustments.

Word Recognition and Word Meaning. Activities in these areas provide teachers with some information about the general operating level of students. Clues from word recognition and word meaning activities can be used as a basis for selection of passages for initial diagnosis in oral and silent reading. Patterns of performance need to be observed in the various reading situations in order to develop sound diagnostic hypotheses. Each behavior observed should be followed by a statement of diagnosis, looking at both strengths and weaknesses. Strengths generally indicate areas in which a student is making a positive effort; therefore, attitudes as well as skills are reflected. Teachers using these suggestions must see them as possible listings of strengths and weaknesses. The following are examples of such observations:

1. The student refuses to pronounce words even after a delay of up to five seconds.

    strengths:　unknown
    weaknesses: may not know the word;
    　　　　　　 may have no apparent use of word attack skills

2. The student hesitates to pronounce a word but finally pronounces it after a delay of between two to five seconds.

    strength:　may be using word attack skills or delayed recall of
    　　　　　　 word form at sight
    weakness:　may not be in sight vocabulary

3. The student partially pronounces the word but fails to pronounce entire word accurately (e.g., *ta* . . . for *table*)

    strength:　uses graphic cues for portion of word pronounced, in
    　　　　　　 this case, initial consonant and vowel sound

weaknesses: may not be in sight vocabulary;

may have difficulty in word attack with unpronounced portion of word, in this case, word ending

4. The student substitutes one word for another while maintaining the basic word meaning (e.g., *kitten* for *cat*)

strength: may have clue to word meaning through association
weakness: may be disregarding graphic cues

5. The student can pronounce a word accurately but does not know its meaning.

strength: uses graphic cues
weaknesses: may need concept development;

may have worked so hard to pronounce the word that simply failed to attend to its meaning

6. The student confuses letter order—reversals (e.g., *was* for *saw, expect* for *except*)

strength: may be observing graphic cues
weaknesses: may have directional confusion (orientation);

may not know the word

Observations noted during word recognition activities should be verified by observation in oral and silent reading activities.

Oral Reading. Observation during oral reading adds the dimension of the use of context. Teachers can observe how students use graphic and semanatic (meaning) cues. The first three behaviors discussed below are considered to be minor and are often the signs of thoughtful oral reading:

1. The student repeats words or phrases. Four types of repetitions should be considered:

a. Student successfully changes first response to match text:

strengths: may be using context (semantic) cues;
may be using graphic cues
weaknesses: unknown

b. Student attempts to correct but is unsuccessful:

strength: may be aware of semantic cues
weakness: may be unable to fully utilize graphic cues in this semantic setting

c. Student simply repeats portion which was initially correct:

strength: may be attempting to improve intonation
weakness: may be biding for time to attack forthcoming segment of the passage

d. Student changes an initially correct response:

strength: may be changing passage into a more familiar language
weakness: may be biding for time to attack forthcoming segment of the passage

2. The student omits words. Two types of omissions should be considered:

a. The omission distorts meaning:

strengths: unknown
weaknesses: may not be reading for meaning;
may not be in sight vocabulary

b. Omission does not distort meaning:

strength: may be reading for meaning
weaknesses: may have too large an eye-voice span;
may not be in sight vocabulary

3. The student inserts words. Two types of insertions should be considered:

a. The insertion distorts meaning:

strengths: unknown
weakness: may not be using semantic cues

b. The insertion does not distort meaning:

strength: may be embellishing the author's meaning
weakness: may have too large an eye-voice span

The remaining observations during oral reading take on more important diagnostic implications:

4. The student substitutes a word or nonword for the word in the passage. When such a substitution occurs, it can be analyzed according to these types of information: graphic, syntactic, and semantic. These behaviors were presented in a theoretical argument by Goodman.[11] Such an analysis considers qualitative as well as quantitative considerations. The qualitative aspects rest heavily with the student's reaction to the passage in a meaningful context.

Example: Student reads, "the big title was"
Text was, "the big table was"
Graphic: initial—accurate
medial—error
final—accurate

---

[11]Kenneth S. Goodman, "Analysis of Oral Reading Miscues: Applied Psycholinguistics," *Reading Research Quarterly* 5 (Fall 1969): 9-30.

Syntactic: accurate, a noun for a noun
Semantic: error, major change in meaning

Example: Student reads, "boy hurried down"
Text was,   "boy hustled down"
Graphic: initial—accurate
         medial—variance
         final—accurate
Syntactic: accurate, a verb for a verb
Semantic: not accurate, but acceptable

These three types of oral reading behavior need to be considered in terms of how they relate to one another. Individually the strengths and weaknesses include:

a. Student fails to use all graphic cues:

   strengths: uses graphic cues for portions of words accurately pronounced;
                 may be using syntactic and semantic cues
   weaknesses: may fail to use all graphic cues available;
                 may not be in sight vocabulary

b. Student fails to use syntactic cues:

   strength: may be using graphic cues
   weaknesses: may fail to use syntactic cues in the language;
                 may not be in sight vocabulary

c. Student fails to use semantic cues:

   strength: may be using graphic and syntactic cues
   weaknesses: may not be in sight vocabulary;
                 may be concentrating on pronunciation instead of meaning

5. The student fails to observe punctuation:

   strengths: unknown
   weaknesses: decoding may be so difficult that punctuation is ignored;
                 may be unaware of the function of punctuation

6. The student observes all punctuation via pauses and inflection:

   strengths: using semantic cues;
                 knows cues implied by punctuation
   weaknesses: unknown

7. The student loses place during oral reading:

   strengths: unknown
   weaknesses: may have directional confusion;

>   may have visual problem;
>   may be overconcentrating on decoding

8. The student reads word-by-word (all words pronounced accurately, but slowly with pauses between them and with much expression):

>   strength: may be using graphic cues
>   weaknesses: may not be using semantic cues;
>   may not have sufficient sight vocabulary

9. The student exhibits difficulty when asked literal questions although accurately pronounced all words:

>   strength: may be using graphic cues
>   weaknesses: decoding may be so "all-consuming" that comprehension does not occur;
>   may have inadequate conceptual development;
>   may have poor verbal memory

Symptoms observed during oral reading should be based upon materials which the student can handle fairly well (accuracy between 90–95 percent). All symptoms observed during attempts to read frustrating material are invalid due to the difficulty of the material, creating unnatural error patterns. (Readers tend to depend more heavily on graphic information when reading frustrating material).

Silent Reading. During silent reading, teachers can observe several overt behaviors which may aid in the total diagnosis:

1. The student moves lips and makes subvocalized sound during silent reading:

>   strength: appears to be working on graphic cues
>   weaknesses: may be overworking decoding;
>   may be trying to remember what is read;
>   may be a habit carried over from excessive oral reading

2. The student points to words with fingers:

>   strength: may be using touch to keep place or to emphasize words
>   weaknesses: orientation skills may need touch support;
>   may be having decoding difficulties

3. The student shows physical signs of reading discomfort (e.g., rubbing of eyes, extreme restlessness, constant adjustment of book).

>   strength: may be persevering with task
>   weaknesses: possible difficulty of material;
>   possible physical defect—vision, nutrition, and the like;
>   possible emotional reaction to frustration

The important diagnostic aspect of silent reading is, of course, the ability of the student to demonstrate an understanding of the author's message. Five important considerations must be noted:

1. What types of questions are to be asked: literal questions which call for facts and details, interpretive questions which call for paraphrasing and drawing inferences, or problem-solving questions which call for critical and creative response and evaluative thinking?
2. What situation is the student facing when answering questions? A recall situation calls for the reading material to be unavailable during questioning. A locate situation encourages the student to find the answer in the reading material. Locating opportunities appear to have a great effect on a student's ability to respond to questions at all levels.
3. Was the student aware of purposes for silent reading?
4. How much exposure has the student had to the reading material? Are the responses expected after a single reading or after study and reexamination of the material? It is obvious that different performances might be expected depending on the amount of exposure to the material.
5. How much time has elapsed between the reading of the material and the student's response to it? If long-term memory is expected, then comprehension responses can be expected to be less accurate.

The following procedure is suggested for silent reading comprehension diagnosis:

1. Have the student read the story for a set purpose.
2. Start questioning in a recall situation and with interpretive questions. Davey found that students answer literal questions more accurately when questioning starts with interpretive questions than they do when questions start with literal questions.[12] Then ask literal and problem-solving questions.
3. On all questions missed in the recall situation, permit students to return to the passage and locate the answers.

In this matter teachers have six types of comprehension scores. Using the number or percent of accurate responses, these scores can be charted as in Table 7.

---

[12]H. Beth Davey, "The Effect of Question Order on Comprehension Test Performance at the Literal and Interpretive Levels," (faculty research paper, Reading Center, University of Maryland, 1975).

TABLE 7

Type of Response	Reading Situations	
	Recall	Locate
Interpretive		
Literal		
Problem Solving		

The following behaviors can be observed during the question-reaction period of a silent reading lesson:

4. The student can decode the material but cannot respond to literal questions in a recall situation:

   strength: may be using graphics, semantic, and syntactic cues
   weaknesses: may have poor (visual) memory;
   may need concept development related to material read;
   may be overconcentrating on graphic cues

5. The student can decode the material and can respond to literal questions in a locate situation:

   strengths: may be using graphic, semantic, and syntactic cues;
   may be able to locate literally stated ideas
   weaknesses: unknown

6. The student can respond to literal understanding questions but cannot interpret those ideas into own words:

   strengths: may be using graphic, semantic, and syntactic cues;
   uses literal understanding
   weaknesses: possible overconcentration on graphic cues;
   possible load difficulty;
   possible failure to reflect on the author's ideas

7. The student can respond literally and can interpret the author's ideas but cannot apply ideas to problem-solving situations:

   strengths: may be using graphic, syntactic, and semantic cues;
   uses literal understanding;
   uses interpretation
   weaknesses: may have problem-solving skills;
   possible misunderstanding of the problem

8. The student can retell the story accurately but cannot answer teacher-made questions relating to it:

strengths: shows literal understanding;
              uses sequence skills
weakness: may have inability to anticipate teacher questions

9. The student can answer teacher-made questions when allowed to study
   and reexamine passage, but not after a single reading:

   strength: gains meaning when allotted sufficient time
   weakness: may need repeated exposure for comprehension

10. The student can answer teacher-made questions immediately after reading
    but is unable to do so a day or so later:

    strength: may have short-term memory
    weakness: may not have adequate long-term memory

11. The student can answer questions covering short passage but is unable to
    do so on longer passages:

    strength: may have short-term memory
    weaknesses: may have inadequate long-term memory;
                 may lack organizational skills

Teachers should collect observational data relating to comprehension over a period of time. A given comprehension failure might be as attributal to story content, reader interest, or reader motivation on a given day as it is to reading ability. Once a consistent pattern is observed, teachers can make diagnostic hypotheses and start to make adjustments in the instructional aspects of the reading program.

Two Cautions

Observation of reading behavior is a learned skill. Consistent practice, the habit of keeping careful records, and double and triple checking of findings are musts. Obviously one repetition in an oral reading situation cannot become a diagnostic hypothesis. A danger also exists that classroom observations will lead to a fractionalized view of the reader. Every reader is more than the sum of skills listed on the preceding pages—a lot more. The classroom teacher in a diagnostic role needs to pull back periodically and observe the whole reader. Such observations might reveal that the reader is always on-task, enjoying the reading activities, helping others, and is happy. Perhaps such observations are more important than a listing of skill strengths and weaknesses. At least they should be recorded as equally important information.

RECORD KEEPING

An essential part of any diagnosis is record keeping. It is often through record keeping that patterns emerge which give insight into the reader's processes.

Records may take the form of Table 5 or individual folders can be maintained on each student. Individual records have the advantage of being open ended so that comments can be added, and information can be adjusted as behaviors change. Table 8 might be adapted for individual record folders.

TABLE 8

Name _____ Age _____ Teacher _____
Grade _____ Date record initiated _____

	Date: ____	Date: ____	Date: ____
Scores:	Score	Score	Score
Word Recognition:			
Oral Reading Accuracy			
Silent Reading			
Recall Comp.			
Locate Comp.			
Strengths:	Strengths	Strengths	Strengths
Word Recognition			
Oral Reading Behavior			
Silent Reading Comp.			
Weaknesses:	Weaknesses	Weaknesses	Weaknesses
Word Recognition			
Oral Reading Behavior			
Silent Reading Comp.			

Comments: _____

Such records are useful during student-teacher conferences and parent conferences and to pass along to the student's next teacher.

QUESTIONS TO PINPOINT DIAGNOSTIC FINDINGS

From word recognition, oral reading, and silent reading data, teachers should seek answers to the following questions:

Skill Area: prereading-readiness skills. If answers to questions in this area are yes, remedial suggestions can be found in Chapter 7.

1. Do language skills appear to be underdeveloped?
2. Do speech skills appear to be underdeveloped?
3. Does dialect usage appear to cause difficulty?
4. Do visual or auditory problems appear to be causing discomfort?
5. Do visual discrimination skills appear to be underdeveloped?
6. Do auditory discrimination skills appear to be underdeveloped?
7. Do reversals occur frequently enough to cause confusion?
8. Does student frequently lose place during reading?

Skill Area: sight vocabulary. If answers to questions in this area are yes, remedial suggestions can be found in Chapter 8.

1. Does student miscall small, similar words?
2. Do words missed represent abstract concepts?
3. Do word meanings appear to be confused?
4. Does student know words in context but not in isolation?
5. Does student appear to know words at end of a lesson, but not the next day?

Skill Area: word attack. If answers to questions in this area are yes, remedial suggestions can be found in Chapter 8.

Phonics:
1. Does student not use graphic cues? Which graphic cues are used?
2. Does student attack small words accurately, but not larger ones?
3. Does student seem to know sound-symbol relationships but seem unable to use them during reading?

Structural:
1. Do words missed contain prefixes or suffixes?
2. Are words missed compound words?

Contexual:
1. Does student appear to ignore syntactic cues?
2. Does student appear to ignore semantic cues?
3. Does student appear to ignore punctuation cues?

Skill Area: comprehension. If answers to questions in this area are yes, remedial suggestions can be found in Chapter 9.

1. Do large units of material seem to interfere with comprehension?
2. Do comprehension difficulties occur with some types of comprehension and not others? (Literal comprehension is weak but interpretive is good.)

3. Does student have difficulty using locating skills?
4. Does student have difficulty with content reading? Why?
5. Does student fail to comprehend most of what is read?

HABITS AND ATTITUDES

An evaluation of student habits and attitudes is an important part of classroom diagnosis. Teachers, through regular observation of student performances, are in the ideal setting to note changes in habits and attitudes. An effort should be made to note effective and ineffective habits which seem to vary considerably from those of the average student. The classroom teacher is likely to be asked by the reading specialist for information concerning habits and attitudes; therefore, observations should be noted carefully. Specifically, classroom teachers should obtain answers to the following questions:

1. What uses do students make of free reading opportunity? Do they appear eager to use free time for reading, or is reading only the result of constant prodding?

2. Do students appear anxious or reluctant to read orally? Silently? Does there appear to be a difference in attitude between oral and silent situations.

3. Are signs of reluctance noticeable in reading situations only or in all learning situations? Students who hesitate in all learning situations must be motivated; whereas those reluctant in reading alone need success and reward in reading.

4. In what reading situations are students most or least effective? Do students tend to enjoy providing answers orally as opposed to writing them? Do questions which call for summaries get better results than specific questions? Students often have developed habits as a result of what has been expected by other teachers.

5. Do students have to be prodded to finish reading assignments? If they cannot work without supervision even when specific assignments have been made, unsupervised reading situations should be avoided in initial remedial instruction.

6. What type of book selections do the students make in the library? Considerable information can be obtained about interests by noticing the types of books chosen from the library. Remedial efforts should start with the type of material in which students have indicated an interest.

Answers to the above questions will become important guides to the initial remedial sessions. Teachers will find it useful to record these findings so that they will have a record of accurate data and be able to inform the reading specialist. Although these questions will be answered for the most part by informal observation, teachers should give them special attention and become active agents in collecting information.

At times, it is not possible to obtain precise yes or no answers to such questions. In these cases, teachers should continue to observe the readers until they can substantiate accurate patterns of errors. Specifically, teachers may provide students with individualized exercises to do independently, go over their responses, and have a short conference about their responses. As a part of informal, on-the-spot diagnosis, this technique can be useful in verifying classroom diagnosis. Suppose, for example, that one has diagnosed irregular patterns of difficulty with final consonant sounds. Several carefully prepared exercises with final consonant sounds can be developed, administered, and analyzed for the purpose of verification. Futher verification can come from information available in school records, from parental interviews, from past observations, from classroom diagnostic tests, and from subsequent instruction. All information, however obtained, should be used to effect an accurate classroom diagnosis.

FOUR FINAL QUESTIONS

Teachers should reflect upon the answers to the following four questions to complete an effective classroom diagnosis and to assist them in establishing more clearly the validity of their findings:

1. Did the students make the same error in both easy and difficult material, or did the observed errors indicate frustration with the material? We are most interested in the errors made at the instructional level, the level at which we hope to make improvement. All readers make errors when reading at their frustration level; these errors, however, normally do not lead to diagnostic conclusions, for these are not the errors upon which remediation is based.

2. Were the errors first interpreted as slowness actually an effort on the part of the reader to be especially careful and precise and to be reflective? Beware of diagnostic conclusions drawn from the students' responses to questions on material read due to slowness, especially when timed standardized tests are used or when testing situations make the reader aware of being evaluated. Many students have been taught to be impulsive with their responses when, in fact, reflective behavior may be considerably more desirable.

3. Can students be helped as a result of classroom diagnosis, or is further diagnosis necessary? Further testing with any of the instruments mentioned under clinical diagnosis may be in order and is appropriate when the teacher

has the knowledge of their proper usage and interpretation and the time to use them. At this point, however, the services of a reading specialist may be required.

4. Did the students appear to concentrate while being directly observed, or did they seem easily distracted? Children who appear to be distracted during observation may have produced unreliable symptoms.

The diagnostic task has been to observe individuals through analysis of symptoms, to associate the symptoms to appropriate skill areas, to determine the significance of the errors, and to organize the information in terms of practical classroom adjustments. On only a few occasions will diagnosis be concluded at this point. An ongoing process, diagnosis will normally continue during the remedial sessions, always attempting to obtain more precise information concerning the readers. Morris feels that this is the important advantage for the classroom teacher. He states, "To the teacher . . . the challenge is to get to grips more directly with the problem and by working with the individual pupil try to understand what is leading him astray."[13] To this can be added: and to determine more precisely his skill, *strengths,* and deficiencies.

EARLY IDENTIFICATION

Teachers are capable of making early identifications of children who are likely to experience difficulty in school. In Maryland, a multidiscipline task force worked two years to develop assessment instruments to identify children with potential learning handicaps. They found the best device for such identification to be systematic teacher observations.[14] At the University of Maryland reading clinic, we found a similar result when asking teachers to identify potential reading problems. They identified them more accurately than did the tests which we administered. In some schools, early identification occurs in kindergarten. When accompanied by specific symptoms, such identification assists teachers to modify educational programs to increase the possibilities of success. Some children might best start with a phonics-based program; others might profit from one that stresses sight learning. Some succeed best when the initial program uses the language-experience approach, and others need multisensory techniques. Such programs have the potential to assist children to get a successful start in school and to avoid several years of failure.

---

[13]Ronald Morris, *Success and Failure in Learning to Read* (London: Oldbourne, 1963), p. 159

[14]*Reading in Maryland* (Baltimore, Md.: Division of Instruction, Maryland State Department of Education, 1974-75).

Several problems are related to early identification programs. First, if they stop with identification, they may do more harm than good. Second, when tests are relied upon heavily, many children become identified erroneously, and others are not identified when they should be. Thirdly, providing teachers with check lists of behaviors which may cause learning problems may result in self-fulfillment. For example, if a teacher is told that children in first grade who make reversals may have serious reading problems, teachers might react to children so identified in such ways that create nonlearning. Finally, parents can be aroused to such a state of anxiety as to alarm the child.

If early identification programs are to be implemented, several safeguards can be applied to avoid the above-mentioned problems. Early identification should never be made using a single testing instrument. Children who have been initially identified should be reevaluated periodically. Early identification programs should be accompanied by instructional adjustments. Parents should be informed of the program and the advantages it offers their children. All early identification programs should be carefully monitored and periodically evaluated to be certain they are effective.

SUMMARY

Classroom diagnosis, involving both diagnostic teaching and formal assessment of the strengths and weaknesses of students, is essential to effective teaching. Awareness of the diagnostic areas and resulting identification of skill needs of students guide reading instruction.

Diagnostic teaching is not easy and is time-consuming. As does most effective teaching, it calls for attention to individual needs of students and requires careful study. Those who use diagnostic teaching find it highly rewarding and extremely effective.

SUGGESTED READINGS

DeBoer, Dorothy L., ed. *Reading Diagnosis and Evaluation*. Newark, Del.: International Reading Association, 1970. Emphasis is on the diagnostic aspects of reading. This IRA collection features early identification, use of testing, and formal approaches.

Durr, William K., ed. *Reading Difficulties*. Newark, Del.: International Reading Association, 1970. The second section, "The Informal Inventories," includes six articles by different authors on the various aspects of informal inventories.

Readers who are unfamiliar with informal techniques will want to study this section.

Farr, Roger. *Reading: What Can Be Measured?* Newark, Del.: International Reading Association, 1969. An excellent paperback which looks at the value and limitations of the various measuring instruments used in reading. Farr has prepared a valuable resource for teachers.

Goodman, Kenneth S. "Analysis of Oral Reading Miscues: Applied Psycholinguistics." *Reading Research Quarterly 5* (Fall 1969): 9-30. Goodman states his case for oral reading analysis in this article. This view of the reader as a processor of language cues is important for those who wish to become skilled diagnostic teachers.

Geyer, James R., and Matanzo, Jane. *Strategies for Classroom Teachers: A Programmed Text.* Columbus, O.: Charles E. Merrill, 1977. For those who want practice coding and analyzing reading behavior, this book may be interesting. Aside from specific practice exercises, case studies are included for prescription writing. Suggested answers are provided throughout.

5

Clinical Diagnosis

Through a program of observation and testing, reading specialists conduct clinical diagnosis. The questions they ask are similar to those asked by the classroom teachers in classroom diagnosis. They need to obtain information about the students' potentials, reading levels, and skill strengths and needs. They are also looking for ways to help the classroom teacher help the students. It is possible that they will even recommend changes in the school program in hopes of preventing certain types of reading difficulties. Ideally clinical diagnosis will not be a one-shot testing activity; rather the reading specialists will conduct follow-ups on their diagnostic findings, following the students' progress in instructional situations.

Saddled with the limitations of time and large numbers of requests, reading specialists usually start clinical diagnosis with some type of screening procedure to gain a quick insight into the approximate difficulty a given reader may be having. At times, a screening can provide enough insight so that further testing is not necessary. Using information from teachers, parents, and the student, reading specialists administer certain tests, analyze the reader's behavior during testing, interpret the results, and attempt to blend all of the data available into a helpful set of recommendations so that the reader can be successful.

THE USE OF TEST DATA

Word Recognition

The first reading test to be administered in a clinical diagnosis is usually one of word recognition. The purpose of such tests is to screen the reader's ability to pronounce accurately words normally found at various grade levels. From a screening of word recognition, reading specialists are able to make the same analysis as that made from direct observation in classroom diagnosis (Chapter 4). It also assists them to make the following two basic judgments concerning the next steps in clinical diagnosis:

1. From the word recognition test (performance), the reading specialist is able to determine reasonable starting levels for oral reading testing. Without this information, it is possible to find oneself administering tests upon which students cannot score at all or upon which they can obtain a nearly perfect score because they are too easy. In neither case will this type of testing produce usable diagnostic information, for tests must be administered upon which students can start with success and upon which they ultimately will encounter difficulty.

2. An analysis of word recognition responses may cause the reading specialist to select certain types of tests for further diagnosis. A very poor performance which shows the reader using no graphic cues may lead the specialist to examine phonics knowledge. On the other hand, a good score on a word recognition test may cause the specialist to skip further analysis in the area of phonics and move on to testing in oral and silent reading situations.

One test of word recognition is the *Botel Reading Inventory.** The "Word Recognition" section of the Botel inventory samples groups of twenty words found in the various basal readers in grades one through four. A student pronounces the word while the examiner records responses. A sample of one-half of the first page of the Botel "Word Recognition" section is shown in Figure 7. Notice that the student's responses must be recorded accurately. In this example, the student made most errors in final consonant sounds and then in vowel sounds. Inner test analysis requires examination and marking of each type of error: *v* stands for vowel, *fc* for final consonant, *ic* for initial consonant, *mc* for medial consonant, and √ for correct response.

Many reading specialists prefer to use informal tests of word recognition. These consist of words randomly selected from basal series which the reader might encounter. A minimum of twenty words per reader level should be used. The more words selected, the more reliable are the test results. The specialist who is inexperienced with informal test construction will find this task quite difficult and may find it more profitable to use ready-made tests. Informal word lists are available and may be used when desired.[1]

Aside from obtaining information concerning starting levels for further testing, word recognition response analysis provides the initial glimpse at the word attack strategies used by the reader.

FIGURE 7

Botel Reading Inventory A
Word Recognition Scoring Sheet

Pupil _____

Date _____

Instructional Levels _____

Teacher _____

A (Pre-Primer)		B (Primer)		C (First)	
Word	*Response*	Word	*Response*	Word	*Response*
1. a	✓	all	✓	about	✓
2. ball	✓	at	✓	as	✓
3. blue ✓	blow	boat fc	boak	be	✓
4. come	✓	but fc	bud	by	✓
5. farther m.	fatter	do	✓	could ✓	cold
6. get	✓	duck	✓	fast ✓	first
7. have fc	half	find fc	fine	friend fc	friet
8. house ✓	horse	girl	✓	guess fc	guest
9. in	✓	he	✓	hen	✓
10. it	✓	kitten ✓	kitton	how fc	hot

SOURCE: Morton Botel, *Botel Reading Inventory* (Chicago: Follett Publishing Co., 1962).

Oral Reading

Next, reading specialists will usually administer a test of oral reading to identify strategies readers use in contextual situations. From oral reading tests, the reading specialists can gather diagnostic information in the same manner as

---

[1]Mary C. Austin; Clifford L. Bush; and Mildred H. Huebner, *Reading Evaluation* (New York: The Ronald Press, 1961), p. 13; and Emmett A. Betts, *Handbook on Corrective Reading for the American Adventure Series* (Chicago: Wheeler Publishing Co., 1956), pp. 37-39.

did classroom teachers when they observed oral reading in the classroom (see Chapter 4). It also enables them to do the following:

1. Conduct an analysis of student responses. As in classroom diagnosis, oral reading provides opportunities to determine the types of cues students use in decoding—graphic, syntactic, and semantic. The analysis of responses in oral reading situations is more useful than analysis from word recognition situations.

2. Further diagnostic information is obtained while determining whether words unknown in word recognition are known when they are seen in their relationship with other words. The ability of the reader to use contextual word attack skills is determined by comparing the word recognition instructional level with the oral reading instructional level. A large difference in favor of oral reading indicates effective use of context. A score difference in favor of word recognition may be an indication of contextual confusion. If the difference is in favor of oral reading, reading specialists become less concerned about the types of errors observed in word recognition, since nearly all of the reading a student does is in contextual situations.

3. Oral reading tests also provide the examiner with insight into the student's reading behavior in school situations. Although this particular diagnostic information may not have a direct relationship to specific remedial procedures, it can provide the reading specialist with an understanding of the child's reaction to oral reading and of the problems which those reactions may be causing in the classroom.

Several tests with oral reading selections and norms for grade equivalents are available (see Appendix A). Although the directions for administration of these tests vary, they have the following basic ingredients: the student reads aloud from graded selections, ranging from simple to difficult; the examiner records the reader's responses as outlined by the manual; scores are based on a frequency count rather than a qualitative analysis; then several comprehension questions are asked which normally provide a measure of the reader's ability to recall specifically stated facts from the story. The value of oral reading comprehension scores is subject to question. During oral reading, most readers are concentrating on pronunciation and fluency. The valuable insights we get from an analysis of oral reading relate to those processes that the reader demonstrates. The skills of comprehension are best measured after silent reading. Why, then, ask questions after oral reading? Starting with purpose-setting questions and following oral reading with those questions helps the students see purpose in their reading.

As with word recognition, many reading specialists prefer to construct informal tests of oral reading. Using the graded materials which the student might be expected to read, passages are selected. Accuracy, if a level of oral reading is desired, is recorded as it is on standardized tests of oral reading. Using informal tests of oral reading during diagnosis offers the advantages of larger selections and a variety of content. A major disadvantage is inherent in the assumption that the graded materials used for the test are, in fact, accurately graded. For example, if a given selection taken from a fifth-grade book is actually at the sixth-grade level, diagnostic conclusions which come from it are faulty. Another limitation relates to how such tests are interpreted. Pikulski states that an informal inventory's usefulness in diagnosis is related to how well the testing material matches the material to be used for instruction.[2] Obviously, if they are mismatched, then interpretation of results is difficult.

Oral reading tests as diagnostic tools are plagued by several limitations. In the first place, there is considerable disagreement about what an oral reading error is. Certainly, one would recognize mispronounced words, hesitancy on unknown words, or disregard of punctuation marks as obvious limitations to effective oral reading, at least as far as the listening audience is concerned. But is it an error when a reader repeats words to correct oral reading mistakes? Is it an error when a student stops to use word attack skills on words not known at sight? Or are these the types of behaviors which we want readers to display? Are all errors of equal importance, or do some interfere with reading efficiency more seriously than others? If weights could be developed for various types of errors, would the same weight hold at various grade levels? For example, would a vowel error made by a first grader be as serious an error as a vowel error made by a fifth grader?

Test constructors, in an effort to standardize oral reading tests, have had to establish some easily recognizable arbitrary standards of accurate and inaccurate oral reading. Although these arbitrary systems vary, most of them include markings similar to those listed in the *Gilmore Oral Reading Test*.[3] Substitutions and mispronunciations are written above the word for which the substitution was made; omissions are circled; repetitions are underlined; words inserted are put in the appropriate place; punctuation which is disregarded is marked by an *x*; hesitations of two seconds or more are marked by a check mark above the word; at five seconds, these words are pronounced for the reader, and two check marks are indicated. Diagnosis, of course, depends upon the accurate marking of errors and a valid interpretation of them. Naturally, the marking system will somewhat control the type of information available for interpretation.

---

[2]John Pikulski, "A Critical Review: Informal Reading Inventories," *Reading Teacher* 28 (November 1974): 143.

[3]"Gilmore Oral Reading Test," *Manual of Directions* (New York: Harcourt Brace Jovanovich, 1952), pp. 8-9.

The following paragraph has been marked according to the system discussed:

A spaceman has stepped onto the surface of the moon.

He is very careful as he steps from his capsule. Live television brings the

moment to the entire population of the earth. It is an exciting moment.

With such marking, a student's reading is recorded. This student hesitated on the word *has* and failed to pronounce the word *stepped* in five seconds, mispronounced *surface* and disregarded the period after *moon*, repeated *He is very*, substituted *telephone* for *television* and *a* for *an*, omitted *entire*, and added *very*. The above paragraph illustrates not only the marking system but also the fact that all errors are not of equal importance. For example: hesitation on the word *has* is not as serious an error as is the failure to pronounce *stepped*.[4] One can also observe reader strengths.

Another limitation of oral reading tests concerns the ability of the examiner to hear and record accurately the errors which the reader is making. Supervised practice is necessary to obtain proficiency in oral reading test administration. It is obvious that if the examiner is not able to hear or record the responses accurately, the results of testing will be invalid. Through practice, competency can be developed to assure satisfactory administration and interpretation of oral reading. However, unsupervised testing without adequate practice can lead to extremely unreliable results.

Another Way to Analyze Oral Reading Behavior. As was discussed in Chapter 4, the work of Kenneth Goodman has influenced the way many are using oral reading in clinical diagnosis.[5] This influence is away from using oral reading to obtain reading level information and toward using it for linguistic processing information. Student responses during oral reading are classified qualitatively in terms of the appropriate use of cues. The coding system mentioned above is also changed to reflect the qualitative classifications.

Many have made adaptations of the ideas of Goodman for clinical use. Staff members at the University of Maryland reading clinic, for example, have adapted his ideas as a way of looking at oral reading behavior (ORB). Those ideas which most directly affect the ability to make useful recommendations to

---

[4]For opportunities to practice oral reading coding, see James Geyer and Jane Matanzo, *Diagnostic and Prescriptive Reading Strategies for Classroom Teachers: A Programmed Text* (Columbus, O.: Charles E. Merrill Publishing Co., 1977).

[5]Kenneth S. Goodman, "Analysis of Oral Reading Miscues: Applied Pycholinguistics," *Reading Research Quarterly* 5 (Fall 1969): 9-30.

teachers were modified and used. Basically, with this approach, every response which is in variance to the text is recorded, leaving one word of text on each side of the variant word, for example:

Text: in *the* street

Student response: in *a* street

Then a judgment is made to classify the student variance as a regression, insertion, omission, or substitution. Regressions are further analyzed to determine:

1. Did student change first response to make correction?
2. Did student appear to attempt a correction but was unsuccessful?
3. Did student simply repeat a portion which was initially correct?
4. Did student change a response that was initially correct?

With such an analysis, one can see that a regression may be classified as good oral reading behavior as well as poor.

Omissions and insertions are judged in terms of whether or not they changed the meaning. If they do not change the meaning, we can assume that the reader is using semantic cues.

Substitutions, the most important student response to be studied, are evaluated as follows:

1. When making the substitution, did the reader use graphic cues? In what way did the reader evidence knowledge of phonics or structural analysis?
2. Did the reader use semantic cues? In what ways did the reader evidence use of the context?
3. Did the reader use syntactic cues? In what ways did the reader evidence knowledge of grammar? If the reader uses semantic cues, one assumes the use of syntatic cues. However, if the reader does not use semantic cues but does use syntatic cues, valuable information is obtained about the student's awareness of language.

Obviously, each of these analyses involves some judgment. But with them the reader can be given credit for oral reading strengths even when responses are at variance with the text. Each of these responses is recorded; then all responses in a category are totaled. As a result, the specialist can say how much of the time a student demonstrates a specific oral reading behavior; for example, when the reader makes substitutions, semantic cues are used effectively 75 percent of the time.

The use of this type of oral reading behavior analysis calls for considerable practice. Examiners are urged to use tape recorders, at least during initial efforts, to record variances for this type of analysis.

The work of Goodman and Burke may be referred to for thosee who want to obtain a detailed explanation of oral reading miscue analysis.[6] It should be cautioned that oral reading diagnosis is of most value for students reading between second- and seventh-grade reading levels. Beginning readers' responses may be related to the method used for instruction. If language-experience has been used, the reader may rely heavily upon semantic cues; if a phonics method has been used, the reader may indicate heavy reliance upon graphic cues. Once the reader is beyond the initial stages of learning to read, one can better determine which cues the reader has picked to rely upon. Older readers probably use very different behaviors in oral and silent reading. Perhaps oral reading analysis becomes less useful as an insight into silent reading behavior as the reader matures. Diagnostic information from oral reading should be interpreted with this caution in mind.

Silent Reading

A starting point for silent reading testing is determined by using data from oral reading testing. Generally, it is desirable to start the student at a point where there will be 100 percent comprehension. Testing continues until comprehension drops below the 70 percent mark. Comprehension is usually analyzed from the answers given to questions; however, retelling and cloze testing are also ways of looking at comprehension.

It is useful to collect three types of information concerning comprehension. First, what is the student's level or performance in recall and in locate situations? Second, what are the student's specific skill strengths and needs? Third, what is the student's attitude toward various types of materials?

Informal Measures. Teacher-made informal inventories can provide information to answer each of the above questions. Carefully selected passages, checked for readability and content, are the base for informal inventories. The passages should be long enough for the student to really be able to react beyond the literal level, and they should contain both narrative and content material.

Level can be determined by using the 70 percent correct figure as a guide. When comprehension falls below this mark, the student is missing too much to be comprehending effectively. Skill strengths can be determined by asking a variety of questions, for example, three literal, three interpretive, three problem solving, and one vocabulary (containing several items).

Once constructed, informal instruments should be field tested before used in diagnosis. With field testing, several things can be determined. Students should find passages to be more difficult as readability levels go higher.

---

[6]Yetta M. Goodman, and Carolyn L. Burke, *Reading Miscue Inventory-Manual* (New York: MacMillan Publishing Co., 1971).

Certain questions may be poorly written, causing confusion. Other questions may be passage independent, that is, the student can answer the question without reading the passage. After field testing, the inventory can be revised, checked again, and then placed into use.

The following procedures are suggested for testing comprehension using informal inventories.

1. Start with a purpose-setting statement. For example, "I want you to read this passage. When you are finished I want you to tell me what you think is the most important idea (or interesting idea) that the author is trying to make."

2. Observe the student during silent reading. Make notes of signs of comfort or discomfort, irritation or enjoyment, speed or slowness, and other outstanding behaviors.

3. When the student has finished, re-ask your purpose-setting question. Students respond better and feel more comfortable when permitted to discuss what they think is important before being asked other questions. Obviously, the examiner should not overly react, positively or negatively, to student responses.

4. Then proceed to ask the interpretive, literal, and problem-solving questions. These are first asked in a recall setting, that is, without the passage available to the student. After all questions are asked, ask the student to locate answers to any questions missed. Using both recall and locate, the examiner will obtain two comprehension scores. The differences can be quite dramatic. Generally, students improve between 30 and 40 percent when permitted to locate answers. Some students improve as much as four and five grade levels.

5. Vocabulary questions such as, "What does the word *bank* mean, as used in the second paragraph?" should always be asked in a locating situation.

By charting the data obtained, the examiner has a useful picture of the student's comprehension skills, as illustrated in Table 9.

TABLE 9

Passage Level	Literal Recall	Literal Locate	Interpretive Recall	Interpretive Locate	P. Solving Recall	P. Solving Locate	Vocab-ulary	Total Recall	Total Locate	
	Comprehension—Number Correct									
5	1	0	0	1	1	0	0	2	1	= 30%
4	1	2	1	1	2	0	0	4	3	= 70%
3–2	2	1	2	1	2	1	1	6	4	= 100%
3–1	3	—	2	1	2	1	1	7	3	= 100%

The examiner can now interpret the chart and discuss the student's comprehension performance on the passages read. Assuming ten questions are asked, three literal, three interpretive, three problem solving, and one vocabulary (maybe more than one question, but counted as one), it is easy to determine percentages. The recall and locate scores should be added to obtain a total number correct. The student in Table 9 could be said to be reading on a 3–1 level when recalling because a 70 percent score was obtained at that level. When permitted to locate, the student could be said to be reading on a 4 level, getting 40 percent through recall and 30 percent through locate. Further analysis can describe the student's specific comprehension skills, in terms of interpretive, literal, and problem solving and also in terms of recall and locate. If some of the passages are on content material and others on narrative, further analysis can be made.

Several test constructors have prepared informal inventories to match certain materials. Austin, Bush, and Huebner prepared one to go with the Allyn & Bacon series readers.[7] Betts prepared one for use with the *American Adventure Series*.[8] Smith et al. developed one for use in the primary grades.[9] And Silvaroli developed one for use in grades two through ten.[10] These inventories are designed for use by classroom teachers who are using those particular materials. They are useful, however, in clinical diagnosis when prescription calls for the use of those materials.

Cloze and Maze Testing. Cloze tests are constructed directly from the material to be used in instruction. Every fifth word is deleted, and the student is to supply the missing word. Accuracy scores of 40 to 44 percent reflect the 70 percent mark (or instructional level) on the tests previously mentioned. Fifty deletions are suggested. These tests are very frustrating, especially when the student is doing poorly.

Cloze tests can be used more informally to determine how well students use syntatic and semantic cues when reading. In these cases, certain words are deleted (for example, all verbs) to see if the students can supply appropriate words.

Maze testing is a modification of cloze procedures.[11] In maze tests, instead of deleting every fifth word, a three-word choice is provided. For example:

---

[7]Mary C. Austin, C. H. Bush, and Mildred H. Huebner, *Reading Evaluation*, (New York: Ronald Press, 1961), Appendix.

[8]Betts, *Handbook on Corrective Reading* . . . , chapter 3.

[9]Nila B. Smith et al., *Graded Selections for Informal Reading Diagnosis* (New York: New York University Press, 1959).

[10]Nicholas J. Silvaroli, *Classroom Reading Inventory*, (Dubuque, Ia.: Wm. C. Brown Publishers, 1973).

[11]John T. Guthrie et al., "The Maze Technique to Assess, Monitor Reading Comprehension," *Reading Teacher* 28, no. 2 (Nov. 1974): 161-68.

street

The boys walked down the house.

table

The student is to select the most appropriate word. In this type of testing, students are expected to score 70 percent accuracy to determine instructional levels.

Many will find cloze and maze tests useful to supplement information obtained from informal inventories.

Standardized Tests. Group standardized tests designed to evaluate reading comprehension are *of* little value in clinical diagnosis. However the reading specialist should be knowledgeable about such tests since scores from them are often in the hands of the classroom teacher or in the student's file.

Several of the better-known group tests of silent reading ability are the following: the *California Achievement Test,* * the *Diagnostic Reading Tests,* * *Durrell Listening-Reading Series,* * the *Gates MacGinitie Reading Survey,* * the *Iowa Test of Basic Skills,* * the *Metropolitan Achievement Tests,* * and the *Stanford Achievement Tests.* * Being silent tests, they may be administered in group situations in which the reader normally is expected to complete the process in a generously allotted time period. Although each of these tests provides a measure of a student's performance in word and paragraph meaning, the differences in the items involved to obtain these scores are great. For example, some tests stress the location of directly stated facts, while others sample the ability to handle main ideas, inferences, map reading, and the like.

Silent reading tests are also plagued with limitations. First, if a student's instructional level is not measured by a silent test, the score obtained will be meaningless. For example, if a reader takes a test designed for intermediate-grade students but cannot read beyond the first-grade level, the resulting test score is likely to be invalid since the test did not measure the instructional level. This type of test indicates only that the student is a poor reader, a fact known before the test was administered, but it gives little useful information beyond that.

Second, the author's definition of comprehension may make a difference in the resulting score. For example, the *California Achievement Test* measures comprehension at the elementary level by combining the ability to follow directions; the ability to read maps, charts, and graphs; and the ability to get meaning from paragraphs. Obviously, that score is not comparable to the score on an achievement test measuring only factual recall paragraph meaning.

Another limitation is that standardized populations vary considerably, resulting in grade equivalent scores which are not always accurate for the reader upon whom the diagnosis is being conducted. Efforts must be made to determine the nature of the standardization population; otherwise, the resulting score cannot be evaluated accurately for a given student.

Finally, the reading specialist should be cautioned about the limitations in using certain silent reading tests to make reliable inner test analysis and diagnosis. On the *California Achievement Test,* for example, students taking the elementary form of the test answer three questions to indicate whether they can determine the main idea. Conclusions based upon student responses to only three questions must be held suspect. If the reading specialist is to interpret this score as an area in which further investigation seems warranted, the test has a useful function. More reliable diagnosis is possible, however, on this same test if one compares the major sections, such as "Following Directions," "Reference Skills," and "Interpretation of Materials." The *Diagnostic Reading Tests* and the *Gates MacGinitie Reading Survey* have entire sections which are devoted to an analysis of a child's competency in specific types of silent reading comprehension. Gates, for example, has separate sections for "Speed and Accuracy," "Level of Comprehension," and "Vocabulary."

Reading specialists will use standardized tests, even when not using them in clinical diagnosis. Such tests can be useful for evaluating groups of students if the objectives of the test match the objectives of the instructional program. They can also be used to screen for particularly low achievers.

Another type of standardized test resembles the informal inventory. Such tests are individually administered, have graded paragraphs, and can be used for oral as well as silent reading. An example of such a test is the *Diagnostic Reading Scales.* * Many clinics use such tests in place of informal inventories or as supplements to them. They can also be used for initial screenings (to be discussed later) and informal inventories for more in-depth study of the student's reading behavior.

Order of Testing

As has been explained, testing usually starts with word recognition, moves to oral reading, then silent reading. The University of Maryland reading clinic staff has experimented with a change in order of testing. There, we start with word recognition, then test for comprehension, and follow that with oral reading testing. This order seems to save time and seems to be less frustrating for the student. Since oral reading performance is used more for analysis of the reader's strategies than for reading levels, this adjusted order of testing seems logical.

HYPOTHESIS FORMATION

After measuring the strengths and weaknesses of the reader in sight vocabulary, oral reading, and silent reading, tentative hypotheses are made. From these hypotheses, the reading specialist obtains clues to the reader's strengths and weaknesses in the skill areas and plans further diagnosis. The procedures here are identical to those used by the teacher in classroom diagnosis. Although the questions asked in relation to each skill area are those asked in classroom diagnosis, the resulting conclusions may culminate in further diagnosis since the reading specialist has more diagnostic tools available and is more qualified to interpret the results. Based upon these tentative hypotheses, the reading specialist now will extend the diagnosis to those skill areas which have been identified as needing further analysis.

Extension of Diagnosis

One of the basic considerations for clinical diagnosis concerns the possibility that a student might have a certain strength in mode of learning. For example, a reader who may learn effectively when tactile experiences are combined with visual stimuli, may not learn through visual stimuli alone. These strengths and weaknesses should serve as guides for instruction.

Learning Modalities. To assess learning modalities, the reading specialist has such tests as the *Mills Learning Methods Tests,* * the *Monroe-Sherman Group Diagnostic Reading Aptitude and Achievement Tests,* * the *Detroit Tests of Learning Aptitude,* the *Gates Associative Learning Test,* and the *Illinois Test of Psycholinguistic Abilities.* * These tests attempt to identify strengths in visual or auditory sensory systems; the Mills test adds tactile and combination techniques. For the severely handicapped, identification of strong learning modalities seems to be especially helpful. Modality identification is illusive, however. The examiner must realize that scores from such tests are just that and that student's may have many strengths not noted when using a specific instrument.

Intellectual Abilities. Diagnosis might also be extended into the area of intellectual abilities. As was discussed in Chapter 3, the WISC and the Binet are most commonly used for these purposes. The *Illinois Test of Psycholinguistic Abilities* (ITPA) claims to provide a different look at the student's linguistic functioning. Newcomer and Hammill caution, however, that the ITPA's value is limited to gathering broad, descriptive information and is seriously limited for specific educational diagnosis.[12] Furthermore, correlations between ITPA subtest scores and reading achievement are very low.

Visual Discrimination. If visual discrimination skills appear to be deficient, the *Monroe-Sherman Group Diagnostic Reading Aptitude and Achievement Tests,* standardized readiness tests, or informal measures can be used for further diagnosis. The clinician should be certain that diagnostic data will aid

---

[12]Phyllis L. Newcomer, and Donald D. Hammill, "ITPA and Academic Achievement: A Survey," *Reading Teacher* 28, no. 8 (May 1975): 731-41.

in the development of an educational prescription. Generally, informal measures are of most value. Informal testing, using a simple passage or an experience story, can be conducted by asking the reader to circle all words which begin with a specific letter after showing the letter, by asking the reader to underline all words which have a certain ending, or by finding specific letters in a paragraph. The advantage of such informal testing is that the actual reading passage is the testing medium.

Auditory Discrimination. If auditory discrimination appears to be the problem, further testing through measures such as the *Wepman Auditory Discrimination Test** appears to be of value. Here, auditory discrimination abilities are identified further as initial sounds, medial sounds, or final sounds. Again, informal measures are equally useful and easily constructed. The clinician can read lists of words in pairs (*cat—fat*) and ask the student to indicate whether they are the same or different. Perhaps a better way to determine auditory discrimination skills is to ask the student to repeat the two words. This eliminates confusion about what is meant by same or different.

Orientation. If the tentative hypothesis identifies the orientation area as a problem in reading, diagnosis often is extended through an evaluation of eye motion during the reading act, normally through careful observation of the student during both oral and silent reading. Do the eyes appear to move with a reasonable number of fixations across the line of print? Do the eyes move backwards, making many regressions? Everyone makes regressions in reading; without experience in observing students in the reading act, it is difficult to diagnose this area accurately. Reading specialists should observe groups of good, fair, and poor readers so that they can learn what is expected in the observation of eye movements. Other observations can lead to suspicions about orientation, for example, behaviors such as peculiar reading position, turning the book, and losing one's place.

Dominance Preference. Another extension of diagnosis of orientation often focuses on the area of dominance preference. After screening hundreds of cases of severely handicapped readers, the staff of the University of Maryland reading clinic found no relationship of dominance to orientation problems, nor did they find any remedial solutions based upon such diagnosis. While many students have symptoms of confused dominance, such cases are not restricted to reading problems. Their conclusion to diagnosis in this controversial area is that there is no justification for continued efforts to link reading difficulties to dominance problems. In fact, such diagnosis often leads educators away from the symptoms which will best offer solutions to the student's educational difficulties.

Sight Vocabulary. If the tentative hypothesis identifies sight vocabulary as the problem area, a more careful analysis of tests previously administered may determine consistent patterns of sight vocabulary errors (see Chapter 4).

Durrell suggests that the word not known at sight should be used to see if the reader can analyze the word using word attack when time is not a factor.[13] In such cases, the word recognition answer sheet will have two columns, one for instant pronunciation and one for delayed pronunciation. Obviously, if the reader does not know the word at sight but does know it when permitted to examine it, that reader has skills to attack the word properly but has not overlearned it to the extent that it can be called a sight word.

Word Attack. If the tentative hypothesis finds the area of word attack in need of further diagnosis, the specialist should analyze the errors made in word recognition and oral reading as was done in the classroom diagnosis (see Chapter 4). There are also tests available for clinical diagnosis which measure specific word attack skill performance. The *Botel Reading Inventory: Phonics Mastery,** the *Diagnostic Reading Test** by Bond, Balow, and Hoyt, the *Roswell-Chall Diagnostic Reading Test of Word Analysis Skills,** and the *Doren Diagnostic Reading Test** are four well-known, quite different evaluations of word attack skills. Each of these tests may be administered to groups of students who respond to oral presentations by the teacher. The Botel test is quite short, the Bond, Balow, and Hoyt test takes about forty-five minutes, and the Doren test takes three hours. The various diagnostic test batteries also contain an analysis of word attack skills; however, they heavily emphasize phonics. Teacher-made criterion-referenced tests of the various word attack skills often provide the best insight into skill strengths and needs in this area. For example, if analysis of word recognition and oral reading responses indicates that the student is having difficulty with word endings, then a test can be constructed which measures only those skills dealing with word endings. A standardized word attack test would seem to be a waste of time in such a case.

Reading specialists generally want to see how well a student with specific word attack problems performs on a spelling test. A test of this nature should be given at the student's instructional level. Through an analysis of spelling errors, the reading specialist can extend the diagnosis and verify previous findings.

The reading specialist is cautioned that many readers have learned to attack words adequately in isolated drill-type exercises but are not capable of performing the same task when they see these words in context. It would be erroneous, therefore, to conclude that students do not have word attack deficiencies simply because they perform successfully on diagnostic tests of word attack skills. Evaluation must be made in an oral reading situation where the student is faced, not with the single unknown word, but with the unknown word in a group of familiar words.

---

[13]Donald D. Durrell, *Manual of Directions: Durrell Analysis of Reading Difficulty* (New York: Harcourt Brace Jovanovich, 1955), p. 14.

Comprehension. If the tentative hypothesis identifies the comprehension area as needing further diagnosis, attention must again be directed to those questions asked in classroom diagnosis (see Chapter 4). Clinical diagnosis will be extended to review the history of the basic types of approaches used in the student's reading instruction. From this type of analysis, it often is possible for the reading specialist to understand gaps in areas of instruction and to suggest remedial programs to fill these gaps. In the area of comprehension, the specialist should establish the answers to four additional questions before proceeding to remediation:

1. Is the reader's poor performance on a comprehension test due basically to weak comprehension skills, or is it more closely related to inadequate vocabulary? One technique for determining the answer to this question is to make a careful comparison between word meaning and paragraph meaning scores. Poorer performance in word meaning usually indicates that a student's vocabulary skills are prohibiting maximum performance in comprehension.

2. Is there a need for further comprehension testing to verify scores upon which there is conflicting evidence? It may be necessary to administer a test which has more items, one which has a better variety of items, or one which measures a certain type of comprehension skill not measured in the previously administered silent reading test. When students have serious comprehension difficulties, the reading specialist seldom will find one silent reading test satisfactory. If another test is administered, the results of that test should undergo the same diagnostic scrutiny as did the previous test. Scores of such tests should not be averaged, however. When more than one test of silent reading is used to diagnose skill strengths and weaknesses, analysis of the responses to types of questions rather than a composite score is critical to clinical diagnosis.

3. Is the reader's poor performance on a comprehension test due basically to reading speed? In classroom diagnosis, the ability to complete the reading assignments in a specific time period was considered; in clinical diagnosis, equal consideration must be given to the reader who fails to complete reading tests in the allotted time or is very slow on untimed tests. There is no possibility of obtaining this information from the grade scores on silent reading tests; rather, a careful inner test analysis will reveal the amount of material covered. A test now is available to determine the flexibility with which a student attacks print designed for different purposes. The *Reading Versatility Test** is designed to provide this type of information.

4. Is the reader's poor comprehension on specific text exercises caused by the lack of experiences in the area of the content of the material being read? It is

easy to understand that a city student unfamiliar with farm life might score poorly on a story test about farming yet be quite capable of comprehending a similar story about city life. Diagnosis, however, is not so easy. While broad areas of experience may be identified, a reader's background of experiences is quite personal and involved.

Reading Habits and Attitudes. If the tentative hypothesis identifies reading habits and attitudes as the problem area, the reading specialist has found that the student has the basic skills to read adequately but does not care to read. This diagnosis involves a careful consideration of the information from the areas of emotional and physical diagnosis. The student may indicate a poor attitude toward school-type tasks and books or physical discomfort. Further evaluation is needed of past efforts made by the school to encourage the student to read, the availability of books in the school and at home, and the general atmosphere which may either encourage or discourage reading in these situations. A student who can read but doesn't normally is not considered in need of a specialist's attention. The reading specialist's obligation is to make specific recommendations to the classroom teacher. Fully aware that interests are of the moment and ever changing, the reading specialist, nevertheless, will attempt to assess the student's interests either formally through an established interest inventory or informally through interest inventories and/or a personal interview with the student, his parents, and his teacher. Many students, although they are reading as well as can be expected, are placed in frustrating reading situations daily in school. It does not take a specialist to realize that reading is not much fun for these students and that they easily might develop a negative attitude toward reading. Information gleaned in such a manner will be important to include in the diagnostic report of a problem reader.

Diagnostic Batteries

There are available for clinical diagnosis a group of tests which, used in a single unit, constitute a diagnostic battery. These tests are designed for use as a rather complete reading analysis. The more prominent of these batteries are the *Durrell Analysis of Reading Difficulties,* * *Gates-McKillop Reading Diagnostic Test,* * *Diagnostic Reading Scales,* * and *Monroe-Sherman Group Diagnostic Reading Aptitude and Achievement Tests.* * The first three are individual in nature, while the last is a group test. A careful examination of these diagnostic batteries is essential for an appropriate selection for clinical diagnosis. The only items that all these tests have in common are measures of silent or oral reading and word attack skills. Some tests also include word recognition, oral reading, arithmetic, spelling, auditory and visual discrimination, and auding. The main advantage of using a diagnostic battery is that the scores of the subtests are more comparable since they are standardized on the same population. Another advantage is that there is one manual and one test to learn to administer and interpret; one does not have the overwhelming job that occurs in some other types of testing combinations. The resulting information will provide an individual analysis of how a student is reading and how the student's skill development is related to total reading scores.

These diagnostic batteries are not without limitations, however. Some are too brief and some are standardized on very small populations, thereby causing reliability problems. Most important, possibly, reading specialists will find that the tests do not measure the types or quantities of skills that they wish to measure, thus causing validity problems. Therefore, in clinical diagnosis, it is unlikely that any one of these diagnostic batteries will be adequate for a complete diagnosis. Note that subtests of diagnostic batteries are recommended for use in specific areas of diagnosis, not for precise scores, but for indicators of strengths and weaknesses which might be studied in more depth.

Diagnostic Teaching

Formulating diagnostic hypotheses from data based on testing situations can lead to a distorted view of the reader. How does the reader operate during instruction? An instructional session provides important data for clinical diagnosis.

Specifically, reading specialists should provide lessons which check their findings concerning reading level, major skill strengths, and major skill needs. For example, if the diagnosis supported an instructional level at 3–1, skill strengths in beginning consonants and directly stated recall, and skill weaknesses in vowels and problem solving, a lesson should be designed to see how the reader operates in each of these areas. Several books, one at the 2–2 level, one at the 3–1 level, and perhaps one at the 3–2 level can be selected with silent reading followed by questioning in the area of strengths and needs. A short phonics lesson can be developed to see how well the reader handles consonants and vowels.

If the hypotheses are confirmed, the diagnosis becomes more certain. However, if the student can perform during instruction, new hypotheses will need to be formulated and tested. Rarely are all hypotheses confirmed. Clinicians who skip the step of diagnostic teaching place themselves in the position of drawing faulty conclusions. Preparing a report on a student which contains faulty conclusions has serious consequences. If specialists expect teachers to use their reports to adjust instruction, they should test their findings in instructional situations. In the reading center at the University of Maryland, we have found diagnostic lessons which follow testing to be of the utmost value.

DIFFICULT DIAGNOSTIC PROBLEMS

The So-called Nonreader

Unfortunately, not all diagnosis falls into neat packages of specific skill deficiencies. A small number of students appear unable to profit from even the best instruction in any of the skill areas. They cannot learn to read by conventional methods. Abrams estimates this population to be less than 1 percent of the total population of disabled readers.[14] While diagnosis of these students may be the basic responsibility of the reading specialist, the entire resources of the school should be consulted.

Commonly referred to as *dyslexic, neurologically deficient, minimally brain damaged,* or as possessing a specific reading disability, nonreaders have disabilities complicated by multiple factors. They are almost always emotionally involved in their gross failure. They are likely to be physically deficient and may appear to be dull. Trying to please the teacher often is no longer of interest to them. Diagnosis has failed to identify a consistent pattern of behaviors. Educators have attempted to teach them by all known methods; each of these methods has failed.

Effective diagnosis calls for an interdisciplinary approach to these students. Every effort should be made to seek out the sources of difficulties. It is often necessary for these students to be diagnosed in clinics which have been established to work efficiently with them. Diagnosis and initial remediation will be accomplished most effectively in these clinic-type situations. Many school districts are establishing special schools for such students. Carefully trained teachers work in coordination with personnel from other disciplines to establish meaningful educational programs for these very troubled learners.

In some cases, despite all efforts, these students continue to fail. Multidisciplinary efforts are continuously explored in hopes of establishing new areas of diagnosis and remediation for them. Screening committees assure that the most appropriate resource personnel work to diagnose and remediate these students. Early identification programs followed by early intervention hold some promise. Multisensory techniques are often employed effectively. But the search continues for diagnostic and instructional techniques which will make school life more pleasant and successful for these students.

The Culturally Different

Another group who appear to be experiencing severe difficulty in traditional programs are those who come from culturally different backgrounds. Their

---

[14]Jules Abrams, "Minimal Brain Dysfunction and Dyslexia," *Reading World* 14, no. 3 (March 1975): 219.

language and their experiences are not likely to correspond to the instructional materials which they are expected to use. Mismatching students from poor-income homes with books designed for middle- and upper-class children has been common.

Diagnostic instruments which use stories based on middle-class concepts (Dick and Jane going on a vacation in the suburbs) put poor students at a disadvantage in the testing situation. Interpretation of low reading and intelligence scores must be in terms of the different cultural backgrounds of the students.

Aside from considerations such as these, culturally different students should be diagnosed using the questions suggested in this chapter. Strengths should be noted and taught too. Deficiencies should be worked with through the student's demonstrated strengths. The accept and challenge philosophy is extremely important for establishing good diagnostic and remedial relationships with these students.

LEVELS OF CLINICAL DIAGNOSIS

Initial Screening

The reading specialist will find that an accurate diagnosis of reading disabilities will take much time and effort. It is unfortunate that time is wasted in clinical diagnosis of large numbers of students who do not have reading problems. These students are referred to reading specialists who have no means of knowing them until the entire diagnosis or a major part of it is complete. It seems advisable, then, that the reading specialist have a technique which will screen students prior to the administration of the entire diagnosis. Thus, the reading specialist can eliminate the long waiting lists of students actually in need of diagnosis.

For these reasons, the concept of "initial screening" is introduced. An initial screening should be a brief, concise evaluation of the reading skills, taking approximately one hour. The following is recommended:

1. A test of verbal ability   (such as the *Peabody Picture Vocabulary Test*)

2. A test of word recognition   (such as *Botel Reading Inventory—Word Recognition*)

3. A test of word meaning   (such as *Botel Reading Inventory—Word Opposite, Reading*)

4. An oral reading test   (such as *Diagnostic Reading Scales*)

5. A phonics test, if necessary   (such as *Botel Reading Inventory—Phonics Mastery*)

6. A test of silent   (such as the *Diagnostic Reading Test*)
   reading

7. Information from the   (such as parental interview)
   parents

8. Information from a
   diagnostic lesson

Approximately one-third of the students referred for clinical diagnosis can be eliminated from complete diagnosis on the basis of an initial screening because their problems are not basically ones of poor reading. Many are referred by parents who have not accepted their children as average students and are anxious to see them earning A's and B's in school. Some are referred for poor grades in school for which there appears, as a result of initial screening, to be no blame on reading skills. The screening often provides enough information to outline an instructional program. The amount of examination time and effort saved by the early identification of these students can be used for more thorough diagnosis of those in real need.

Classroom teachers who have had the opportunity to use initial screening techniques in college courses have found them usable in classroom diagnosis; however, initial screening is recommended as a classroom diagnostic technique only if the teacher has had supervised experience with the administration and interpretation of the specific instruments suggested.

Selective Testing

Selective studies can be conducted for one of two reasons. First, during instruction a reading specialist often finds a student's responses to be conflicting. It may appear, for example, that silent reading comprehension has been underrated by the screening. Selective testing is advised. Second, selective testing may be necessary if diagnostic results in one area or another are conflicting. For example, if the school reports that the student has low average I.Q., but the verbal ability test finds him to be high average, further testing is advised. Apparently, in neither situation did the initial screening provide enough information for accurate diagnosis. However, the reading specialist can identify the area in need of further testing. Selective testing follows the principle of maintaining efficiency (that is, not overtesting).

Since reporting is important, the reading specialist should prepare a report on the selective testing. Such a report should include the reasons for testing, the test scores, and a test interpretation. If the testing results in a changed instructional prescription, that also should be included in the report.

Case Study

Occasionally a full case study seems necessary to complete a diagnostic evaluation. To develop a full case study, in-depth testing is required in the areas of intelligence, verbal performance, auditory skills, visual skills, word recognition, oral reading behavior, silent reading comprehension, and word attack skills. To these are added medical reports and a developmental history as well as detailed information from both the school and the home.

The decision to proceed with a full case study will stem from lack of information on the student and failure of the initial screening to identify satisfactorily the student's strengths and weaknesses. Every aspect of the student's educational development, along with an evaluation of intellectual, emotional, and physical development, is needed. Due to the time needed, the expense, and the coordination of efforts, case studies are reserved for those students in most need.

Case Reporting

As in classroom diagnosis, the information accumulated in a clinical diagnosis is useless unless it can be organized so that it is readily understood.

A case report is the typical approach to preparing diagnostic information for clinical use. Although the precise form may vary, the following format should be used so that persons unfamiliar with this student can make optimum use of case information:

1. The first page should contain a concise summary of the essential data included in the report (that is, name, age, address, and school of the student, degree of reading retardation, and a summary statement of the diagnostic findings, including intellectual, physical, emotional, and educational diagnosis).

2. The first page should be followed by as many pages of explanation as necessary. The explanation should include all test scores, the dates upon which they were administered, and the name of the test administrator, as well as diagnostic interpretations of the test performance and evaluations of the student's responses. It also should include data from screening tests and referral reports. It is here that the relative importance of each piece of data is evaluated and interrelated and that causative factors may be identified.

3. A page or two of complete description of the successes of the diagnostic lesson should be the contents of the third section.

4. The last page of the case report should be reserved for specific recommendations and referrals. Recommendations should include those to the clinic, the classroom teacher, and the parents specifying preventive as well as remedial procedures.

It is useful to explain the report to the teacher in a face-to-face interview. Teachers nearly always have questions about the report which can be answered during the interview. It is more likely that the report has been understood by the teacher if it has been discussed.

Not long ago, parents were not given specific information concerning test results. Today that has changed. Not only have parents become aware of the need for such information, they have rights to it. It is essential to give parents copies of anything sent to teachers. If reports are misfiled or lost, parents have copies to replace those lost. Furthermore, parents can often implement adjustments at home to assist with the correction of difficulties.

Since reports often contain technical language, it is helpful to parents to give them the report during a conference. In this manner, technical language can be explained and questions can be answered.

PITFALLS OF DIAGNOSIS

Both clinical and classroom diagnosis may be plagued by certain pitfalls. They include the following:

1. Overgeneralization: The tendency to use total test scores without examination of the pattern of test scores; the tendency to draw conclusions before all facts are in; the tendency to rely upon the first significant symptom; and the tendency to hazard guesses outside the professional field are all examples of overgeneralizing in diagnosis. Overgeneralizing can be controlled, in part, by making couched statements when all data is not available. For example, instead of saying that a student has a poor home life, one might say that from the data available the home conditions bear watching as a possible cause of the student's educational development. More than merely playing with words, couched statements protect the educational diagnostician and lead to more accurate reporting of diagnostic results.

2. Overextension of diagnosis: Extending diagnosis beyond that which will help arrive at an accurate picture of the student may cause the student to become overconcerned about the reading problem and is a waste of time. In commenting on the disadvantages of extended diagnostic periods, Strang concludes, "He may feel more strongly than ever that something may be wrong with him.[15] Overextension of diagnosis occurs more commonly in the clinic than in the classroom, for it is in the clinic that the most careful study of the reader is conducted and a variety of tests are available. Some clinics suggest that each student receive a complete diagnostic analysis regardless of needs. This can only be justified in the interest of gathering research data; however, the expense to the student must always be considered, for not all students can accept large quantities of diagnosis.

[15]Ruth Strang, *Diagnostic Teaching of Reading* (New York: McGraw-Hill, 1969), p. 8.

Nevertheless, every effort must be made to arrive at a true picture of the problem. Through the use of initial screenings, selective studies, and in-depth case studies, diagnosticians have choices available and can avoid overextension of diagnosis.

3. Abbreviated diagnosis: A hurried diagnosis often does not investigate a given reading problem properly. Insufficient diagnosis is most common in the classroom where lack of time and materials exert constant pressure upon the teacher's efforts. Regardless of the limitations of the classroom situation, the teacher must use all available data to insure that the information obtained is reliable and valid. Through abbreviated diagnosis, it is common to jump to wrong conclusions and, in effect, to waste large amounts of time which would have been saved through a more thorough diagnosis. If diagnosticians include the diagnostic teaching lesson as part of their diagnosis, the chance of an abbreviated diagnosis is lessened, for in a diagnostic lesson unknown factors come to light.

4. Overstepping professional boundaries: There is a tendency for educators to make statements which are beyond the professional boundaries of their preparation. The diagnostician must refrain from playing psychiatrist or medical doctor and, instead, must refer willingly when necessary. As with overgeneralizing, couching terms in a diagnostic report that goes beyond the field of education will help avoid overstepping professional boundaries. For example, if a telebinocular examination indicates the need for referral, the clinician might write that poor performance on test four of the telebinocular indicates the need for a professional visual examination. That type of statement is more appropriate than one stating that the poor score on the telebinocular indicates visual problems which need professional attention.

5. Unfounded statements of fact: In direct relation to the preceding pitfalls are positive, factual statements made by educators based on evidence which does not justify that strong a statement. The couching of terms to indicate areas of suspicion where more testing may be needed or areas where referral is necessary will be beneficial to all those who are attempting to arrive at a student's problem. An examiner must be certain that positive statements concerning a student's problem are backed by highly reliable data.

6. Isolation of factors: Isolated pieces of diagnostic data, test scores, and the like must not be examined without consideration for their relationship to the entire diagnosis. It is not unusual for the significance of particular data to be lessened when it is placed in the total picture of a student's reading problem. A single piece of data or a single test score used in isolation is likely to lead to a distorted picture of the problem. Even in the classroom, where time and materials are at a premium, this pitfall should be avoided.

7. Previous bias: The examiner must be alert to the possible interference of data which is tainted by bias. Bias is often found in the remarks of parents or teachers and can have a definite effect on the direction the diagnosis may take. To circumvent this effect, the examiner may intentionally avoid the evaluation of data from the parents and teachers until tentative hypotheses are reached.

SUMMARY

It is through mutual awareness of the specific diagnostic responsibilities of the classroom teacher and the reading specialist that both can perform diagnosis most efficiently. Working with a reader in a classroom group and working with a reader individually outside the classroom call for quite different diagnostic responsibilities and approaches. The realization of these differences enables educators to diagnose problem readers effectively.

Following the observation of the student in reading situations or following testing, diagnosis takes the form of questions which are designed to lead the classroom teacher and the reading specialist to adjustments in instruction. The fact that clinical diagnosis goes further than the classroom teacher can go must not deter the teacher from doing whatever is possible for the student in the classroom.

Diagnosis, to be most useful, must be recorded and interpreted accurately to the individuals concerned, whether they are teachers or parents. All diagnosis need not culminate in an in-depth case study. The choices among initial screenings, selective studies, and in-depth studies places the reading specialist in a flexible diagnostic role.

Finally, diagnosis does not terminate within a given period but continues as long as an educator is working with the student. The continuous nature of diagnosis enables the educator to determine the precise program which will best help the student toward improved reading.

SUGGESTED READINGS

Abrams, Jules. "Minimal Brain Dysfunction and Dyslexia." *Reading World* 14, no. 3 (March (1975): 219-27. A useful discussion, this article places these terms in perspective for reading teachers and classroom teachers.

Buros, Oscar K. *Reading Tests & Reviews, 1 & 2.* Highland Park, N. J.: Gryphon, 1975, 1968. This publication is a listing of all available reading tests available as of 1968. Most tests receive critical reviews. An essential book for those selecting testing instruments in reading.

Farr, Roger. *Reading: What Can Be Measured?* Newark, Del.: International Reading Association, 1967. Chapters 2 and 3 discuss the use and misuse of available testing instruments in reading. Readers are encouraged to study Farr's discussion.

Goodman, Kenneth S. "Analysis of Oral Reading Miscues: Applied Psycholinguistics." *Reading Research Quarterly* 5 (Fall 1969): 9-30.

Harris, Albert J. *How To Increase Reading Ability,* 4th ed. New York: David McKay Co., 1970. Chapters 7 and 8 present rather interesting discussions of the topics discussed under educational diagnosis. Harris' book is considered required reading by all those seriously interested in the diagnosis of reading problems.

Geyer, James R., and Matanzo, Jane. *Strategies for Classroom Teachers: A Programmed Text.* Columbus, O.: Charles E. Merrill Publishing Co., 1977. The opportunity for specific practice in various parts of diagnosis and prescription is provided in this book. Reading specialists would do well to have worked through all aspects presented by Geyer and Matanzo.

Kolson, Clifford J., and Kaluger, George. *Clinical Aspects of Remedial Reading.* Springfield, Ill.: Charles C Thomas, 1964. Chapters 3, 4, and 6 discuss diagnosis of reading problems from the most difficult to the not so serious. This book limits itself to clinical diagnosis and would be most interesting to the reading specialist.

Strang, Ruth. *Diagnostic Teaching of Reading,* p. 8. New York: McGraw-Hill, 1964. In Chapters 3 through 7, diagnostic techniques are presented which have application to classroom as well as clinical situations. There are specific suggestions for working with older children in diagnostic situations.

6

Remediation— Some Insights

Remediation of reading problems is not, as many believe, based upon mysterious techniques which are impossible for the classroom teacher to understand. Rather, remediation is based upon sound instructional principles focused upon the strengths and needs of the students on the basis of careful diagnosis. Since remediation calls for skillful teaching, it is assumed that anyone who works in a remedial program is a skilled teacher who keeps up-to-date by reading and studying.

As previously discussed in diagnosis, there is seldom *one* cause of reading problems; therefore, there is seldom one approach to the solution of such problems. On this point, the public has often been led to believe the opposite, thereby causing pressure to be placed upon educators to teach by certain methods. That there is seldom one satisfactory remedial approach, however, in no way justifies using a little of all known teaching techniques; this is called the "shotgun" approach. Rather, remediation must be in direct response to diagnostic conclusions, necessitating the use of the most suitable educational techniques as solutions to the diagnostic conclusions. These conclusions contain information concerning skill strengths as well as needs.

GUIDELINES FOR REMEDIATION

By adhering to the following three guidelines, teachers will find remediation most effective.

Remediation must guarantee immediate success. In the remedial program, initial instruction should culminate in a successful, satisfying experience. In this way, students who have experienced frequent failure in reading begin the remedial program with the attitude that this educational experience will be both different and rewarding. Without this attitude, the best remedial efforts are often wasted. Successful learning situations also are assured by directing activities toward those learning activities which the diagnosis has indicated are the students' strengths and interests. It is recommended that all the early lessons be directed toward student strengths. As remediation progresses, the percentage of time devoted to strengths is likely to decrease. When the students start to ask for instruction in the areas of their weaknesses, changes in instructional strategy can take place. However, it is recommended that throughout the entire program, a large portion of every lesson be directed to strengths.

Remedial successes must be illustrated to the student. It is not enough that a reader be started at the right level and experience a successful situation; successes must be presented so that awareness of those successes is assured. As students progress, charts, graphs, word files, and specific teacher praise comments can be used to illustrate successes.

Remediation must provide for transfer to actual reading situations. There will be occasions in a remedial program where isolated drill in various areas will be required; however, drill activities should always come from contextual reading material and should always conclude in contextual reading situations. The overlearning of all skills takes place best in actual reading situations.

Types of Remediation

Unlike diagnosis, classroom and clinical remediation involve the same teaching strategies. The students need individualized instruction. Instruction is based on sound learning theory, and is constantly adjusted to students' responses. While remediation in a clinical setting may be easier due to small numbers of students in a group, the strategies used do not differ. There are no materials, no techniques, and no learning theories which are reserved for the clinical setting. In fact, the opposite may be true. Many teachers are able and willing to apply skills learned in a clinical setting to their classrooms. Many reading specialists find it useful to conduct remedial efforts without taking the readers from their classrooms. In this manner, teachers can easily pick up teaching strategies used by the reading specialist. And, to the surprise of some, reading specialists can often learn a great deal from the classroom teacher's teaching strategies.

Considerations for Starting Remediation

Several types of planning strategies need to be considered as one enters into remedial programs. These strategies have been found to make a difference between success and failure when instructing handicapped readers.

Assure Positive Attitude. Remedial activities, while based on diagnosis, should concentrate on the interests of students. The sense of self-worth must be developed early. Helping readers to realize success with materials which are of interest has tremendous impact. The "I can't do it," attitude quickly turns around to "I can do it." We don't talk handicapped readers into feeling good about themselves; we make certain that success experiences are realized. We also make certain that those experiences are important to the student. The use of newspapers, auto magazines, model construction, and cooking are examples of reading activities which generally have high interest. One student, reportedly not able to read above the third-grade level, could read football articles in the *Washington Post* at a high level of comprehension. The following suggestions can be used as starter ideas.

1. When students perform successfully, let them teach that activity to another.
2. Provide rewards for successful performance.
3. Build small-group rapport. "We can read—we are worthwhile."
4. Provide teaming situations for successful learning. Let pairs of readers work toward an objective.
5. Make certain the students know the objectives and know when they have reached them.
6. Keep parents and other teachers informed about success experiences so that they may reinforce them.

Plan for a Balanced Program. Two types of balance make remedial programs effective. The first type is a balance between reading narrative types of material and reading content material. As students see reading skills transferred to content material, the realization develops that they can be successful in science and social studies types of activities and that success in school is possible.

Another type of balance is that of skills and reading. Each skills lesson must result in a successful reading activity. Actually, three steps are appropriate:

1. Skills lessons
2. Practice lessons utilizing those skills
3. Free reading, applying those skills

Without these types of balance, remedial instruction can become segmented and can distort the purposes for learning to read well. Success in phonics lessons is useless unless those learned skills can be applied in free reading. Teachers need to plan for balance in order to assure a complete remedial program.

Plan for Student Decision Making. No better way for a student to be enthusiastic about the lesson than to be involved in setting objectives, selecting activities, and participating in evaluation. Many handicapped readers sit through activities designed to improve their reading skills but have no idea where the lesson is designed to lead them.

During orientation activities to a given lesson, students should be free to add objectives and question others. This is not to say that students make all decisions, but they can have input. Generally students are inclined to put forth more effort once they understand why they are doing a given activity.

Contracting to complete a certain number of activities in a certain amount of time has great impact. The teacher provides a list of possible activities which will satisfy skill drill, skill practice, and free reading. From this list, the students and teacher pick those which are of most interest and appear to be most possible for them. The concept of negotiation is important. Both the students and the teacher have input. At times, some activities are required; at other times, two activities are selected from a list of five. Or, at other times, students might have completely free choice. A form such as Figure 8 is useful.

The student is instructed to self-evaluate by placing a smile or frown in the little box beside the activity completed. When all agreed-upon activities are completed, no further work is assigned. The payoff for completing assignments must not be more assignments.

The teacher and students now discuss the quality of the completed activities and plan for tomorrow's lessons. Activities positively evaluated should be discussed in terms of what made the students feel good about them. Ones negatively evaluated should also be discussed. The important point is that students should not be made to feel badly about an honest evaluation. Use their reactions as clues in future planning. Experience with such contracts shows that many students become more and more positive about reading, and it is not uncommon for them to ask for more activities—a good sign that reading is becoming interesting and worthwhile.

The students now feel very involved with their lessons. They become trusting and enthusiastic. The teacher, always in control, now knows what does and does not interest the students; therefore, better planning results.

Conduct Task Analysis. When students have difficulty with a given activity, task analysis can be used as a diagnostic teaching tool. Task analysis asks the teacher to consider which subskills might be missing in order for the student to

FIGURE 8

Name _____   Date _____

Pick one activity from box 1, 2, 3.
Pick one activity from box 4, 5, 6.
Pick one activity from box 7, 8, 9.
Activity 10 is required.

1. Play initial consonant game.	2. Teach consonants to your partner.
3. Complete skills sheet on consonants.	4. Find words beginning with s, t, c, b on page 34.
5. Read story about Pat the Rat.	6. Read aloud with teacher.
7. Read story from book on library shelf.	8. Make display advertising book you are reading.
9. Read aloud with your partner from book of your choice.	10. Participate in ten-minute sustained silent reading.

complete the given task. Since all students master skills in very personal ways, pat formulas for why a given student cannot respond are of little use. The efforts in this direction by the University of Maryland reading center were stimulated by the ideas of Ladd.[1] Here is how we have applied those ideas:[2]

Step 1   A problem is identified.
        Example:[3] A student cannot respond satisfactorily to questioning about the material read, even when reading silently.

Step 2   The teacher is to determine the strengths and weaknesses the student has in this skill area.
        Example: Can read orally with satisfactory accuracy at the fourth-grade level.

---

[1]Eleanor Ladd, "Task Analysis," *Reading: What Is It All About* (Clemson, S.C.: Clemson University, 1975), pp. 68-77.

[2]Robert M. Wilson, "Comprehension Diagnosis Via Task Analysis," *Reading World* 14, no. 3 (March 1975): 178-79.

[3]Examples are abbreviated, not including all possible entries.

Cannot answer literal questions asked of him from this material.

Can answer literal questions when working from the third-grade level.

Step 3   The teacher makes a series of hypotheses concerning the possible reasons for this difficulty.

Example: The student is not interested in the material.

The passage is too long.

The questions are threatening.

The student does not have purpose for reading.

Step 4   Through diagnostic teaching, the teacher tests each hypothesis.

Example: For the first hypothesis, the reader might attempt to determine the student's interest areas and find material at the fourth-grade level which is of interest. For the second hypothesis, the teacher might break the passage into smaller parts, asking the questions following each part.

Step 5   The teacher keeps a record of each diagnostic lesson and forms a tentative conclusion to be tested in further instruction.

Example: This student responded well when material was in the area of sports and motorcycles. He also responded better when he jotted down his purposes for reading before he started. Passage length adjustment did not change his ability to comprehend, and the questions did not seem threatening in this new situation.

Of course task analysis is the strategy that has been used by good teachers for a long time. But we have found it helpful to formalize the process in this manner so that all can profit from its power as a diagnostic tool.

The value of task analysis for reading diagnosis is increased by the fact that people do not all learn through the same set of subskills. What stops one person from comprehending a given passage is different from what stops another. And what one person needs as a subskill to read better might well be a subskill that another person does not need. Task analysis provides a highly suitable, flexible strategy for getting at the unique learning styles of each reader.

Get Others Involved. When working with handicapped readers, teachers must utilize all the resources available. The answer to a given student's problem might best be solved by involving a physical education teacher, a speech therapist, the parents, a psychologist, or the family doctor. Even if others do not have suggestions for helping such students, communication channels should be open so that all involved are informed. Many a good instructional program has become ineffective when others are working at crossed purposes.

Peers can work with a given reader by teaming with her on activities which she cannot do by herself. They can also conduct some of the time-consuming, drill-type activities; they too can profit from the student's strengths. For example, I worked with a boy who always was the poorest in every activity. He always saw himself as a follower, never as a leader. As a field trip approached, he was taken on a "dry run" to familiarize him with the features of the field trip. He became excited and served as a group leader on the actual field trip. The other children appreciated his leadership and assistance. By getting everyone involved, the teacher can change a student's life from one of failure and frustration to one of success and excitement.

By considering the above-mentioned ideas prior to initiating a remedial program, teachers can make adjustments that provide for a greater chance of success.

The Older Handicapped Reader

Secondary school students with serious reading problems require special consideration when planning a remedial program. Materials for instruction and instructional techniques need to be selected in terms of appeal for the secondary student. Driver's manuals, job information, consumer education materials, and newspaper articles are examples of appealing materials. We have found it best to let these students bring to class the materials they need to be able to read.

Contracting with these students also has appeal. The contracts differ from those used with younger students in that the secondary students are more involved with the decisions made in each part of the contract, i.e., planning, selecting activities, and evaluating. We have also found secondary students with severe reading problems to be excellent tutors for younger students. They take great pride in such roles and obtain excellent results. As is commonly reported, they probably learn more than the student being tutored. It also helps to organize instructional activities around problems which the students have identified as important to them. Secondary students can get turned on to reading when the learning activities have immediate application in their lives.

Continuing to teach the same reading skills which these students have had forced upon them for years is seldom effective. Instead of isolated phonics, keep instruction at the word and phrase level at a minimum. Instead of seeking to retain details, engage the student in discussion of important ideas. Relate reading skills to those academic subjects which are of interest. Help them see reading as a key to success in school.

While all of the above suggestions have application to students of all ages, they have particular application to secondary students with severe reading problems, because almost all of these students have been turned off to school and to reading. The teacher has to work first on attitude and self-concept. A little reading success with the right types of materials can start changing negative attitudes.

SUMMARY

Effective remedial programs focus on the self-concept of the student. Strengths must be practiced, recognized, and approved. Students must be decision makers in their instructional activities along with the teacher. All school resources must be utilized to assist handicapped readers to realize they can and do read.

SUGGESTED READINGS

Gambrell, Linda B., and Wilson, Robert M. *Focusing on the Strengths of Children.* Belmont, Calif.: Fearon Publishers, 1973. Detailed accounts for techniques for focusing on strengths of all students are provided. Ideas for making school enjoyable are throughout.

Gates, Arthur I. *The Improvement of Reading.* New York: The Macmillan Co., 1947. Gates devotes Chapter 5 to the establishment of a remedial program. The reader who desires more information will find this a suitable reference.

Kaluger, George, and Kolson, Clifford J. *Reading & Learning Disabilities.* Columbus, Ohio: Charles E. Merrill Publishing Co., 1969. In Chapter 8, the authors suggest techniques for starting a reader in a remedial program. With an approach differing from those suggested in this chapter, the authors explain the necessity for establishing rapport.

Wilson, Robert M., and Gambrell, Linda B. *Contract Teaching.* Silver Spring, Md.: Reading Education Inc., 1975. Numerous examples of contract teaching with detailed explanations are included. Record-keeping strategies and reinforcement techniques make this a useful source.

7

Remedial Activities in Readiness Skills

There are some handicapped readers who need to have readiness skills refined. Some of these readers seem immature; others appear to be dull. Some need time to develop, and others need instruction. Readiness activities for handicapped readers are similar to readiness activities for beginning readers.

LANGUAGE

Language difficulties can result from three different causes: the student's language does not match the language of the school; it is underdeveloped due to a limited experiential language background; or it reflects limited intellectual development.

Language Mismatching

Students whose language differs from that used in school and in the materials of instruction are often found in remedial reading classes. Their difficulty lies in attempting to learn to read a language which differs to some degree from the one they speak. How seriously the problem of mismatching affects reading ability is uncertain; however, one might safely assume that it causes a degree of discomfort which, when coupled with other learning difficulties, can interfere with learning to read easily. Of course, many students with mismatched language do learn to read effectively.

Instruction must start with acceptance of their language by the teacher. Genuine respect for the language which all students bring to school is extremely important. Attacks and criticisms of one's language is personally intolerable, for they attack not only the student but his family and his friends. Specifically, the teacher should demonstrate acceptance by:

1. Responding to the language without initial correction.
2. Responding to the student's thoughts with enthusiasm regardless of his language form.
3. Not repeating the student's response in a correcting effort.
4. Permitting the student to write his language without correction.

The premise upon which such suggestions are based is that anyone can work better and faster with a student who feels comfortable and accepted. However, teachers demonstrate considerable concern about these techniques because they feel that they are responsible for improving language. But the concept of "improving" in itself implies nonacceptance. The teacher must recognize the students' language as being good for them and acceptable for their purposes.[1] The teacher also can help students to become aware of other language forms in addition to those more commonly used in school. Most importantly, students must feel accepted so that they can receive further instruction. Specifically, the following instruction techniques are suggested:

1. When using prepared materials, accept students' use of dialect. If the sentence is "I see two dogs," and a student says, "I see two dog," accept it without correction. By so doing, meaning is being stressed and language is accepted.
2. Use language-experience stories which children can dictate to you (see page 149 for specifics on the use of language experience). In writing student contributions, be certain to spell words accurately (e.g., if a student says, "da dog," write, "the dog"). When the student reads the story aloud, he will probably say, "da dog" and that should be acceptable. Teachers should not change the syntax. (For example, if a student says, "I

---

[1]Kenneth S. Goodman, "Dialect Rejection and Reading," *Reading Research Quarterly,* Summer 1970, p. 603.

ain't got none,'' it should be written as he says it). To change the syntax to 'I don't have any'' is a correction and denies the principle of acceptance.

3. Structure numerous opportunities for students to hear and to respond to language which is commonly found in books and is used in other segments of our society, through the following methods:

   a. Read to them. Read every day. Read good literature. Talk with them about what you have read. Let them discuss it with you.

   b. Always serve as a model. Enunciate precisely and use standard English forms. Teach students to respond to your language. Use of tape recorders to provide stories and directions for activities can provide even more model opportunities.

   c. Provide structured lessons to develop students' abilities to use the language they will find elsewhere in society and particularly in school. Feigenbaum suggests the following three steps:[2]

      (1) *Auditory discrimination:* Help the student to hear differences in language form. Take one type of difference (negation, for example) and say, ''Tell me whether these two sentences sound exactly alike or different: 1. I ain't got none. 2. I don't have any.'' As the students develop auditory discrimination skills between their language and school language, move to step two.

      (2) *Identification of school language:* From the two sentences, help the students to pick the one they are most likely to hear the teacher use or to read in books. Auditory awareness of school language is not difficult to develop but is not to be assumed merely from the ability to discriminate auditorily.

      (3) *Dialect transfer:* Say one sentence and have the students respond in the other language. Such transfer should be practiced both ways (i.e., from home language to school language and the reverse). For example, the teacher says, ''I ain't got none,'' and the students attempt to put the expression into school language. Then the teacher uses school language, and the students respond in their language. When conducting structured lessons, the teacher should start with a structure common to the students' language and stay with one structure until dialect transfer is mastered before selecting another. All lessons must be conducted without reference to right and wrong or good and bad.

---

[2]Irwin Feigenbaum, ''The Use of Nonstandard English in Teaching Standard: Contrast and Comparison,'' *Teaching Standard English in the Inner City* (Washington, D.C.: Center for Applied Linguistics, 1970), pp. 87-104.

Once dialect transfer is mastered, the teacher should encourage the students to use school language in school but should not encourage them to use it in their informal conversations at play or at home. As students with language mismatch problems gain skill in dialect transfer, instruction with materials using school language can be used effectively.

Underdeveloped Language

Students who come to school seriously deficient in experiences simply do not have the conceptual framework to work effectively in reading. Those from isolated rural poverty areas and those from severe poverty areas in large cities might be considered as representing these types of students. In the following discussion, it is assumed that these types of students lack experiences but not mental ability. They may appear to be dull because they fail to understand situations which are comprehended commonly. They may not know about mountains, lakes, automobiles, and airplanes. Specific educational adjustments include:

1. Emphasis on the creation of language experiences. Everything that happens during the school day is discussed. Linking language directly to the experiences of students helps them to develop concepts for the things they are encountering. Trips, pictures, films, and tapes can be used in the development of language experiences. Activities within the classroom, special programs in the school, and visitors in the classroom also stimulate language. Every experience must be discussed, for language should be a constant part of the experience. For example, it is not enough for a class to make a trip to the zoo. The students should talk about what they are experiencing, and the teacher should bombard them with language explanations of what they are experiencing.

2. Starting with the language-experience approach. As it does for students with different dialects, the language-experience approach assures a successful start in reading since the language students encounter is their own.

3. Employment of available commercial programs. Several companies have commercial programs designed to facilitate language development. Most of these programs involve stimulation with pictures, tapes, or films. Teachers are directed to help students explain what they are seeing or hearing. Vocabulary is developed as they listen to each other and to the teacher. Synonym and antonym activities also stretch students' conceptual framework.

4. Continuous language exposure. Activities which permit students to talk with one another and to listen to the teacher make language improvement possible. Activities such as role playing in which students are encouraged

to act out roles of story characters or persons whom they admire stimulate students to talk with each other. A telephone corner with toy phones can be used to stimulate talking. Perhaps an older buddy can come to the room to talk about an exciting experience. Activities that stimulate one-to-one conversations are needed in abundance for those with underdeveloped language backgrounds. Activities through which teachers can encourage students to talk include: a question chair placed close to the teacher's work area (a student with a question comes to the chair, and the teacher talks with him), simple repetition games which call for students to repeat what the teacher has said, and eating lunch and chatting with several students every day. Activities such as these place value on language as communication and expose students to modeled language. However, since reading is *not* withheld until large vocabularies are developed, it is important to remember that the language bombardment concept must continue for several years.

Intellectual Development

There are some who have language problems which stem from slow intellectual development. They may be six years old but have slowed intellectual development so that they react to language like four year olds. Many of these children have compounding problems, such as poor motor coordination or physical defects. Although many find their way into programs for the mentally retarded, many others are in the classroom, and teachers must learn how to work with them.

As a first suggestion, every teacher is encouraged to view each student as a developmental human who is as much as he can be. Therefore, the teacher should work with him from where he is in his development. Accept him. Categorizing him through name calling or special grouping does not indicate acceptance and is of limited value. At the same time, expectations in terms of rate of learning, quantity of learning, and retention ability should be realistic. Programs must be adjusted for these students in order to utilize their strengths. Patience and many rewards for successful performances should be predominant. Successes must be highlighted, and failures must be minimized or ignored.

Regardless of the type of language deficiency, the student's education must continue. No excuses, no "cop-outs." Starting points must be identified, and progress should be documented. The teacher should keep in mind that all students can learn and that all can profit from reading programs if the programs are adjusted to their strengths.

The classifications for language deficiencies suggested in this chapter are not as clear-cut as they might seem. Many students might be handicapped by two or by all three types of language limitations. But these students can learn.

Educators cannot use language development as an excuse for not teaching; students cannot use it as an excuse for not learning.

The developmental nature of language is obvious. That students have language indicates that they have developed their language to some degree. Teachers must start with what the students have, make them feel comfortable, illustrate to them that learning is possible and fun, and be pleased with successes that occur.

AUDITORY DIFFICULTIES

Many students enter school without the necessary auditory skills to profit from normal instruction. When ignored by the teacher, these auditory skills can remain undeveloped, thus causing considerable discomfort to the struggling reader. For this discussion on remediation, auditory skills will be classified in two general areas: hearing problems and auditory discrimination problems.

Hearing Problems

While teachers can do nothing to correct hearing problems aside from referring the student to a hearing specialist, they can make temporary classroom adjustments to facilitate a comfortable learning situation:

1. They can arrange the seating so that the students with hearing problems are close to the teacher during group instruction.
2. Teachers should stand close to those students' desks during group instruction and should increase their volume so that students with hearing problems can hear the instructions. They can also face the children, thereby providing opportunity for lip reading.
3. Creating a buddy system is helpful. When a student does not hear the teacher or the other students, his buddy can repeat the information and help him to understand it.
4. When possible, visual learning activities (i.e., reading instead of listening) should be stressed. Instruction for independent work should be written, as should rules, regulations, and announcements. The writing can be on the board, on chart paper, or in personal notes to students with hearing problems.

Auditory Discrimination

It is common to find students with normal hearing skills but underdeveloped auditory discrimination skills. They have difficulty distinguishing one sound from another. Their difficulty is likely to be easily recognized as speech impairment or trouble with phonics. That students come to school with most speech skills developed would lead one to believe that their auditory discrimination skills are also developed. However, for teachers with students with underdeveloped articulation skills or who are not in the habit of listening carefully, the following suggestions can be of value:

1. Request the assistance of a speech therapist who can work with the students, help you to diagnose the child's difficulty, or offer suggestions for classroom adjustments.

2. Serve as a speech model. Enunciate distinctly and read with articulate speech patterns.

3. Provide exercises which stress gross auditory differences. For example:

   Tell me whether the words which I repeat are the same or different:

   > *catch—catch*
   > *big—dog*
   > *many—some*

   Tell me whether the first sound you hear in the words which I repeat are the same or different:

   > *big—big*
   > *butter—lettuce*
   > *boy—sail*

4. Gradually provide exercises involving finer auditory discriminations. For example:

   Tell me whether the words which I repeat are the same or different:

   > *catch—catch*
   > *corn—scorn*
   > *can—tan*

   Tell me whether the first sound you hear in the following words is the same or different:

   > *big—pig*
   > *bite—tight*
   > *best—best*

5. Provide exercises which demand longer auditory memory. For example:

   Listen to the first word which I give you. Then tell me whether the following words are the same or different:

   > *pig: pig—small—big—pig—dig*

   Listen to the first sound in the word I give you. Then tell me which of the following words have the same beginning sound:

   > *pig: bite—pick—pencil—dig—picnic*

6. Provide exercises which call for listening for sound in different parts of the word. For example:

> Listen for words which end in the same sound as the word *pig:*
>
> dig—ditch—park—twig—dog

7. Provide exercises which indicate the ability to hear rhyming words. For example:

> Listen to the first word I give you and tell me whether the following words rhyme with that word:
>
> cat: rat—sat—pot—pat

8. Provide a stimulus word and ask the student to say some words which rhyme. For example:

> Listen to the first word I give you and tell me some words that rhyme with it:
>
> cat: _____ _____ _____ _____ _____

Techniques for conducting drill lessons such as those suggested above can include: placing items on tape and having students do the exercises independently, having an aide or a skilled student read what you have prepared, calling the students who need such work to you while the others are working independently. The point is that the students need daily practice to assist them in the development of the auditory discrimination skills. As the skills are mastered, periodic review is necessary. It is also necessary to review the skills prior to the development of phonics lessons. Auditory discrimination skills are easily developed. Furthermore, skills which have been taught can be reinforced through game activities.[3,4]

Some students will not respond to the activities suggested above due to serious problems in auditory orientation. These students need in-depth training in a cooperative effort among the reading teacher, the classroom teacher, and the speech teacher. Phonics instruction, for them, should be withheld until a thorough program in auditory sequencing has been completed. They have difficulty distinguishing initial, medial, and final sounds as they hear them. They also have difficulty associating auditory with visual sequences. Understandably these are different skills. Auditory sequences occur in time while visual sequences occur in space. That most students come to school with these skills in hand causes some teachers to assume that all students have them. Programs such as *Auditory Discrimination in Depth** provide instruction in sound formation, sound sequences, and sound placement. These programs

---

[3]David Russell and Etta E. Karp, *Reading Aids Through the Grades* and *Listening Aids Through the Grades* (New York: Teachers College, Columbia University, 1951).

[4]Arthur Heilman, *Phonics We Use, Learning Games Kit* (Chicago: Lyons and Carnaham, 1968).

require one-to-one instruction and complete cooperation of all who work with the student. The results have been rewarding in the few cases I have seen the program in operation.

VISUAL DIFFICULTIES

As is true of auditory problems, visual problems also can be grouped into two categories: those dealing with the skills and functions of vision and those dealing with visual discrimination. Numerous students find giving visual attention difficult either as the result of a physical disability or of a developmental lag.

Problems in Vision

Visual problems can be adjusted and corrected by vision specialists. The teacher, in the meantime, must work with those students daily. Several suggestions are offered for helping students with vision problems:

1. Arrange seating so that the reader has the best light, the least glare, and the optimum distance for his difficulty. Those who are farsighted can sit in the back of the instructional area and those who are nearsighted can sit in the front.
2. When writing on the board, use larger letter size than usual.
3. Supplement writing on the board or on chart paper by providing auditory reinforcement.
4. Use the buddy system. By working with a student who has normal sight, a student with visual difficulties can seek help when his vision keeps him from getting needed material.
5. Stress auditory learning. A student with visual problems might respond better to a phonics approach or to sound reinforcement. Tracing also helps, for it develops within the reader opportunities for reinforcing his weak visual skills.
6. Make visual activity periods of short duration. When students show signs of discomfort (e.g., rubbing of eyes and inattentiveness), they should be released from the visual tasks involved in reading.

Adjustments such as those suggested above are not the answer to the basic problem but are adjustments which can make learning both possible and comfortable for a student.

Visual Discrimination

Difficulties with visual discrimination skills are usually the result of either a lack of experience or an inability to attend to the task. In either case, successful experience can usually develop comfort in visual discrimination skills. The following suggestions can be of value in developing visual discrimination skills:

1. Start with the language of the students. As they talk, write down what they say. For example, if a student wanted to talk about what he saw on his way to school, the following story might develop:

   > I saw a big dog.
   > His name was Rex.
   > The dog frightened many of us.
   > But I picked up a stick and scared the dog.
   > Everyone thinks I am very brave.
   > Do you?

   Once the story is written, two copies are prepared for each student, one to use for visual discrimination activities and one to save for reading. On the copy which the children can mark, the following activities can be tried.

   a. Ask the students to pick words which they know. Write the words on cards and then have them find the words in the story. They do not need to say them, but they do have to match them.

   b. Write the letter s on a card and ask the students to underline that letter every time they see it in the story.

   c. Ask the students to circle all the words that begin with the letter a. (Give them a cards.)

   d. Write a phrase on cards. Have the students find it in the story and draw two lines under it.

   e. Ask the students to draw a box around every word that ends with the letter e. (Give the students e cards.)

   From story copy which has been duplicated, have the students cut out words and phrases and match them with the story on chart paper. Such an activity enhances transfer from activities at the seat to activities at the board. Depending upon the story, there are many visual discrimination activities which can help students develop the required skills. Matching, seeing letters in words, finding letters in specific parts of words, and finding groups of words in a certain order are but a few examples. By asking the students to do something different in each activity (i.e., underlining, circling, drawing a box, and so on), the teacher can see easily how well each activity has been completed. As is true with auditory discrimination, start with gross discriminations and move to fine discriminations. For example, beginning with the letter *s* is easier than starting with *d*. Finding a word is easier than finding a letter; finding a letter or a group of letters in a certain position in a word is even more difficult. Discover where the students are in the development of visual discrimination abilities and work from there. It is also important to give a stimulus with which the students are to work visually. Auditory reinforcements are fine, but the activities must be visual to visual (i.e., the students see a word on a card and matches it with a word on the board).

2. Word cards (i.e., cards on which the students have written words mastered) can be used to develop visual discrimination skills. For example, ask the students to:

   a. find all the words in their files that end in *e*, like at*e*.

   b. find all the words that end in *ing*, like walk*ing*.

   c. find all the words that have double consonants, like te*ll*.

   The suggestions for such activities could be endless, but two points about them are important: (1) you are working with visual clues and from words which the students know, and (2), through teaching from strengths, students can develop strong visual discrimination skills.

3. Provide an area in the room where several magazines are collected. Instruct the readers to look through the magazine ads for examples of certain kinds of words (e.g., words about people, words which describe things, etc.). Provide a visual stimulus (e.g., a pair of scissors or some paste, and a place to post these words when found).

4. Game-type activities hold considerable merit in developing visual discrimination, just as they do in developing auditory discrimination. Suggestions can be found in Russell.[5] For example, give the students a set of cards with letters on them. Start with a small group of letters, such as *s, t,* and *w*. Hold up a letter and have them hold up the same letter. Then hold up two letters and have them hold up the same two letters in the same sequence. Such an activity gradually can be increased in difficulty, thus developing the attention to detail and visual discrimination skills needed for reading. Once the game idea is developed, students can play the game without direct teacher supervision.

5. Commercially prepared materials are available in several forms. Workbook-type activities, spirit duplication master sheets, and pencil-paper activities are common. Many such activities start with form identification. For example, five balls are placed on a sheet; four of them are green and

---

[5]Russell and Karp, *Reading Aids Through the Grades*.

one is red. Students are to mark the one that is different. However, such activities should be reserved for only the most severely handicapped and even then seem to be of questionable value in the reading process. Several of the more popular commercial materials are listed in Appendix B. However, teachers themselves can make materials which are more relevant and more related to the reading process with relatively small commitments of time and energy. Students respond very well to such homemade materials.

While making materials for students to use in visual discrimination activities, several precautions are necessary:

1. Printing should be done very carefully; however, typing is preferred.
2. Only printing should be used on working copies. These copies should contain no art work, pictures, or other types of distractions.
3. At first, small amounts of print should be used on a page. Do not smother the reader with too many words and sentences.
4. Make activities short and, if possible, self-correcting. Provide answer keys or models of marked copies.
5. Make the print of beginning activities look like that which the children are accustomed to seeing. For very young children, each new sentence should start a new line. With older students, material can appear in paragraph form. To make the material too much like a preprimer is insulting to older students.
6. Always end the activity with a reading of the story. If the students cannot read it, read it to them. Always bring the activity back to reading for thought. Discuss the story and its meanings with the students.
7. When students do well, tell them so. Praise for legitimate successes is important in all drill work, but do not praise incomplete or inaccurate work. Instead, restructure the activity so that students can complete it and then praise them.

Continue with visual discrimination activities as the students begin to read. Review as well as more advanced activities should be part of the visual discrimination program until students are operating with comfort.

ORIENTATION

Orientation difficulties are reflected by an inability to visually follow the print in words or sentences. Orientation skills are commonly listed under visual discrimination; however, difficulties in this area seem to be peculiar enough to justify separate classification. As has been stated, visual discrimination skills are related to seeing likenesses and differences, while orientation skills are concerned with the left-to-right controlled visual movements necessary for effective reading.

It is generally acknowledged that readers' orientation errors cannot be corrected by simply calling the errors to their attention. Remedial procedures in the area of orientation skills are most effective when they help students feel the comfort and success that accompanies correct orientation and when they provide practice to extend the skill into a habit.

Three specific questions are asked for correction of orientation problems:

1. Does the student exhibit visual difficulty in following the print from left-to-right?
2. Does the student habitually reverse words and letters?
3. Does the student habitually lose his place?

The framework of remediation will involve dealing with these questions in terms of instruction.

The symptoms suggested by these questions are closely related at times for they all pertain to directional attack on the printed page. As a result, remedial techniques are often quite similar. However, these areas are differentiated here in an effort to make remediation as understandable as possible.

Failure to Move Left-to-Right

This is a problem that normally can be traced to a faulty habit and, therefore, is usually alleviated by concentrated practice to correct the habit. Many suggestions for improved left-to-right movement across the printed page are available in the manuals of the basal readers. The following specific suggestions have worked well with those who need more practice than that suggested in these manuals:

1. Utilize opportunities for writing experience. It is through writing that students can clearly see the necessity of the left-to-right formation of words across the line. Students should observe the teacher writing on the board, and those who are able to write should be given every opportunity to do so.
2. Illustrate that sentences involve a left-to-right progression of words. An initial approach would be to have the students write sentences containing their sight words, thereby actively involving them in developing effective left-to-right sequence. An understanding of this concept is demonstrated when students are able to create their own sentences from their resource of sight words.

3. Have students point to words while reading. In this respect, the finger is used as a crutch until the *habit* of left-to-right eye movements can be developed more fully.

4. Utilize choral reading activities. A dividend added to the obvious advantages of choral reading is the opportunity for students to experience in a group a feeling for the flow of words from left-to-right. Reading orally in unison with the teacher or with others also is helpful in the same way. There should be one good model of oral reading in the group. Sentences from experience stories can be cut into word cards and reassembled to match the original sentence.

5. The *Michigan Tracking* program has been useful in working with students with severe orientation problems. These materials are constructed to teach readers to move from left to right and from the top of the page to the bottom. Students must complete the entire activity in order. If they miss one item, the materials are constructed so that they cannot finish.

    The concept of tracking can be adapted to any materials. For example, take any unit of print and provide a sentence to look for:

    Look for: See the dog run

    Unit of print: I have a dog. You can *see* him on Saturday. He can run into *the* house. My *dog* can *run* very fast.

6. Mechanical aids are available to help children with orientation skills. Tracking, for example, can be reinforced by the use of the *Controlled Reader.*** Children watch a story from a film, which is paced either a line at a time or by a left-to-right exposure control and which can be regulated for speed. Mechanical aids can help motivate the children to attempt activities which are otherwise rather dull. However, when one considers the costs of such devices and the excitement that can be created with teacher-made materials, it would appear that the use of machines in remedial reading is of a seriously limited value. First, they place readers in reading situations which are unreal. Reading is not a mechanically paced activity; rather, it is a stop-and-go activity. Readers stop to use word attack skills and to reread certain passages; they then go quickly to other sections. That all words and phrases deserve the same amount of reading time must be seriously questioned. When mechanical aids are used, they should be followed by practice with normal reading materials without the use of the aid. In such a way, students are assisted in transferring from practice situations to real reading situations.

Tendency to Reverse Letters, Words, and Phrases

While normal for some beginning readers, the tendency to reverse letters, words, and phrases is one of the common orientation difficulties, particularly

FIGURE 9

Sample of Word Tracking

1. The man walked.

She This The Them
me may mad man
talked waked walked walled

2. Joe ran here.

Jim Joe John Jack
run ray ran ram
there then head here

3. Dad is big.

Day Dad Dab Dog
it at as is
bag buy big bog

4. Boys play ball.

Bugs Bays Buys Boys
plan play park page
bill pull ball balk

5. I saw birds.

A I It As
was say way saw
bids birds burst birch

Fill in:

Boys _____ ball.
Joe _____ here.
The man _____ .

_____ saw birds.
Dad is _____ .
Min_____Sec_____ .

6. Girls, go home.

Grills Girls Guys Goods
go got get golf
house horse home come

7. Look at him.

Cook Lake Took Look
it as at is
his her him hem

8. Are you there?

Car Are Far Tar
one your you once
here then were there

9. Who was that?

Why How Who What
saw was way wash
this then that they

10. Call her up.

Came Tell Tall Call
him her has his
up on down in

Fill in:

Who was _____ ?
Call her _____ ?
Girls, _____ home.

_____ at him.
Are _____ there?
Min_____Sec_____ .

SOURCE: *Word Tracking* by Donald E. P. Smith. Reprinted by permission of the author.

with young problem readers. Different from following left-to-right across a line, reversals involve inappropriate left-to-right progression in words and phrases within a line. The reader not only must consciously attack words from left to right but must develop this attack into a habit. After awareness is developed, the problem can be solved by specific practice:

1. Kindergarten and first-grade teachers should emphasize directional progression both directly and subtly. Through writing on the board in front of children and calling their attention to the direction that the letters flow to form a word, the teacher can give the children opportunities to grasp this concept. The children may also write on the board, for there is less tendency to make directional errors when doing board work. It should be noted that this is a more difficult concept for some to grasp than is the left-to-right movement across a line of print, especially when whole word techniques have been stressed in initial instruction. The sense of touch involved in writing easily confused words reinforces the left-to-right progression within words. When individual language-experience stories are being written, the teacher should sit beside each child so that the child can watch the words being formed. By sitting across the table, the child watches the words being formed right-to-left instead of left-to-right. If the teacher types the story, the child should sit at the typewriter to watch the words form.

2. Phonics lessons also provide opportunity for the reinforcement of proper progression through words, particularly in initial and final consonant substitution activities where the position of the letters in words is emphasized. In phonics lessons, where stress is being placed upon the initial sounds in words, it is often possible to place words on the board to illustrate the similarities or differences in the initial sounds. This practice, of course, emphasizes the left-to-right concept as it applies to word attack.

3. Spelling activities, where the concept of the position of the letters in each word is of primary importance, are excellent times for reinforcing the proper image of the word. Through the spelling of confused words, the teacher is able to reinforce the proper sequence of letters.

4. Students also may be encouraged to trace words that are missed so that they may feel the left-to-right progression. As the students trace the words, they are expected to pronounce them correctly. If they cannot do this, the problem is more likely one of inadequate sight vocabulary. Special instructions for the kinesthetic technique follow:[6]

---

[6]Grace Fernald, *Remedial Techniques in Basic School Subjects* (New York: McGraw-Hill, 1943), Chapter 5.

a. The reader is exposed to the word symbol and its pronunciation. (That these words are usually taken from the reader's experience stories implies that he knows their meanings.)

b. The reader is directed to trace the word while saying it. (This tracing procedure is to be repeated until it appears that the reader has mastered the word. The teacher demonstrates as often as necessary when beginning this approach.) Fernald notes that finger contact with the letters is essential, especially in these early stages.

c. The reader then is directed to reproduce the word without the copy, again pronouncing it as he says it. It should be noted that this technique is not one in which the reader spells the word or sounds the letters; rather, it is a whole word technique. The advantages of the tracing technique are not limited to orientation skills; other uses will be noted under sight vocabulary and word attack where a more detailed explanation is presented.

Teachers will find several variations of the kinesthetic technique in the literature. Some prefer that all tracing be done in sand; some prefer the use of a blackboard; others feel that tracing the word in large copy is entirely adequate. Some suggest that the word be printed, providing the best transfer to actual reading. Others prefer that the word be written in script to reinforce the flow and connection between the letters. Regardless of the system, the left-to-right progression of the words is reinforced, and the reader, sensing the total results of his efforts, often learns to pronounce words properly.

Teachers will find many opportunities in other reading activities to reinforce left-to-right progressions through words. It goes without saying that every opportunity should be utilized.

Tendency to Omit Words
without Distorting Context

Omissions are generally made unknowingly. Therefore, the first remedial activity is to call attention to the fact that although the omission has *not* interfered with comprehension, the reading has *not* been accurate. It should be understood that, in these cases, we assume that the students have read the words prior to pronouncing them and, while not distorting the context, have failed to recall the precise words of the author:

1. Effective utilization can be made of a tape recorder for students with this type of difficulty. Having taped an oral reading selection, the student

listens carefully to the tape while following the story with his eyes. He then marks each word that was omitted. (Students are generally surprised to find that they make the many omissions that they do.) Then the student attempts to reread the story without omitting any words. He listens to the new tape while following the story; again, he marks omissions. We often find that students are able to make conscious corrections, although this technique may need to be repeated several times to develop satisfactory performance.[7] Self-diagnosis helps to emphasize to the students their reading strengths and needs. Followed by practice and reevaluation, it tends to correct most omission errors.

2. The reading impress method has value for students who make many omissions.[8] With the impress method, the teacher and the student read in unison. The student is reinforced by the teacher's voice.

Habitual Loss of One's Place

This reading behavior might be related to a visual problem; therefore, it first would be advisable to check for signs of ocular difficulty manifested by other symptoms (see Chapter 3). If there is no indication that the difficulty is visual, the student should be given instruction.

When readers lose their places during reading, they might be having difficulty following the line of print or with their return sweep. As a reader moves from line to line, his eyes sweep back across the page. Many readers find that movement difficult.

For either of the above reasons, use of a line holder of some type is suggested. An index card will do just fine. Some instruct students to point to the first word in the line. It is more desirable to use line holders than to encourage the student to point to individual words; however, at times, pointing is necessary. Pointing to words can lead to word-by-word reading and can slow the pace of reading greatly. The use of all line holders should be dropped as soon as the student becomes comfortable and is able to read without losing his place.

Those who lose their places during reading might also be indicating a lack of interest and might not be paying attention. These students need to be involved in setting the objectives for their lessons and in selecting materials for instruction. These are attention-getting strategies and tend to increase reader awareness of the need to stay with the lesson. At other times, the tempo of the lesson encourages some minds to wander. As the teacher stops to assist a

---

[7]Robert M. Wilson, "Oral Reading Is Fun," *Reading Teacher,* October 1965, pp. 41-43.
[8]Paul M. Hollingsworth, "An Experiment With The Impress Methods of Teaching Reading," *Reading Teacher,* November 1970, pp. 112-14.

reader having difficulty, other students may mentally slip away. Teacher awareness of the lesson tempo should help to alleviate such problems.

The Seriously Disoriented Reader

Some students display serious difficulties in all of the readiness areas. Their orientation to the printed page is so distorted that there is little chance of their learning to read. Their problem is usually complicated by inability to remember sight words and to understand the relationship between letters and sounds. Several suggestions are offered for working with students who have these types of problems:

1. Physical and psychological assessments should be conducted so that problems in these areas can be understood and adjustments can be made. If no problems are identified as a result of these assessments, the problem is with the school program.

2. A school screening committee should gather as much data as possible including observation of the student during instructional periods. With all of the resources of the school available, the screening committee makes decisions concerning which resources can best assist the student. A plan is implemented and periodic evaluation of progress keeps the screening committee informed and able to make future decisions.

3. Some schools have special programs for these seriously handicapped readers. Instructors with special training direct the learning of such students. Experienced nursery school and kindergarten teachers might have highly useful instructional suggestions. Persons trained in the use of the Gillingham technique also might be called upon.[9] Local college personnel who operate clinics and who work with seriously handicapped readers might offer program suggestions and work with specially identified children.

4. Means for providing large amounts of individual attention often need to be developed. Teacher aides, parents, volunteers, and, at times, a peer tutor can assist the teacher. They can help students as they work independently from the teacher. They can assist them to avoid practicing faulty learning habits, and they can help build a sense of self-worth and success that these students need so badly.

5. Teachers will need to provide communication with parents. Naturally parents become anxious about their children's problems. They also become easy targets for people who have all of the answers. Expensive tutorial

---

[9]Anna Gillingham and Bessie W. Stillman, *Remedial Training* (Cambridge, Mass.: Educators Publishing Service, 1960).

programs, often operated in the interests of profit instead of the reader, are easy to find. By helping the parents to understand the problem and realize the efforts being made by school personnel, much of the anxiety can be reduced.

SUMMARY

The activities involved in readiness instruction are not limited to primary-grade teachers. Teachers at all levels must be skilled in identification and treatment of the types of problems discussed in this chapter. Reading specialists must know how to obtain maximum help for teachers who can't reach students because of readiness limitations. In most cases, there is no reason why reading instruction, directed to the strengths of students, cannot proceed while readiness programs are being conducted. Of course, the effort must be to assist the student in becoming the most successful learner possible.

SUGGESTED READINGS

Coley, Joan, and Gambrell, Linda. *Programmed Reading Vocabulary for Teachers.* Columbus, O.: Charles E. Merrill Publishing Co., 1977. This book presents a quick overview of the basics of sight vocabulary which all teachers need to know. It is especially useful for those who feel uncertain about terminology and teaching strategies.

Fernald, Grace. *Remedial Techniques in Basic School Subjects.* Chapter 5. New York: McGraw-Hill Book Co., 1943. The advantages and specific techniques of the tracing technique are presented in these pages. The reader will find this presentation interesting and complete.

Hall, MaryAnne. *Teaching Reading as a Language Experience,* 2nd ed. Columbus, Ohio: Charles E. Merrill Publishing Co., 1976. This book provides a basic background for those unfamiliar with the possibilities for using the language-experience approach in remediation. Chapter 7 deals specifically with the teaching of prereading skills through the language-experience approach.

Hymes, James L., Jr. *Before the Child Reads.* New York: Row, Peterson & Co., 1958. Hymes presents the point of view of an experienced educator of young children. His chapter "You Do Not Have to 'Build' 'Readiness,'" while concerned with preschool children, should be considered required reading.

Kephart, Newell C. *The Slow Learner in the Classroom.* Columbus, Ohio: Charles E. Merrill Publishing Co., 1971. The reader will find interesting reading covering completely the motor readiness needs of youngsters. Particular attention is given to motor skills which the author sees as being related to success in learning.

Monroe, Marion, and Rogers, Bernice. *Foundations for Reading,* Chapters 1-5. Chicago: Scott Foresman and Co., 1964. The authors' have presented a series of chapters relating to the beginning processes of reading. The educator who is attempting remediation without a thorough understanding of this initial process will find this reading very profitable.

8

Remedial Activities for Word Recognition and Word Meaning

Sight vocabulary and word attack skills are needed for word recognition and word meaning. These areas usually receive major emphasis in remedial programs since many students are hindered from reading successfully due to handicaps in word recognition and word meaning.

THE LANGUAGE-EXPERIENCE APPROACH

Of first priority in remediation of vocabulary problems is common agreement about how the language-experience approach fits into a remedial situation. Use of the language-experience approach includes the following possibilities:

1. Following an experience with one student or a group of students, generate a discussion concerning the experience. The students are encouraged to talk about what they saw or did, about how it made them feel, and about the meaning the experience had for them.
2. Following free discussion, direct the students to tell a story about the experience. Ask for contributions and write exactly what they say. Always

PIZZA

1. Preheat oven to 425° F.

2. Put pizza flour mix in a small bowl. PIZZA FLOUR MIX

3. Add ½ cup very warm water to mix. Stir with spoon until all flour particles are moistened. Then stir vigorously for 25 strokes.

4. Cover bowl. Let stand in warm place for 5 minutes.

5. Using shortening, grease well a 14" pizza pan or an 11" x 14" rectangle on a cookie sheet.

6. Grease fingers them lightly Spread pizza edges of pan. up edges ¼" to rim.

7. Pour canned sauce over t

Following direction activities can come naturally from the language-experience approach.

spell words correctly but do not change the contributor's sentence structure. Some guidelines for writing stories are:

a. Encourage all students to contribute.

b. In the beginning, use some type of identification for each individual's contribution [e.g., "Donald said, 'I see a big dog' " or "I see a big dog" (Donald)].

c. Read what has been written immediately following the writing of each sentence. Next, have the student who gave the sentence read it; then, the entire group.

d. For very young readers, start every new sentence on a new line. For older readers, write in paragraphs.

e. Begin by making stories rather short. If the students have more to say, write the story on two pages with only a few lines on each page. Those with serious reading problems can become discouraged with too much print on a single page.

f. Have students watch as the story is written. Call attention to the formation of words as they are written.

g. As students develop skill with beginning consonants, invite them to help with the spelling of words (e.g., "How would I begin the word *boy*?").

3. After the story is written, have the students read it in unison several times.

4. Duplicate the story as soon as possible, making at least two copies for each student. One copy can be placed in a folder to become the reading material for the students. The second copy can be used for skill development.

5. Skill can be developed from language-experience stories in a variety of ways. In Chapter 7, using language-experience stories to develop visual, discrimination, auditory discrimination, and orientation skills was discussed. Skills in vocabulary can be developed as follows:

   a. Have the students mark all the words which they know. Then have them put several of these words in a private word box or word bank. The students' word banks provide a natural opportunity for meaningful word drills.

   b. Students can practice their known words in pairs or in small groups. They can match words in their word bank with words in their stories. They can select words for classification as action words, as naming words, as people words, as words beginnng with specific letters, and so on.

   c. Once a group of words is developed, students can use their word banks to help them with spelling activities. They can use them to build sentences, make crossword puzzles, and many other activities.

   d. Add words to the students' banks occasionally. When the word *and* or *the* occurs again and again in a story, but has not been choosen for placement in the word banks, call it to the students' attention. Such service words will be needed in future reading and in vocabulary activities.

6. Comprehension activities can also be developed from language-experience stories (see Chapter 9).

The suggestions listed above in no way cover all the possibilities for uses of the language-experience approach in remediation. Additional specific suggestions are provided under various remedial areas in this and other chapters. Those unfamiliar with the language-experience approach will want to study the books of Stauffer and Hall listed in the Suggested Readings at the end of this chapter.

REMEDIATION IN SIGHT VOCABULARY

Sight vocabulary involves the skills of instant word pronunciation and word meaning. While the remedial approaches to sight vocabulary problems are presented in terms of the questions asked in diagnosis, it must be remembered that the end goal of sight vocabulary is the decoding and association of the word in a line of print, in a sentence, or in a paragraph rather than in isolation, for word meaning depends on relationships with other words.

Remedial procedures will be developed in direct reply to the questions asked under the diagnosis of sight vocabulary difficulties. Specifically, those questions are:

1. Does the student miss small graphically similar words?
2. Do words missed represent abstract concepts?
3. Do word meanings appear to be confused?
4. Does the student know words in context but not in isolation?
5. Does the student appear to know words at the end of a lesson but not the next day?

These deficiencies seldom appear alone; rather, they are interrelated. The purpose in establishing the answers to the questions is to determine in which areas the interrelationship has taken place and to emphasize these areas in remediation. Through examination it can clearly be seen, for example, that small, graphically similar words are often words with abstract meanings which require dual remedial considerations.

Small, Graphically Similar Words

Does the student miss small, graphically similar words or does he falter on words that are obviously different? Quite often, handicapped readers will miss small words which are minimal in configurational differences (e.g., *when* and *where*) while effectively attacking larger and more obviously different words (e.g., *elephant* and *Christmas*). The latter is considered a skill in sight vocabulary, while the former is normally a problem in word attack, especially if the words missed are at or below the instructional level. The major point is to work from the reader's strengths. If the student can work with words of maximal differences, the teacher should provide more exercises with those types of words, moving gradually to words that are more similar until skill with those words is developed. Then, the student should move to words even more alike until skill with words which have minimal graphic differences has been developed.

Ultimately, the student must receive instruction in the discrimination of words that are minimally different. These exercises should be conducted in phrase and sentence form so that the reader realizes that the minimal difference distorts not only the pronunciation but the meaning of the words as well: "We took the dig [instead of *dog*] for a walk." To clarify these similarities and differences in minimally different words, it is sometimes feasible to pull these words from context for study (*dig–dog*). Any exercise, however, should be followed by return to context.

In the early grades, the teacher may use experience charts to illustrate the need for careful visual discrimination of minimally different words. In these situations, the teacher should take every opportunity to emphasize how words of similar configuration actually differ in both form and meaning, using the reader's own language contributions as examples. For instance, when writing a student's story, the teacher should look for opportunities to demonstrate how certain words look alike or different.

Using words from the students' word banks (i.e., words which are already known) illustrates teaching to strengths. Locating words in the banks which look very much alike, pronouncing them, noting meanings, using them in sentences, and noting how they look alike and different is extremely useful. Attention should be given to differences in all parts of the words—initial, medial, and final.

Programmed materials are available that are particularly adaptable to the classroom for use in remediation of this type of skill deficiency. These materials can aid the student to observe differences in words which are alike except for minimal graphic differences (e.g., *hat* and *bat*). As an example of these materials, *Programmed Reading*** contains a series of exercises through which the reader can develop skill with a minimum amount of teacher supervision. Note the sample on page 141. The student must look at the pictures, read the sentence or partial sentence, and use closure to obtain the correct code and message. These exercises progress from the elementary type seen in Figure 11 to complete stories. The forced-choice closure concept is maintained at all levels (i.e., the reader selects from a limited number of appropriate responses).

The student is reinforced by the appearance of the correct answer after each frame or after each page, depending upon how much material the teacher feels the reader can handle without reinforcement. The skills developed in the workbooks are transferred to reading in prepared *Storybooks,*** containing stories with minimally different words. Although it is unlikely that these materials will satisfy the total reading needs of the reader, they are particularly useful when working with minimal differences.

The linguistic approach can be adapted to almost any type of material, for example, word banks which add a personalized aspect and the programmed materials mentioned above. The *Let's Read* books** and *The Merrill Linguistic Readers*** are prepared linguistic materials for beginning reading, appropriate for individualized instruction of students with serious reading problems. Both of these approaches have in common a controlled vocabulary of minimally different words, the controlled initial presentation of words with consistent vowel and consonant sounds, and an absence of pictures so that correct visual perception is necessary for accurate decoding. A similar approach, *The Linguistic Readers,* varies somewhat from those mentioned above but does maintain the necessity for visual perception of minimal differences. An example of adaptations of the above for instruction is thoroughly described by Botel.[1]

Abstract Concepts

It is common for students to find it particularly difficult to remember words which represent abstract concepts (e.g., *when, these, if, those*). Emphasis in remediation for students with this type of difficulty should focus on the word as it appears in context, for it is from context that the function of these words can be understood. Furthermore, since there is seldom a reading situation in which these words are used in isolation, they should not be taught in isolation.

Once again, experience-story approaches are of particular value in the development of this type of reading sight vocabulary. Students use these words to formulate their experience stories, providing a natural opportunity for instruction in the service and function of these words as the student uses them. Although the experience-story approach will probably be used more frequently with the younger reader, considerable success with this type of approach has been found with older students as well. It is in experience-story reading that we can be certain that all words used have meaning for the readers since they are their contributions. Through these materials, the use and nature of abstract words can be effectively illustrated.

Again, word-bank words which carry little meaning of their own (*and, the, of,* and the like) are known to students and can be developed into meaningful activities. For example, using *and, the,* and *of* from a word bank, ask which word would fit in the blank: bread _____ butter, I see _____ man, and on top _____ the table. The use of such modified closure activities develops skills in the use of abstract words.

Sight vocabulary drills with abstract concepts are most effective when the words are used in phrases (e.g., *in a good spirit*). Prepared phrase cards with the more commonly used word combinations are available in the Dolch game** (e.g., *Match, Basic Sight Cards)* series. There is little or no justification for sight word drill with these words in isolation, for when they are extracted from context, any meaning the word contains is lost.

After a certain amount of sight vocabulary has been developed, students may build sentences from word cards. Here emphasis should be placed upon the function of the abstract word as created by the student. With this activity, the unknown word is not placed in a definition situation; rather, it appears in a

---

[1]Morton Botel, *Forming and Re-Forming the Reading Language Arts Curriculum* (Curriculum Development Associates, 1975).

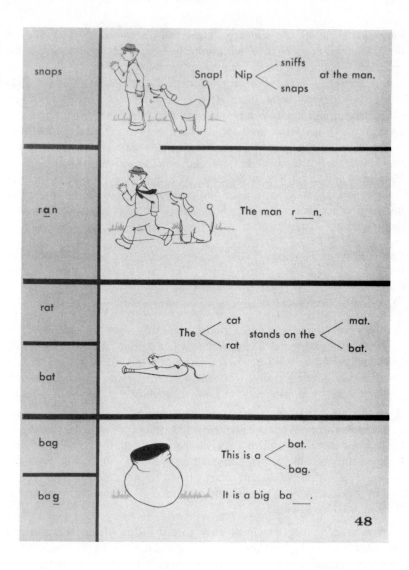

FIGURE 11

Sample Page of a Programmed Reader (Photograph with Permission
of Webster Division, McGraw-Hill)

functional situation, the sentence. Intentional distortions of these types of words in context may be used to illustrate their importance. For example, the text reads, ''In the table is a lot of money.'' We change it to read, ''On the table is a lot of money.'' The students either describe or illustrate how the slight change has affected the meaning of the sentence.

Such word games as Word Lotto, which use abstract words, can be used successfully to reinforce words which have been previously learned (i.e., words from students' word banks). Word games are highly motivating and tend to take the drill atmosphere from reinforcement activities. Games such as Checkers can be used with words taped on each square. As players move or jump opponents, they are expected to pronounce the words on the spaces involved. Students become so enthusiastic about such activities that they ignore the drill nature involved.

Confused Word Meanings

Remedial instruction in this very important area must be precluded by the following two considerations:

1. There are situations in which students, for one reason or another, fail to develop a background of experiences which permits them to associate the meaning with the word they have pronounced. If this deficiency is chronic, remediation, of necessity, will consist of experiential language development rather than instruction in sight vocabulary.

2. We find numerous students who have little trouble pronouncing the words they see in print. Although they know the meaning of a word and can use it in a sentence, they fail to associate the word with the correct meaning, apparently because of preoccupation with word pronunciation. Remedial activities with these students, then, should be in the area of sight vocabulary where they must be taught to be conscious of what the word *says* as well as how it *sounds*.

As has been stated previously, every word drill should end with the word in context. In this way, the precise meaning and function of the word are best understood; readers with this deficiency must have context emphasized even more precisely. The students begin by reading easy material and demonstrating their knowledge of the words in question by paraphrasing the author's words. Specific mention of this technique will be discussed in Chapter 9.

It is often useful to establish whether the students know the meaning of a word through definition. If they do, it is not the meaning of the word as such that is causing the problem, but the use of the word in a particular contextual situation. The presentation of the word in various settings is then appropriate.

Since students already understand the meaning of the pronounced words, experience stories using the students' own wording again play an important role in remedial efforts. Teachers of elementary school children are urged to provide numerous opportunities for group experience stories in which there is an association between the experiences of the group and the words which represent those experiences. This is a golden opportunity to create situations in which students learn from one another. Frequently we find students reacting better to the responses of their peers than to teacher efforts. Two sources of activities to assist students to develop word meaning skills are Heilman and Holmes[2] for the younger student and Dale and O'Rourke[3] for the more mature student.

Although frequently not included as a remedial technique, the dictionary is of particular assistance to older students. Their knowledge of the correct pronunciation of a word in print permits them to use the dictionary to find meanings efficiently; they may, incidentally, develop a habit of consulting the dictionary for unknown words. Techniques for use with the dictionary are discussed in the section "Remediation in Word Attack."

Although it is fine to talk about building experiences to develop listening and speaking vocabularies, it is another thing to build such a program (refer to Chapter 7). The *Peabody Language Development Kits*** contain programs for numerous lessons in language development. Teachers may find this type of program a guide for the entire school year. Among the experiences included with these kits are following directions, brainstorming, critical thinking, memorizing, rhyming, and listening. Pictures, objects, and tapes are used to enrich the child's experiential background.

The *Building Pre-reading Skills Kit-A-Language*** provides the teacher with another program for language development. It consists of pictures through which vocabulary can be stimulated, synonyms developed, and language-experience stories drawn.

For the reader seriously handicapped by the inability to associate, the *Non-oral Reading*** approach may contain the requisites for initial instruction. This approach bypasses completely the vocalization of the printed word and emphasizes instead the word's association with a pictured concept. The task is to match the printed symbol with a picture representing the concept for that symbol. This direct association from print to concept minimizes the importance of pronunciation for those who have been overdrilled in it.

Teachers will also find it useful to have the student respond directly through physical activity to such printed word commands as "jump up," and "shake hands." This approach also minimizes vocalization of the printed word, emphasizing again the meaning of the word through the student's response. The *Nichols Tachistoscope Slides*** developed for this purpose

[2]Arthur W. Heilman, *Smuggling Language into the Teaching of Reading* (Columbus, O.: Charles E. Merrill, 1972).

[3]Edgar Dale, and Joseph O'Rourke, *Techniques of Teaching Vocabulary* (Palo Alto, Calif.: Field Educational Publications, 1971).

By placing word bank words on a checker board, it is possible to make drill exercises an enjoyable activity for students.

appear to be effective in establishing the importance of the concepts covered by words.

Collecting words from the word bank in categories can also help to stress word meanings. For example, to collect action words, the student must think of word meaning, not just pronunciation. Words which are names of things can be matched with the action words to make short sentences (e.g., *dogs run, ducks talk, horses jump*). Students can look at the sentences which they have built to determine which ones make sense. This is an extremely meaningful activity. In addition, stimulating students with incomplete sentences, such as "I like to _____" makes the learning personal and, therefore, more interesting.

Teachers also may use initial sight vocabulary exercises consisting of nouns, adjectives, and verbs which can be pictured. The Dolch *Picture Word Cards*,** containing ninety-six of these types of words, may be used. Several matching-type games involve a student's matching a picture with a printed word, thereby indicating understanding of the meaning of the word in a game-like activity which is self-motivating. *Picture Word Puzzles*** provides similar reinforcement with children having association deficiencies.

Active participation can be achieved by having students build sentences from the words which they know. After known words are placed on cards, the cards are scrambled and the students are asked to build specific sentences or to build sentences of their choosing. The *Linguistic Block Series*** can be used in the same manner with the blank block for words in the students' personal vocabularies.

Meaning in Context

Students who know words in context but not in isolation are telling you that context aids their reading. Being aware of the function of words in their language and aware of sentence meaning, these students are using desirable word attack processes. Since most words are encountered in context, this problem should not be considered critical.

Occasionally, however, a word is faced in isolation and recognition is crucial, e.g., *stop, danger, women.* Such words should be taught in context, then pulled from context and attention placed on meaning. Since meaning clues seem to aid this type of reader, the stress on meaning should also help. These words should also be encountered in real life whenever possible. Find a stop sign and see if students know the word when they see it at a street corner.

Sometimes the reverse is true, the student knows the word in isolation but not in context. While such cases are rare, some consideration should be given to the problem. Usually this happens when the use of the word has been changed from what students had known. If students learned the word *bank* as a basketball term and then encountered it in the following sentence, "I can *bank* on you," they might not understand it. In such a case it would be correct to say that the students did not have the word *bank* as used in the sentence above as a sight word; so they did not know the word in isolation. Some readers have difficulty with certain types of print. Small print on a crowded page can cause them some confusion. The teacher can encourage these students to frame the word by blocking out all of the other words. If the other words were distractors, then the student should now be able to read the word and proceed with the reading of the passage. By starting vocabulary instruction with words in context, this problem should not occur.

Learning Not Retained

Of all of the problems with sight vocabulary, students' knowing words at the end of a lesson but not the next day is surely the most frustrating to teachers. Thinking that the students had learned the words, the teacher plans the next lesson using those learned words as a base. Then the students become confused for, in fact, they had not remembered those words from the previous lesson. The solution for such problems is elusive because there are several causes which may be operating alone or in combination.

Teachers may be asking the students to learn too many sight words in a given lesson. Pacing then must be adjusted. In remedial situations, the teacher and the student should negotiate the pace of sight words to be learned. If the teacher feels that a given student can learn about four words a day and the student says, "I think I can learn three a day," then three should be the agreement with an added, "And be certain to learn them well." If this adjustment helps the students to know their sight words, then a suitable pace for successful learning has been found. Of course there are easy words (*elephant, Halloween*), and there are difficult words (*there, their*). Pace, therefore, might need to be adjusted daily depending on the difficulty of the words to be remembered. The point is to be certain that the students learn what they study. The resulting success is not contrived, but real, and can be acknowledged as such.

Another problem might be that the students have not had enough opportunities to encounter the new words. We have all encountered the problem of thinking we had mastered something only to find out that it had slipped our memory. Repeated exposure to such information enables us to recall it clearly. For students who forget easily, it is often necessary to structure extra practice. Games, learning centers, and working with peers can be ways of helping students retain what they initially respond to. Remembering that some need more exposure to sight words than others, such practice should be individually prescribed.

Still another possible explanation is that the teacher has assumed too much when planning to use yesterday's words as a base for today's lesson. A quick review of the materials which have been assumed to have been learned will quickly let the teacher know if the base is solid or not. If not, a brief review lesson should strengthen the ability of students to recall the sight words so that the base for the lesson is established.

Some students need more sensory reinforcement for learning sight words than do others. The VAKT technique, for example, can be used to help some students remember sight words. This technique is discussed in detail on page 142.

Finally, one wants to be certain that the students have learned the words in a contextual situation. If the students' word cards have only the word in the front of a card, then sentences using that word created by the students should be placed on the back of the card. If students do not seem to be able to respond to a word, they can turn the card over and see it in a familiar context. In this manner, they can work with word cards without teacher help even when they run into difficulty.

Additional Considerations in Sight Vocabulary

The following aspects of remediation of sight vocabulary problems should be carefully understood by any person conducting remediation in this area.

The Need to Tell Students the Word. The teacher will find many situations in which it is advisable to tell the students unknown words. Although normally teachers should not provide unknown words, they will often find that students are in situations where they simply do not have the skills needed to attack unknown words. In these cases, telling them the word will permit them to move along with the context of the story, focusing attention on those words they have the skills to attack effectively. In such cases, the teachers need not feel guilty about telling students words, nor should they make the students feel this way.

The Need for Overlearning. The very nature of sight vocabulary (instant recognition and meaning) implies that it must be overlearned. Overlearning, not to be conducted in isolated drill activities, is most effective when the reader has opportunities to use the word again and again in context. Many remedial efforts fail because they do not provide for the overlearning of sight vocabulary words in context. Experience stories, trade books, and similar materials are available to facilitate transfer for students with serious limitations.

Reinforcement of sight vocabulary through the use of word banks exemplifies the concept of accept and challenge and meets the need for overlearning. Several suggestions for the use of word banks as reinforcers are:

1. Find all the words that begin like _____ or end like _____.
2. Find all the words that rhyme with _____.
3. Find all the words that are one syllable words or two syllable words, and so on.
4. Find all the words that are examples of _____ (a given generalization).
5. Find all the words that contain silent letters or blends or digraphs and so on.

Likewise, games, either commercially developed or not, make overlearning exciting and funfilled. Games which follow the pattern of a race track and involve the spinning of a wheel or the rolling of dice can be used. Each block on the race track can require the student to demonstrate a skill: initial consonant substitution, syllabication, or vowel knowledge. Remember that the element of chance enters into game activities; a loss is not a matter of intellectual inabilities, but luck. Teachers should be certain that the chance factor is obvious in all games used for these purposes.

Competitive games add enrichment to otherwise
boring phonics activities.

Every remedial session should provide opportunities for the students to read materials of their own choosing. Perhaps as much as 25 percent of the remedial time can be wisely spent on such activities. It is through a great deal of reading that readers become comfortable with words which they will meet over and over again. Overlearning is often interpreted as a drill-and-grill type activity. Obviously, the more motivation an activity has, the less it will be viewed as a chore.

Segmentation of Skills. Again the teacher is reminded that students often see no connection between the learning of a sight vocabulary and reading. I recall the student who asked if the difference between second and third grade were three work sheets a day instead of two. While a humorous accounting of a student's perception, it is also distressing. Efforts to link sight vocabulary training to actual reading situations are essential. Students should be asked why they think they are studying these words. Their verbalization of how sight vocabulary fits into reading helps teachers to know how well their students understand the purposes for a given activity.

Word Length and Sound Length. Some seriously handicapped readers might look at a word such as *mow* and call it *motorcycle*. These readers have not made an association between sound length and word length. Consequently, they have a slim possibility of making progress in sight vocabulary development without an intervention program in awareness of sound and graphic relationships. We are not talking about phonics here, rather an awareness that long-sounding words will appear to be longer in print than short-sounding words. While it amazes mature readers that some students have difficulty in this area, the fact remains that they do. Instruction is directed to the problem by discussing the facts with the students and then providing exercises with extreme examples *(mow–motorcycle)* and moving toward instruction with minor changes *(mow–mower)*.

Motivation Techniques

The often subtle development of power in sight vocabulary needs to be illustrated to problem readers so that they may be encouraged by their progress. The following techniques have been found to be particularly helpful:

1. Transferring every lesson to contextual situations illustrates that the effort the students are making in sight vocabulary is, in effect, making them better readers. Particularly with older students, this in itself is often ample motivation.

2. Recording experience stories in booklet form is of interest to younger students, for they can see progress merely by the quantity of the material they have been able to learn to read. The sight vocabulary implications of that quantity can be pointed out if need be to the student.

3. Charts illustrating the goals toward which the student will work in sight vocabulary seem to trigger some students' efforts to achieve better performance. Ultimately, it is desirable that intrinsic motivation fulfill the function of such charts, and they should never place one reader in competition with another. An illustration of success through the use of charts must be carefully planned. Objectives must be short term and within the realistic grasp of the student. Charts which emphasize long-range goals can discourage as well as encourage students. During a moon shot, University of Maryland clinicians raced their students in vocabulary development against the astronauts. The students won the race, and the short-term nature (eight days) of the chart made it worthwhile. Such charts should never place one reader in competition with another.

4. Sight vocabulary cards maintained in a file or on a ring illustrate visually to students that they have accumulated a number of useful words through which they can become better readers. These words should not be listed in isolation; rather, they should appear in a sentence with the word highlighted. This use of word banks illustrates the concept of acceptance and challenge and teaching to strengths.

In several of the techniques above, games have been suggested for teaching purposes. These appear to hold the student's interest and to establish a degree of motivation, while assisting the student to develop sight vocabulary.

As has been mentioned, the use of contracts through which students regulate their learning to some degree are of particular value. The completion of a contract is motivation in itself. Of course, specially constructed rewards and motivational devices can be built in. For example, contract completion can result in an immediate reward through free-reading time, praise, and other encouragement. The motivation to strive for future efforts is built-in and automatic.

REMEDIATION IN WORD ATTACK

Word attack skills include those techniques which enable students to pronounce words not in their sight vocabularies and to understand them as they are used in contextual situations without teacher assistance.

Many handicapped readers have serious difficulties with word attack skills; so many remedial programs concentrate upon them heavily. Consequently, an abundance of materials is available to teachers for use in word attack, and there are many approaches to the problem recommended in the professional literature. With this wealth of information, it is very easy for teachers to overemphasize instruction in word attack skills. Heilman proposes, "The optimum amount of phonics instruction that a child should receive is the minimum amount he needs to become an independent reader."[4] Following such advice should lessen the possibilities of overemphasis. Another danger related to word attack instruction is that it often occurs in isolation—away from context. Students often fail to see the purposes for such lessons and interest starts to lag. Ending all word attack lessons in context where students can see how what they have learned has helped them to read better is strongly advised.

In the discussion on the use of criterion referenced tests in Chapter 4, teachers were warned against testing too many objectives. Some programs that accompany CRT lock students into learning a specific set of subskills prior to moving to the next level. Since these subskills seem to concentrate on word attack skills, the problem is greatest in this area. The fact is that different students need different amounts and types of phonics instruction. Care should be taken to avoid use of programs which lock students into specific learning sequences. Remedial programs in word attack should be designed to foster independence in reading, not merely proficiency in word attack drills.

[4]Arthur W. Heilman, *Phonics in Proper Perspective,* 3d ed. (Columbus, O.: Charles E. Merrill, 1976), p. 17.

Because there are various methods for attacking words not known at sight, educational focus should be on those word attack skills which assist the reader in attacking words most efficiently in terms of time and most consistently in terms of application. Once overlearned, efficiency in word attack should have the same aim as did sight vocabulary (i.e., to decode the word and associate its meaning instantly to the context in which it occurs).

As indicated in the diagnosis of the problem reader, word attack falls into three major categories: phonics clues, structural clues, and contextual clues. Dictionary skills, a fourth category of word attack that normally is not considered of remedial necessity, at times need development in remedial programs.

Discovery Technique

It must be assumed that most students referred for remedial help have had instruction in word attack skills. That those skills have not been mastered indicates clearly that the instructional efforts have failed. Therefore, part of the reason for failure in learning word attack skills must be attributed to the technique of instruction. Throughout this chapter, the *discovery technique* will be mentioned as a solution to specific problems.[5] A brief review of the discovery technique and some of its possibilities are included as a preface to the discussion of remediation in word attack:

1. Present word patterns which contain the visual clues desired for instruction. For example (using known words):

    index   picnic   pencil   chapter

2. Direct the students to observe, visually, the patterns in the words. For example:

    a. place a *v* above each vowel.

    v v
    index

    b. place a *c* above each consonant between the vowels.

    vccv
    index

    c. divide the word into syllables

    vc cv
    in/dex

3. Have the students form generalizations in their own words. For example, one student might say, ''vc/cv''; another might say, ''When you have vccv divide between the *c*'s,'' concerning the patterns and the syllabication above. Any appropriate response is acceptable. Teachers should avoid forcing their wording on the students.

---

[5]Morton Botel, *How to Teach Reading* (Chicago: Follett Publishing Corp., 1968), p. 64.

4. Have the students turn to material which they are reading to collect words which fit the pattern. For example, refer to a specific page in a book on which you know there are five words which fit the pattern. The students might also find words in their word banks which fit the pattern.

The major advantages of the discovery technique include the active response needed by the students, the acceptance of their wording for the generalization, and the impact which results from forming a generalization through the use of visual clues. Teachers may choose to vary the approach at times; in fact, Botel suggests that steps three and four be reversed from the way the technique is described above. Other variations might include the following: a discussion of exceptions to the generalization, help in beginning the wording (e.g., "When a word contains the pattern . . . ."), and directed activities from word lists to determine the ability of the students to discriminate the visual pattern. Although the discovery technique takes more time than simply telling the students, the lasting effects of the learning are extremely valuable.

Phonics Clues

Remedial efforts in the area of phonics will, again, be in terms of the questions asked following diagnosis:

1. Does the student appear not to use graphic cues?
2. Does the student attack small words accurately but not large ones?
3. Does the student seem to know sound-symbol relationships but seem unable to use them during reading?

Although in diagnosis the skills of phonics have been delegated to three precise areas (sound of letters, syllabication, and blending), it is necessary that the remedial program combine these areas for instructional purposes. The functional use of phonics skills involves the ability of the reader to divide the word into syllables, sound the letters, blend the sounds into a recognizable word, and check the derived pronunciation in the context from which the word was taken.

Auditory discrimination skills are considered essential to success in phonics instruction. These skills were discussed in Chapter 7. However, with serious handicapped readers any phonics instruction should start with auditory discrimination activities. Make it a policy not to assume prior learning in this area.

Graphic Cues. Does the student appear not to use graphic cues? Which graphic cues are used accurately? For each student, the teacher should have a list of all known strengths in the area of phonics. This information has been accumulated during oral reading testing and specific testing in the area of phonics. All phonics lessons should start with these strengths. As new skills are mastered, an adjustment should be made to the list of strengths for each student. In this way, the teacher always has an accounting of each student's phonics knowledge.

Then a plan for instruction is made. Plans should include the approach to be used to teach the skills, methods for practicing the skills, and procedures for using the skill.

Plans for teaching the skill. The decision whether to teach phonics from whole words or in isolation basically is reserved for the teacher. In either case, the major decision concerns which approach best suits the student's strengths. Both will call for providing ample opportunity for all students to demonstrate their skills rather than their weaknesses, and the suitability of either approach will depend upon the following:

1. The teacher's familiarity with a given technique combined with the availability of materials and results obtained through its use. Although teachers generally work best with familiar techniques and materials, new methods and ideas should not be overlooked. Inflexible and inappropriate teaching can result from the failure to adapt. It is therefore very important for teachers to be as objective as possible in their assessments of the materials and techniques which can be used most effectively.

2. The student's previous experience and reaction to that technique. If, after good instruction, a student fails with a given technique and develops a negative attitude toward it, another approach may be more desirable.

If available information concerning the student's initial introduction to phonics (a whole word method, for example) determines that this instruction was of satisfactory quality, it is correct for the teacher or reading specialist to select the other approach (sounds in isolation), for it can be assumed that, even with good instruction, the first technique was not effective. This type of selection requires an awareness of the techniques used in both approaches. Again caution is advised, for if the student has profited by a previous method, it is justifiable to build upon what the student has learned (i.e., strengths). In these cases, a reteaching of a previously taught method may be called for, or it may be appropriate to use the same method with minor modifications. Assessments are often difficult and can best be made only by placing the students in instructional situations and evaluating their performance. Check the suggested readings at the end of this chapter for several sources of recommended techniques for the teaching of the sounds of the various letters and letter combinations.

Students should be alert to the idea that, each time they decode a word, the sounds which are uttered should be associated with a meaningful concept. As part of each phonics lesson, techniques must be used to facilitate this alertness. The students should be required to put the pronounced word in a sentence or the teacher might present words in which classification is possible (e.g., things we do at school and names of animals). In either case, attention is called to the fact that the pronounced word has meaning as well as sound.

Several approaches for instruction are:

1. Discovery approach. In phonics instruction the discovery approach is used to help students develop an awareness of the consistent sound-graphic relationship. The teacher starts with visual and auditory stimulation:

   Let's read these words:

   see   sit   sox   sun

   Listen carefully to the first sound in each word. They all start with the same sound. Let's hear it. What letter do each of these words start with?

   Once the students have an awareness of the relationship between the letter *s* and the sound it represents, the teacher has several choices:

   Look in your word banks and see how many words you can find which start with the letter *s*. Pronounce these words and see if they all have the sound which *see, sit, sox,* and *sun* start with.

   Or, look in your book on page 10. There are three words that start with *s*. Find them and let's see if they start with the sound we hear at the beginning of *see, sit, sox,* and *sun*.

   Or, I'll give you some word endings. You place the *s* sound in front and let's see which ones make real words:

   s-and   s-at   s-im   s-oz

2. Tempo is important. These steps can be dragged out to a point that makes instruction boring. Make this instruction snappy and move on to the generalization step:

   Let's all try to say in our own words what we have learned today.

   Teachers should check each effort and help students to clarify the generalization. A student might write, "When a word starts with the letter *s*, it will start like the word sat." At this point, instruction is over and students go into a practice activity.

3. Word families. Many students develop excellent word attack skills quickly through the use of word families and initial consonant substitution. After some instruction on the initial sounds, then words can be built quickly.

   You now know the initial sounds that the letters *t, s, f,* and *p* represent. This word ending is *-at*. Put your consonant in front and see how many make real words:

   t-at   s-at   f-at   p-at

Attention is placed on two aspects of reading in these activities: initial consonant substitution is easy and quick and when students pronounce words they should always make a check to be sure the word has meaning for them. Then use other word families such as *-in, -and, -et*. Control the pace so that your students are not overwhelmed but keep it moving in a snappy, interesting way.

4. *Speech-to-Print Phonics.*** A commercially prepared program which uses some of all of the above, *Speech to Print Phonics* has been used with handicapped readers with success. The program features learning several sounds, applying them through substitution, checking for meaning, and using repetition. These materials can be used with groups or individually.

5. *Gillingham.*** Some readers need more sensory reinforcement than others. *Gillingham* presents a program for teaching and reinforcing sounds through kinesthetic techniques. This program features spelling as well as reading.

If none of the above instructional techniques are effective, the teacher is encouraged to employ task analysis techniques (see Chapter 6). Since all learners respond in terms of their uniqueness, it may be that some logical explanation exists for a reading difficulty. We might ask, what can the students do?

1. Respond to first sounds, final, medial?
2. Recognize familiar parts in unknown words?
3. Know the meaning of the word when it is read? to them?
4. Find the word in a dictionary?
5. Distinguish sounds when words are read to them?
6. Respond to word when it is placed in context?

From such a list of questions, strengths and instructional needs can be recorded.

Practicing learned skills. Practice sessions allow students to work with what they have learned so that they can gain a degree of comfort with the skill. The following are suggestions for practicing learned skills:

1. Games. Teacher-made or commercially developed games can be used to let students practice what they have learned. *SRA Word Games,* ** *Phonics We Use Learning Games,* ** *Vowel* and *Consonant Lotto***are examples of packaged kits that are available. After instruction, students play those games which contain the skills they have learned. Teacher-made games, although time-consuming to construct, can be made to relate directly to the skills of a given lesson.

2. Learning centers. Self-directed activities which relate to skills learned can be made available. Small groups or individual students can work through centers, practicing their new skills. Centers can be either self-correcting or they can be checked by the teacher. They are generally on topics of interest to the students and add the dimension of attention getting.

A learning center using clothespins and pizza plate provides manipulative activities which are self-correcting.

3. Tutoring. As soon as a skill is determined to be mastered, it is useful for the students to teach the skill to someone else. It does not matter if the other person knows the skill or not. By practicing the teaching of a skill which has been recently learned, the student is going through the process in the teacher's seat. Students love it and they learn from it.

4. Work sheets. Some workbooks contain highly useful activities which can be used for follow-up practice. *Phonics Skilltests,*** *Phonics We Use,*** and *Working with Sounds*** are a few of the many commercial materials available for practice sessions. It is better to pull the pages needed rather than to overwhelm the students with the workbook.

Try to make practice sessions short in duration and interesting. By paying attention to the students as they practice, teachers can prevent student frustration. If the practice activity is too difficult, it should be adjusted so that the students experience success. We do not want the students to be practicing mistakes.

Using learned skills. After instruction and practice, students should have opportunities to use their new skills in the reading situation. Each remedial session generally should end with a period of silent reading in order to communicate to the students that the reason for their effort is to make it possible for them to read on their own. Once they get the idea, these reading periods are cherished by the students.

Attacking Small and Large Words. Many students can use phonics for word attack with small words but have difficulty using it with large words. This is, in part, because small words tend to be more consistent. However, many students do not have useful ways to get large words into smaller parts. Instructional strategies, practice ideas, and procedures for use must be considered.

Instructional strategies. It is imperative to remember that students will need to use *syllabication* when they come to words of two or more syllables which they cannot pronounce at sight or through the use of other word attack techniques. An illustration of the difficulty of this task may be seen when an adult looks at the following nonsense words and attempts to pronounce them:

sogtel	*sog-tel*
akot	*a-kot*
sognochest	*sog-no-chest*

It should be realized that when students attack words which they do not know at sight, their procedure is likely to be to divide the word into syllables and to pronounce the syllable without intensive phonic analysis. A highly valuable word attack technique, syllabication is of particular value to older students. The teaching of the generalizations necessary for accurate syllabication is important. For students who have had this instruction in their normal classroom situations and have failed to respond to it, use discovery techniques.

The number of generalizations necessary may vary with the needs of the students in relation to the types of words they meet at their instructional level. The following three generalizations are *essential* for all students in learning the syllabication of words.

1. The vowel-consonant-vowel generalization. When a word has the structure v-c-v, syllable division is usually between the first vowel and the consonant.

$$v \quad cv$$
Example: (*over* = *o/ver*)

However, vowels which are followed by a consonant *r* form an exception to the v/cv generalization, the *r* going with the preceding vowel.

$$vc \quad v$$
Example: (*carol* = *car/ol*)

2. The vowel-consonant-consonant-vowel generalization. When a word has the structure v-c-c-v, syllable division is usually between the consonants.

vc cv

Example: (*picnic* = *pic/nic*)

However blends and digraphs are treated as one consonant.

v c v

Example: (*achieve* = *a/chieve*)

3. The consonant *le* generalization. When a word ends in the structure consonant plus *le,* those three letters form the last syllable.

c=le

Example: (*ankle* = *an/kle*)

For students who fail to understand syllabication at this point, the Fernald technique with a modification for emphasis on the syllables of words may be used to direct them to substitute the pronunciation of *syllables* in all steps that require them to pronounce the *word*.[6] Although this technique will not teach the student how to divide words into syllables, its value is in assisting them to grasp the concept of syllabication.

Once the word has been dissected, either through syllabication or through the actual sounding of each letter of the syllable, the students must be able to *blend* these sounds and to obtain a *pronunciation* with which they can associate a meaning. Again, classroom and clinical techniques are similar.

When difficulty with blending arises, the student must be given ample opportunity to divide known words into syllables and then to blend these sounds in order to obtain a feeling for blending. It is clear that the blending of sounds and syllables is an inherent part of each lesson in which the student learns the sound or divides the word into syllables.

There are several phonics approaches which simplify the problem of blending and pronunciation by teaching the sounds as units rather than in isolated pronunciation. In the following case, for example, the sound of *b* will be taught in the initial position as it relates to the various vowels: *ba, be, bi, bo, bu.* This then is immediately substituted in word-building exercises:

bad   *bit*   *but*
beg   *boss*

Cordts presents in detail the techniques and philosophy of a blending approach to the teaching of phonics.[7]

---

[6]Grace Fernald, *Remedial Techniques in Basic School Subjects* (New York: McGraw-Hill Book Co., 1943), Part II.

[7]See Suggested Readings and Appendix B.

Structural Clues

Deficiencies in the ability to attack compound words are generally not too serious, for students easily can be taught to pronounce the words if they know the parts. If they do not know the parts, the problem is probably inadequate sight vocabulary. Although prefixes cause more difficulty than compound words, the fact that they are (1) at the beginning of the word; (2) usually a separate, easily pronounceable syllable; and (3) concerned with a meaning which directly alters the base word makes them easier to learn and causes less difficulty in remedial reading. However, in the case of suffixes, where the above three factors are often missing, many students experience difficulty. It is with suffixes that the service of the base word is most likely to change, even though a precise difference in meaning is not evident. Note that in the following words when the suffix is removed, the spelling and configuration of the base word is distorted, causing an additional complication in the study of suffixes:

> *run   running   runn-ing*
> *hope   hoping   hop-ing*

The discovery technique is again suggested for its advantage in making students generalize structural patterns from known words.[8] This technique is equally applicable to difficulties with prefixes, suffixes, or compound words. In teaching the decoding and interpretation of the prefix *un,* for example, it may be best to follow a procedure similar to this:

1. Present the word *happy* in a sentence.   *John is happy.*

2. Change the word to *unhappy.*   *John is unhappy.*

3. Have the students generalize the difference in meaning.

4. Present several other words in a similar manner.

5. Have the students generalize by answering the question, "What does *un* generally do to the meaning of a word to which it is prefixed?"

6. Collect word patterns of this type and see if they apply to the generalization.

7. Note that *un* has a sound which is consistent and that it changes the meaning of the words to which it is attached.

8. As the students read, their attention should be called to words prefixed by *un.* They should determine if these words fit the generalization.

Word wheels which contain the base word easily can be made; as they move the wheel, the students add either the prefix or the suffix to the base

---

[8]Botel, *How to Teach Reading,* p. 40.

word. Suggestions for these can be found in Russell and Karp's *Reading Aids Through the Grades*[9] The teacher is cautioned in the construction of such reinforcement devices to be certain that the problem is not one of the student's not knowing the base word and to be alert to the spelling changes which occur when the suffix is added. Prepared exercises of this type are found in materials such as the *Classroom Reading Clinic*. In this kit, word wheels, upon which base words are altered by prefixes and suffixes, provide ready-made reinforcement exercises.

Sound-Symbol Relationships. Does the student seem to know sound-symbol relationships but seem unable to use them during reading? Many students seem to have this difficulty; so it is a problem well-known to teachers. During skills lessons the students seem to respond accurately but there is no carry-over to reading.

One possible explanation is that instruction was not followed by opportunities for the use of the newly learned skill. Through disuse, the skill gradually becomes weakened and then lost. Each lesson must be followed by reading practice, and in some cases it might be well for that practice to be monitored by the teacher so that the transfer of the skill to reading can be verified.

Another explanation might be that the students have received conflicting advice about how to use their new skills. One teacher might suggest starting with the initial consonant, another might suggest using a dictionary, and parents might tell them to spell the unknown word. While many readers weather such conflicting advice, the handicapped reader can become thoroughly confused.

It is useful to establish a minimal strategy for attacking an unknown word. All teachers working with a group of students agree to the strategy and use it with the students. Parents and librarians are also informed of it and use it. In this way, the student is seeing that what is learned in reading classes is important throughout the school and even at home. The strategy that any group of teachers would develop should relate to what they stress during instruction. The following is an example of such a strategy:

When you come to a word you do not know:

1. Read on and look for clues.

2. Frame the word.

3. Try the first sound.

4. Divide the word into smaller parts.

5. Consult.

---

[9]David H. Russell and Etta E. Karp, *Reading Aids Through the Grades* (New York: Columbia University Press, 1951).

Here the students are asked to use context clues first, configuration clues second, phonics third, syllabication fourth, and then either use a dictionary or ask someone for help. Teachers should then teach each of these strategies. Students have cards they can refer to with the strategies written on them. They can use these for bookmarks. Teachers post the strategies in each room, the media center, and send a copy home, plus emphasize the strategy in every lesson. The students get the idea that what they have worked so hard to learn has application for reading.

Using a minimal strategy does not limit those students who have more skills which they can use. It simply gets the handicapped reader started on the road to independence in reading through word attack.

Practice. Practice activities for structural skills do not differ from those which followed phonics instruction. Games, learning centers, tutoring, and practice sheets are appropriate here also. For older students *Tactics in Reading*** and *Basic Reading Skills*** provide mature activities for practice.

Using learned skills. Again, the reading time provided at the end of practice sessions is important for the students to develop the understanding that all of these activities have but one purpose—to make reading a more enjoyable and successful experience.

Context Clues

Authors provide context clues by the redundancy in their writing and through deliberate attempts to help the reader. Readers pick up on those clues through the use of their knowledge of syntax, semantics, and pronunciation. Just how does a reader gain these skills for use in reading? Probably the best way is to read a great deal. Read all types of material: fiction, content, newspapers, poetry, and magazines. Obviously seriously handicapped readers run into difficulty because there is very little for them to read for practice. However, reading a variety of materials is the best way to learn to use context clues. Questions to ask to determine problems with context clues include:

1. Does the student appear to ignore syntactic cues?
2. Does the student appear to ignore semantic cues?
3. Does the student appear to ignore punctuation cues?

Ignoring Syntactic Clues. Students who make substitutions but use the correct part of speech in the substitution are telling us that they understand the language but are missing the exact word. Those who substitute the incorrect part of speech are telling us the material is so strange to them that they cannot even see it as their language. The very first task is to make adjustments in material to determine if the students continue to misuse syntactic cues on easier material or material which is of higher interest to them. If adjustment of materials eliminates the problem, then practice in reading should be provided in that type of material.

If students continue to substitute incorrect parts of speech, then direct instruction in simple closure activities is appropriate. Students may be asked to discuss which words might fit in this blank:

Mary has a _____ baseball bat.

Answers such as *new, big, large, small, green, yellow,* and *nice* can be accepted and discussed as to why they fit. Then other parts of speech can be eliminated, and the practice can continue. Students enjoy the open-ended type of response and can quickly become aware of the syntactic cues which our language offers.

Ignoring Semantic Cues. If readers substitute with words which do not distort meaning, they are on their way to reading success. However, if they distort meaning with their substitutions, then they are missing the ideas of the author. Again, the first adjustment must be with the materials to see if easier materials and materials of more interest can correct the errors. Such adjustments almost always work. If the readers are over their heads in concepts or technical vocabulary, there is little chance of using context effectively. Smith talks of readers using prediction as a technique to develop awareness of meaning.[10] For example, read these sentences to the students:

The team had their high scorer under the basket. The score was 96–94 with three seconds left. Jim thought, ''Wow, what a _____ game.''

Then ask, ''What words would fit and what words would be wrong? Why?''

The same types of activities can be used in silent reading. Let groups of students work together to determine which word can be used and why. Authors provide semantic cues in all types of reading.

Some commercial materials may assist the teacher in providing many experiences of this type. *Using the Context** provides numerous activities at various grade levels.

For mature readers use newspaper articles and words which can be supplied if the context is understood. Students are excited about such adult-like reading and quickly understand how the use of context clues is more than a guessing game.

Ignoring Punctuation Cues. Punctuation errors are often due to the frustration level of the material rather than failure to observe punctuation. If this is true,

---

[10]Frank Smith, ''The Role of Prediction in Reading,'' *Elementary English* 52, no. 3 (March 1975): 305-11.

directed activity to observe the markings will be useless, and time may be spent more wisely on other skill areas with materials of the proper level. However, if the error is due to lack of knowledge about the use of punctuation marks, instruction is needed.

Choral reading or reading in unison is an effective, subtle way for students to obtain a feeling for the function of punctuation marks. Following group oral reading, the students' attention should be called to the fact that punctuation marks have different functions and call for different inflections. Listening to good oral reading on a tape recorder will also assist readers to become aware of the need to observe punctuation marks in their reading materials.

Opportunities for students to follow the teacher's reading to determine observance of correct punctuation also may be used effectively. Intentionally distorting the punctuation, the teacher can ask students to explain what this does to the ideas of the author. When used sparingly, this technique works well with those having trouble hearing their own punctuation errors.

Activities such as the following are interesting for students and create an awareness for observation of punctuation marks:

Read the following sentences:

Nancy is bright. Jim is in love.
Nancy is bright? Jim is in love?

One of the difficulties with English is that punctuation marks might be far removed from where the student must make the proper inflection. Wouldn't it be easier if we could write it:

? Nancy is bright

Then the reader would know the statement was to be a question.

When readers have difficulty using punctuation it is almost always because the materials are too strange or too difficult. Teachers should make certain that practice activities always involve appropriate materials which reduce frustration.

Use of Dictionaries

Dictionary skills are excellent, indispensable word attack techniques. Students with reading problems may benefit from dictionary instruction; however, special help for problem readers usually does not result from a limitation of dictionary skills alone. Work in programming has produced two publications which may be of use in either remediation, *Lessons for Self-Instruction in Basic Skills*** and *David Discovers the Dictionary*.** The appeal of these programs to remediation is their individualized approach, which requires a minimum of teacher supervision to assist the student in acquiring the skills necessary to use the dictionary.

Provide a dictionary for every reader. When word attack problems occur, let students use the dictionaries. The habit and the skills needed are quickly formed and lead the readers to independence. Of course dictionaries require the use of alphabetizing skills and locating skills. But these can easily be taught and readers can gain self-esteem from the independence which results.

Motivation

By far the strongest motivation for students in the study of word attack skills is being able to see how this knowledge and skill enable them to become more independent in their reading. It is essential, therefore, for students to be put in the situation of transferring learned skills to context in every lesson if possible. Game-type activities, as suggested, make the reinforcement of these skills more informal and pleasurable.

The discovery technique has motivational appeal, especially to some of the older students who need work in word attack. The idea of generalizing the concepts of word attack with a minimum of teacher supervision usually becomes a highly motivating situation.

Graphic illustrations of progress usually help to motivate. Teacher-made materials designed to illustrate established goals and the student's achievement within the scope and capabilities are effective motivating devices too.

Programmed materials with immediate feedback are interesting to students and contain inherent motivational appeal. These materials, designed to reinforce correct and alter incorrect responses, establish situations in which the reader eventually will be successful—a desirable outcome in all types of remedial programs.

SUMMARY

The remedial techniques to be used in the area of vocabulary deficiencies, whether sight vocabulary or word attack, are based on diagnostic findings. Once these deficiencies are determined, educators have a variety of approaches in remediation from which to choose. Starting with those which they believe will serve most adequately, educators remain alert during instruction to the possibility that the original approach may need to be modified as instruction continues.

Constant awareness of the value of incorporating skill activities into contextual situations is the responsibility of both the teacher and the reading specialist. Continued drill, without well-developed transfer opportunities, is of little value.

SUGGESTED READINGS

Botel, Morton. *How to Teach Reading,* Chapters 3 and 5. Chicago: Follett Publishing Co., 1968. In this well-written book, Botel presents the "discovery" and "spelling" mastery techniques for use in sight vocabulary and word attack lessons. The reader will find this a practical guide to developmental as well as remedial activities.

Burmeister, Lou E. "Usefulness of Phonic Generalizations." *The Reading Teacher,* January 1968, pp. 349-59. This article reviews the research on phonics generalizations. A reading of this review is essential prior to work with children in a program which concentrates on phonics and the use of phonics.

Clymer, Theodore. "The Utility of Phonics Generalizations in the Primary Grades." *The Reading Teacher,* January 1963, pp. 252-58. This article discusses how functional the generalizations commonly taught to children are in terms of the number of times the generalizations hold true and the number of words to which they apply.

Coley, Joan, and Gambrell, Linda. *Programmed Reading Vocabulary for Teachers.* Columbus, O.: Charles E. Merrill Publishing Co., 1977. This book presents the basic knowledge a teacher must have to work with students in the area of sight vocabulary. The material is presented in programmed format.

Cordts, Anna D. *Phonics for the Reading Teacher.* New York: Holt, Rinehart and Winston, 1965. This entire book is devoted to a description and explanation of a method of teaching phonics which reduces the necessity for extra blending of isolated sounds. The reader will find this technique valuable in working with many problem readers.

Forte, Imogene et al. *Center Stuff.* Nashville, Tenn. Incentive Publication, 1973. A useful collection of ideas for developing centers on many topics.

Fries, Charles C. *Linguistics and Reading.* New York: Holt, Rinehart and Winston, 1963. One explanation for the linguistic involvement in the teaching of reading can be found in this book. For those who have difficulty understanding the linguist, this book is a good introduction. Teachers of problem readers must acquaint themselves with the works of the linguists.

Hall, MaryAnne. *Teaching Reading as a Language Experience.* 2d ed. Columbus, O.: Charles E. Merrill Publishing Co., 1976. This book presents basic information for teachers concerning the nature and uses of language experience as an approach to reading instruction.

Heilman, Arthur W. *Phonics in Proper Perspective.* 3d ed. Columbus, O.: Charles E. Merrill Publishing Co., 1976. Heilman has combined as assessment of the place of phonics with a survey of the skills to be taught and has included examples and appropriate word lists. The educator who works with problem readers will find this book or one like it indispensable in working with phonics.

Herrick, Virgil E., and Nerbovig, Marcella. *Using Experience Charts with Children.* Columbus, O.: Charles E. Merrill Publishing Co., 1964. This booklet will provide the reader with many suggestions concerning the construction and use of experience charts. The classroom teacher should find these suggestions easily applicable to this group.

Lee, Dorris M., and Allen, R. V. *Learning to Read Through Experience.* New York: Appleton-Century-Crofts, 1963. A combination of philosophy and techniques, this book is a must for those who plan to work with seriously handicapped children. As indicated, this approach will be of particular value with many children, and the book will provide the educator with a thorough background from which to work.

Stauffer, Russell. *The Language-Experience Approach to the Teaching of Reading.* New York: Harper & Row, 1970. Chapters 1, 2, and 3 discuss the theory and uses of language-experience approaches. Chapter 10 discusses special uses of language experience including clinical cases.

Waynant, Louise R., and Wilson, Robert M. *Learning Centers . . . A Guide to Effective Use.* Paoli, Pa.: Instructo, 1974. Provides numerous ideas about the construction and use of learning centers. Those who want to use learning centers in remedial programs will find this book useful.

Wilson, Robert M., and Hall, MaryAnne. *Programmed Word Attack for Teachers.* 2d ed. Columbus, O.: Charles E. Merrill Publishing Co., 1974. This book presents the basic knowledge about word attack needed by teachers for instruction. The material is presented in a programmed format followed by tests which enable teachers to demonstrate their knowledge of word attack skills.

9

Remedial Activities for Comprehension Skills

Comprehension is a thinking activity in which readers must interpret the association of various sets of ideas and link those interpretations to their backgrounds of experiences, resulting in the reception of a message. No one receives the precise message of an author. Sometimes it is the fault of the author for writing vaguely, leaving too much for inference, for example. Sometimes it is the fault of the reader, losing concentration or having limited experiential background, for example. If comprehension fails during teacher-directed activities, the fault could also be with the teaching strategies employed. This chapter will concentrate on the last reason, for in a remedial program the assumption is that the teacher is involved in developing instructional adjustments to create a successful learning environment. Naturally such adjustments might include the use of alternate materials and the building of background experiences.

Instruction in the area of comprehension is highly rewarding for students and teachers. It is here that ideas are discussed and students begin to see the reading process as communication. Note that during the previous discussions of sight vocabulary and word attack attention to meaning was constantly stressed. Obviously, then, comprehension is not a set of separate skills, but a part of the involved reading process.

Success with reading comprehension is enhanced by experiences in reading. Good readers who read and enjoy reading become better readers. Poor readers who lack essential reading skills, tend not to read much, do not enjoy it much, and tend to become poorer readers. One of the major tasks in reading comprehension instruction is to turn that latter cycle around and help poor readers enjoy the process. As they begin to read more, comprehension skills will improve. Remedial programs should provide experiences with a variety of reading materials and a variety of instructional techniques to increase the reading background of the reader.

INSTRUCTIONAL STRATEGIES

Prior to a discussion of the questions asked during diagnosis a brief review of some important instructional strategies may be of some help. These strategies include the directed reading-thinking activity, establishment of mental set, types of questioning situations, adjustment of materials, wait time, and task analysis.

The Directed Reading-Thinking Activity (D-R-T-A)

Stauffer has developed an instructional strategy which focuses on the teacher's role in directing reading as a thinking activity.[1] This strategy can be used with a large group of students or can be adapted to individualized instruction. The steps include:

1. Identifying purposes for reading
2. Guiding the adjustment of rate to purposes and materials
3. Observing the reading
4. Developing comprehension
5. Providing fundamental skill-training activities[2]

These steps must be understood by the teacher of handicapped readers. If this brief discussion does not adequately inform you, review Stauffer's work.

Stauffer's D-R-T-A emphasizes the place of the student in the learning process. His rationale includes a list of assumptions about what students can do. The student then is very involved in each step of the lesson; the teacher is

---

[1]Stauffer, Russell G., *Teaching Reading As A Thinking Process*, Harper & Row, New York, 1969.
[2]Ibid, p. 12.

seen as a member of the group but not the authoritarian figure. For example, in setting purposes, the students are taught to make observations about the materials and set their purposes and then read to satisfy those purposes. The teacher is on hand to guide and assist, but not to dominate. This process and view of the reader and the teacher are essential, basic understandings for anyone entering into remedial instruction.

Establishment of Mental Set

Closely linked to the ideas related to the D-R-T-A is the importance of the mental set of the students. If students see reading lessons as activities in which their performances are being checked and tested then it is quite possible that the mental set for the activity will be one of, ''Well, here we go again, I hope I can answer the teacher's questions.'' On the other hand, if students learn to see reading lessons as activities in which they are reading for their own purposes and in which they will have opportunities to discuss and share what they have found in the passage, their mental sets might well change to, ''I have some control and I have some useful ideas to give to the group.''

The set or attitude that students have at entry to a given lesson is all important to their performance in the lesson. Therefore, questioning will be discussed throughout this chapter, and some very specific strategies will be presented to help establish a favorable mental set. Remedial comprehension lessons should be altered to reduce the amount of direct teacher questions, particularly those of the literal type.

Types of Questioning Situations

Two situations exist for the students to answer questions. One is a recall situation in which the reading materials are not available to the students. The other is a locate situation in which students can use the reading materials to locate answers to questions. Many regular classroom activities have stressed the recall situation which involves not only reading comprehension but memory abilities as well.

However, remedial lessons should focus on locating skills. What the students need to be able to do is use the reading material to either find or check their answers. Students can answer about 30 percent more questions when locating than when recalling. Since remedial lessons should focus on strengths, locating is desirable.

In working with adults discussing the advantages and limitations of recall and locate situations, I often give them some material to read. Their responses are considerably improved when they are allowed to keep the material during questioning. Students have probably read the materials if they can locate the answers. If teachers want to test how well students remember what they have read, then they should call it a memory training activity and not reading comprehension. By stressing locating instead of recalling students are encouraged to learn how to use reading materials. They begin to see books are resource materials which can be reexamined, and, consequently, they develop mature reading skills.

We all maintain some type of professional and personal library in our homes. We maintain those libraries because we enjoy the privilege of rereading something which was of interest or because we need to locate information which has slipped our memory. And, after reading an interesting story in a book or the newspaper, we do not want to be expected to remember details for others to question. Similarly, in the establishment of mental set, recall calls for the student to remember as much as possible during the questioning period; locate calls for the student to be able to use the reading material during questioning.

Adjustment of Materials

Except for periods of self-selection, materials for instruction are chosen by the teacher. If the materials are too difficult or lacking in interest, it is essential to change them. Instead of trying to force students through such materials, the teacher needs to be aware of means of either adjusting the materials or getting different ones.

A materials section is included in Appendix B. Teachers should become familiar with these and other materials so that selections can be made for various students. Other materials may need to be rewritten to reduce either concept load or vocabulary difficulty. See page 206 for a discussion of the use of survival and functional reading materials during remediation.

Wait Time

The work of Rowe on the topic of wait time should be considered by all teachers but particularly by those working with handicapped readers.[3] Rowe found that teachers tend to give very little wait time, that is, the time between asking a question and calling for an answer. One second was the average wait time. By training teachers to wait for three seconds or longer, Rowe found that student responses increased and were more complete.

Rowe also found that the amount of time between the student's answering a question and the teacher's responding to the answer was very short. When teachers waited after a student responded, the student tended to expand the first response, and other students tended to interact without teacher interruption.

---

[3]Rowe, Mary Budd, *Teaching Science as Continuous Inquiry* (New York: McGraw-Hill, 1973), pp. 242-66.

All those inclined to work with handicapped readers should become familiar with the works of Rowe and incorporate wait time as an important factor in remedial lessons.

Task Analysis

Task analysis, as discussed in Chapter 6, has special application to reading comprehension. It can lead teachers to make appropriate adjustments when students become overwhelmed in a comprehension lesson and are unable to respond. Briefly, what can the students do and what seems to be the difficulty? Hypothesize several adjustments which you think can improve the learning situation. Check out each one through diagnostic teaching, and then alter your instructional plan.

Of all of the areas in which task analysis has been useful, it is most useful when severe comprehension problems are encountered.

SPECIFIC REMEDIAL ACTIVITIES IN COMPREHENSION

As in other skill areas, remedial efforts in reading comprehension will be discussed in terms of the questions asked as a result of diagnosis:

1. Do large units of material seem to interfere with comprehension?
2. Do comprehension difficulties occur with some types of comprehension and not others?
3. Does the student have difficulty using locating skills?
4. Does the student have difficulty reading content material? Why?
5. Does the student fail to comprehend most of what is read?

It is most likely that, if a comprehension difficulty exists, there will be no one answer. For example, the student having difficulty with locating skills will likely have difficulty in reading content materials also. By continuing to look at reading as a complex process, teachers realize that single solutions are unlikely.

Large Units of Materials

The improvement of reading skills depends on the student's ability to respond to units of print of increasing length. In diagnosis it is easy to note whether the reader's comprehension is limited basically to sentences, paragraphs, or to larger units. In these cases the problem is one of not being able to recognize the relationship between units of varying sizes and the flow of ideas created by the author.

All remedial approaches must start at the instructional or independent level. When the difficulty is related to the size of the unit, the instructional level should be the largest unit each student can handle effectively. Using the D-R-T-A, teachers can help students set objectives for reasonable amounts of material. Students quickly become aware of the amounts of materials they can handle and learn to set objectives accordingly.

The paragraph appears to be a reasonable starting place, usually containing one major idea and some supporting details. Helping students to understand paragraph structure through identification of the topic sentence is also useful.

Materials such as *SRA Reading Laboratories*** provide smaller units of material at lower levels but manage to maintain interest. Students can set purposes for such reading and read to answer their purposes, not just to answer the questions on the card. Some materials have numbered paragraphs at easier levels. Locating skills can be taught by asking question in relation to the paragraph number. In this manner, the students are helped to locate the area in which the answer can be found—a real time-saver for beginning instruction.

Teachers can also adjust the amount of material included in experience stories. If a long story is dictated, the teacher can place it on two or three sheets, making parts 1, 2, and 3. Students can respond to each section and finally to the entire story.

Highly motivating teacher-made materials easily can be developed to help students handle large quantities of material. For example, a TV guide from the Sunday newspaper can be used to help students handle varying amounts of printed material and to respond to tasks of varying difficulty. Students can be asked:

1. What show is offered on Channel 4 at seven o'clock on Tuesday evening?
2. What sports events are offered on Saturday?
3. Select four movies you would like to watch during the week.
4. What shows are featured at eight o'clock each day?
5. Take 1½ hours per night and schedule your own television watching for the week.

The use of newspaper articles, want ads, telephone yellow pages, cookbooks, shop manuals, catalogues, encyclopedias, and dictionaries can be developed similarly by starting with a specific activity requiring a minimum of reading and moving toward extended activities requiring considerable reading. Students in remedial programs can relate easily and enthusiastically to materials such as these, even though they might tend to be disinterested in book reading. Some of these types of materials contain very small quantities of print and are, therefore, ideally suited for students who have difficulties with larger units.

Difficulties with Some Types of Comprehension

Teachers use questions to determine the ability of students to respond to various types of comprehension activities. When responding to teacher questioning students may indicate strengths and needs based upon the type of questions being asked. The type of question and the type of response needs careful consideration prior to discussion of remedial activities. All too often, the type of question asked in commercially prepared materials is designed to obtain specific facts from the story (literal understanding). When working with groups of students, questions at the literal level can be asked of the entire group at one time. Using Durrell's** idea of every-pupil-response cards, all can quickly respond to literal questions. Each reader, for example, has a card stating *yes* and one stating *no*. The teacher can select five or ten important details from the story and ask questions calling for a yes or no answer. Cards with names of story characters, dates, and numbers to indicate choices in multiple choice questions also can be used. The teacher notes all of the responses and directs rereading or reformulates questions when responses are inaccurate. Literal understanding can be checked in a short period of time, leaving more time for questions and activities of the interpretive and problem-solving types. While literal comprehension is extremely important, the time normally allocated for it is out of proportion to its importance.

When interpretive questions are asked, the reader is expected to respond by paraphrasing the ideas of the author. Such questions as the following might be asked:

1. In your own words state the main idea of the story.
2. How would you summarize the author's major point?
3. Why did the major character lose his temper?

Questioning at the interpretation level requires that the readers draw upon their fields of experience to interpret the author's words. While interested in accurate interpretation, the teacher *must not* have a preconceived statement of the answer. Readers interpret in the best way they can and their efforts must be accepted. If answers contain inaccuracies, there is the possibility of inaccurate reading or of an inappropriate background of experiences. In either case, inaccuracy calls for reteaching rather than criticism.

When questioned at the problem-solving level, students are expected to think beyond the content of the story, applying either critical- or creative-thinking skills to the author's ideas through such questions as the following:

1. What would you have done if you were Jim?   (creative)
2. Did Jim make a good decision? Why?   (critical)
3. Can you think of a better ending for the story?   (creative)
4. What reasons can you give for father's actions?   (critical)

Obviously, questioning at the critical- and creative-thinking levels calls for even more openness on the part of the teacher. When the teacher asks critical questions, the students must have understood the author, must be able to interpret the author, and must apply their experiences in order to analyze what has happened. The students' answers may differ from the one which the teacher has in mind and still may be accurate. If reasoning is not clear, probing questions assist students to seek alternatives.

In creative thinking, any answer given is acceptable and correct. Students are being asked to create, and what they create is good. Students tend to enjoy creative activities and, when their answers are accepted, tend to become more creative. For example, ask a group of students to think of a new title for a story with the idea of making the story into a television show. Tell them the title should attract attention. They usually start with rather traditional titles but soon open up as they see the teacher accepting all of their responses.

Questions asked by the teacher are important, but even more important, perhaps, are the teacher's responses to the students' efforts. Accepting, probing, reteaching, and making reading activities exciting for students depend upon the teacher's attitude toward the responses of those students. Students also will learn to accept and to value a variety of peer responses as they see the teacher accepting them. For those in need of further explanation of the types of comprehension, *Programmed Comprehension for Teachers* may be a useful source of information.[4]

In discussing the three types of comprehension in terms of remediation, they will be in the order of interpretive, literal, and problem solving.

Interpretive. The importance of interpretive comprehension is the key to success with literal comprehension. It is suggested that teachers start by eliciting from the students which ideas they think are important or interesting. Such a start on a comprehension lesson tends to create a thinking atmosphere instead of a testing one. The teacher is encouraged to accept all suggestions, noting them on the chalk board. Some might be quite divergent from the message in the passage, but it is important to know what the various students gathered as the important message. Without comment each idea is recorded. After several ideas have been suggested, the students are now encouraged to

---

[4]Robert M. Wilson and Linda B. Gambrell, *Programmed Comprehension for Teachers*, (Columbus, O.: Charles E. Merrill, 1976).

pick the one they really think was most important. The opportunity to change ones' mind is likely to enhance the thinking process.

Next, pairs of students are formed according to agreement about the important idea. Their task is to go back through the passage to find support statements or proof for the idea selected. It is useful to provide a format sheet such as the following:

1. _____ (Important idea)

   a. _____ Support

   b. _____ Support

   c. _____ Support

This procedure can be repeated in long passages of several paragraphs, since their might be several important ideas. Students can then discuss or otherwise share their efforts. Aside from giving students practice in the important skill of outlining, this approach has several advantages:

1. The locating of literal facts has a purpose, the purpose selected by the students.
2. Students learn to locate swiftly and accurately since the location is specified.
3. On-task behavior is promoted since students are working in areas of their choice.
4. Poor choices for what was important are clearly illustrated to students since they have difficulty finding support.
5. Students accustomed to this approach perform well in literal comprehension activities which might follow.

Throughout this activity students are encouraged to paraphrase instead of using the exact words of the author. Those reading above the second-grade level can work effectively in this manner and learn to direct themselves after four or five lessons.

Other strategies for developing interpretive skills can be developed through some of the following suggestions. Closure activities are excellent means of helping students develop awareness of interpretation. Given the cloze activity:

Mike is a _____ football player.

groups of students can see how many words they can fit into the blank and still have the sentence make sense. To do so calls for awareness of the meaning of the rest of the sentence. Later, a full sentence can be provided, and students can add words that do not change the meaning, for example:

Pat is a tennis player.

Pat is a *tremendous* tennis player.

Using brainstorming, glosseries, or dictionaries, students can build many sentences without significantly changing the meaning of the sample sentence.

After experience stories are written, the teacher can write the same story while paraphrasing the student's stories. Students match the specific section of the teacher's story with their own. Once that skill is developed students can work in teams, paraphrasing their own stories.

Since interpretation involves the ability to relate one's thinking to that of the author, the first step of the D-R-T-A will need emphasis. Reading purposes will stress such activities as summarizing, reading between the lines, and determining the main idea instead of reading for details or facts. The first step of the D-R-T-A is also the place for building a background for the story. Pictures, discussions, film strips, and motion pictures might be used to assure that the students have experiences with the story's concepts. At other times, the simple procedure of using several of the terms in the story and of discussing situations using those terms assists the students when they meet the terms in the story.

Building a story into a motion picture by identifying the three most important scenes and then formulating a selling title for the movie is motivating and is a subtle way of stressing main idea. If interest is high, several students might develop a play or a movie from the story. When stressing interpretation, students perform their roles without reading lines from their books. Paraphrasing, inferring, and selecting the main idea will be essential. Many students demonstrate such skills in highly unique ways; for example, they might make a comic strip from a favorite story by creating both comic pictures and captions. Of course, acceptance of such efforts is the key to encouraging students to continue trying.

Analysis of the topic sentence in a paragraph can also develop interpretation skills. The topic sentence contains the main idea. By stating the topic sentence in their own words, the students are studying both main idea and paraphrasing. An independent activity can involve matching cut-out topic sentences with appropriate paragraphs.

Open-ended questions which call for summarizing can be developed and can result in performances acceptable at many levels of refinement. For example, a summary could be a word, a phrase, a sentence, a paragraph, or several paragraphs. Summaries can be either written or oral and can be either drawn or acted out. By changing the activity, teachers can maintain student interest while continuing to develop the same skill.

Students can learn from their peers if they are grouped so that readers having difficulty paraphrasing can work with those who are quite good at it. They can work in teams of two or three to come up with an answer to a teacher's posed question. By teaming students carefully, all will be able to make contributions to the final product. Pairing of students does not necessarily teach independence, but it often helps students overcome the feeling of frustration, of giving up, or of simply not understanding what is going on. It also assists in making them active rather than passive learners.

With older students, questions can be written (e.g., multiple-choice questions) relating to the content of the story but changing the author's wording. In such cases, teachers do the paraphrasing by means of the way in which they ask questions. The student's task is to match the paraphrased idea to the author's idea. Thus, they see that the same idea may be expressed in several different ways.

Sometimes a simple probing question can be helpful. For example, if a student answers with the precise words of the author, the teacher can respond, "Yes, that is correct. Now let's try to think of other ways to say the same thing." So, if the author has written, "The general led a successful charge," the teacher might suggest that the students attempt to say the same thing using another word for *successful*.

When inferences are stressed as an interpretation skill, the teacher must be aware of two types of inferences. One the author provides intentionally, while the other is developed by the reader. For example, some authors lead the reader to a conclusion without actually stating it. Since inferring involves reading between the lines, the teacher should talk with students about it in exactly those terms.

Ideas such as mood, time, danger, and happiness are often only implied by the author. Questions such as "How do you think the player felt after the game?" "When in history did the story take place?" and "Would you consider the people to be in danger?" are examples of questions which stimulate students to infer. Each question can be followed by probing. "What did the author say to make you think that?" The probing activity helps students to clarify their own thinking and understanding of how others have reacted to the same story they have read.

Cartoons can be used in activities for paraphrasing, obtaining the main ideas, and developing inference skills. For example, using three or four cartoons on the same subject, the teacher can have groups of students write captions for the cartoons and then let other groups try to match the captions with the pictures. Such an activity can be developed at many levels, all of which can be highly motivating.

When students have severe difficulty with interpretation of written material, the teacher should start with picture interpretation, help the students look at pictures which have story possibilities in terms of what they can see in the picture, and, then, move to interpretation. For example, the teacher can ask, "How do you think the children feel?" "How is that street different from the street you live on?" and "Make up a title for the picture." Once students have skills in picture interpretation, these responses should be developed into experience stories.

When a reading specialist draws experience stories from pictures, both literal understanding and interpretation responses should be developed. To modify the language-experience approach in order to develop interpretation, students can be asked to change a sentence without changing the meaning, change a word without changing the meaning, identify the sentences which describe the picture and those which interpret the picture, and discuss the main ideas. By moving from pictures to language-experience stories, reading specialists can make a natural transition from vicarious experiences to reading. The next step is to move to stories written by others.

Perhaps groups of students can write stories about the same picture. These stories can be compared using the above questions. When students are successful with the stories of others, they are indicating that they are ready to start with other printed material.

Literal. Literal comprehension calls for the student to locate or recall specific facts or sequences from the passage read. Again, it is encouraged that all literal comprehension occur in the locate situation. Since a fact or sequence question has a right or wrong answer, the students have no resource in a recall situation but to know the answer or not. However, when permitted to locate, if they do not remember the answer they have a way to find it. The comprehension strategy suggested at the beginning of the interpretive section is also very useful in helping students become aware of how to find important facts in a story.

Pointing out the important information via italicized print, boldface type, information repeated for stress, and illustrated information highlights clues to important details to be remembered. Perhaps more subtle but equally useful are clues which words contain. Descriptive adjectives, proper nouns, action verbs, and the like all call attention to those types of details which should receive more careful attention. For example:

The *large house burned* in the middle of the *night*.

Most basal material is well designed to develop understanding skills. The classroom teacher using basal materials first must be certain that the student is working at the appropriate level and then select those lessons which appear to be most useful.

Understanding sequences causes considerable difficulty for many students. When this skill is deficient, students are limited in their ability to handle content-type materials and to fully appreciate reading of longer units. The thought processes needed involve perceiving groups of items that are related in time (i.e., one comes first, then the next, and so on). Initially, students must obtain sequencing practice from such activities as following oral directions, doing independent work from oral and written instruction, or discussing events from a story which has been read to them by another.

To aid development of sequencing, it is normal to start with a sequence of two events and to advance to more involved sequences after that is understood. For example, begin with two events which are clearly representative of the beginning and ending of the story. When the students can perform with two events (i.e., when they can tell which one came first), add a third event, then a fourth, and so on. Starting with many events to place in sequence tends to smother readers with choices and does not lead to effective sequencing.

Placing comics taken from the Sunday newspaper in sequence is a motivating technique for teaching sequences. Start with obvious sequences and move toward more subtle ones. If they are cut apart and pasted to cards, the comics are quite durable. Numbers on the backs of the cards to indicate the sequence make the activity self-correcting. Obviously, a teacher can build many sequence activities from comics in a short time and with little expenditure of school funds. Teachers can also develop sequence activities from newspaper headlines. Students can read the headlines and place the events (recent to their experiences) in order. They can also match the headlines with newspaper pictures which they have placed in sequence.

Some experience stories can be cut into parts. When experience stories are stimulated by photographs taken during a trip, the photos can be arranged in sequence, topics can be written for each picture, and then topics can be arranged in order. Students can thus arrange the parts to make a sequential story.

Directing the students' attention to sequencing clues used by authors for emphasis is usually of some value. Items that are numbered, steps in a process, dates, the mention of time, and the use of sequence words (e.g., *afterwards, before, during*) are all indications that the author feels the sequence of events is of particular importance.

The development of consciousness of sequence often is done best by more subtle means. We might attempt to direct the student to the idea of making a movie in which three or four scenes are to be produced by asking, ''What is the order of scenes so that the audience will understand the story?'' Many teachers have used the technique of asking the students to retell the story successfully. However, it is important to realize that the reader who is deficient in the sequencing skill may experience considerable difficulty in telling the story in sequence and may merely relate the details indiscriminately instead. In such cases locating sequential events is preferred.

Although initial instruction in this area is conducted wisely at easy reading levels, it is necessary to move to the instructional level, for it is at this level that the student is most likely to see the necessity for concentration in order to reach desired goals.

Often, full attention is lacking when students are limited to working on easy material which does not require concentration. The *Reading Skilltexts,*** *Reading for Meaning,*** *SRA Reading Laboratories,*** *Working with Sounds,*** *Reader's Digest Skill Builders,*** and the *Standard Test Lessons in Reading*** are examples of the types of readily available materials assigned for literal understanding. It is a mistake to drill students in materials without immediate teacher follow-up to evaluate and redirect, since in the case of continued failure, materials can soon become burdensome and disinteresting. By correcting errors immediately, the likelihood of reinforcing correct responses is enhanced. Of course, it is usually better to provide answer keys so that students can check their own work. When they check their own answers, reinforcement possibilities increase. They are more involved in the appropriateness of their work; their responses are reinforced immediately; and they can look for the correct answer when they cannot figure it out from the question asked. Self-correction is a highly desirable activity for students and saves teachers considerable time. It is important to remember that when a check exists in a practice situation (not a testing situation), students can use several routes to answers. They can figure out the answer themselves; they can ask someone else; or they can look on an answer sheet.

We often start with experience stories in which the student is asked to explain how to do something, such as build a model airplane, and then is directed to sequence the steps. When possible, the teacher can obtain funds to purchase car, ship, or airplane models and help students to see the importance of sequences by working with them to construct models using the sequential directions on the box.

Problem Solving. Students usually are not classified as being in need of remedial assistance if their only difficulty is in the area of problem solving. However, problem-solving activities ought to be considered necessary and valuable in remedial situations. Such activities involve the reader in a reaction to the message of the author. The reaction takes on one of two forms, either critical or creative. A critical reaction calls for convergent-thinking activities. The author's ideas are challenged, defended, and evaluated. Creative reactions call for divergent-thinking activities. The ideas of the author form a base from which new ideas can be developed.

When students set their own purposes, their choice is frequently at the problem-solving level. They want to know how to use a piece of equipment, or they want to challenge the ideas of the author. When they make such choices they should be encouraged and also made aware that they are illustrating mature thinking behavior.

Newspaper reading is a natural activity for problem-solving lessons. Generally, the headlines are stated in such a way that the students either wonder what the problem is or what the solution is. The articles also lend themselves to scanning since they are generally written from the most important to the least important facts. Students can be encouraged to take sides on issues and find support for their side in news articles and editorials. Students' questions can be developed with teacher assistance. Do you agree with the author's position? Is the story true? Were the people justified in doing what they did? Each of these questions can be backed by other questions such as, "Why?" or "Why not?"

Problem solving can also be stimulated by working in pairs or small groups. In groups, students get a chance to try out their thinking without committing themselves to a specific point of view. It is often through give-and-take discussions that problem-solving skills are refined.

Students often see problem-solving activities which are related to content subjects, such as history, as highly relevant. This gives the classroom teacher an opportunity to use content materials as reading instructional materials. Thus, the students are helped in two school subjects at once. It is also a technique to prepare students for lessons focusing on materials which they have difficulty reading.

Myers and Torrance have developed a series of critical and creative activities for use at various classroom levels. Students enjoy working with these materials. For example, one activity involves asking, "What would happen if it always rained on Saturday?"[5]

With picture interpretation, problem-solving questions are asked about action pictures (e.g., "How would you feel if you were there?" or "What do you think will happen next?"). As students develop skill in responding to problem-solving questions concerning pictures, they can create the language-experience stories. Once several groups of students have worked on the same picture, stories can be compared, read, and discussed. The use of materials

---

[5]R. E. Myers and E. Paul Torrance, *For Those Who Wonder* (Boston: Ginn and Co., 1966), p. 1.

such as *Tweedy*** transparencies bring action and life to pictures. Even very young readers find these transparencies stimulating and thought provoking. Older students respond to them equally well, and the teacher can move from discussion to writing activities using the transparencies as a basis for instruction. Then, moving to very easy reading material, the teacher can help the students develop problem-solving skills by using the writings of others. With older students, newspaper advertisements and television commercials are helpful to stimulate problem-solving-type thinking. The teacher can ask students what this written material is really saying. What words are used to influence? Is the ad truthful? Why or why not? How would a competitor rewrite the ad? Basic to all of the above steps should be the teacher's reading to the students. Students can watch the book, looking at words and pictures.

Role playing is also useful for students who have difficulty reacting to reading creatively. They can be helped to respond creatively through materials such as *Teaching Reading Through Creative Movement,*** which consists of records with voice, music, and stories, permitting a considerable amount of action. As students become freer in creative expression, they can react to many things which they read. After the creative expression, discussions about why they feel the way they do make a logical transition to creative discussions.

Difficulty Using Locating Skills

Locating information is a learned skill. It does not help handicapped readers much to simply allow them to use the book to answer questions. Instead some systematic instruction is necessary coupled with large amounts of practice.

By starting with materials of high interest and with the objective of trying to obtain literal information, the chances of success are enhanced. Record club memberships, cooking instructions, and local map reading are the kinds of material which can get students accustomed to locating information. Then paragraph-size passages can be introduced.

In longer passages, encourage students to think first about whether the information needed is in the front, toward the middle, or at the end of the passage. Considerable time can be saved if students do not have to start searching in the beginning for information that occurs toward the end of the passage. Obviously the mental set for locating can be developed. Instead of trying to recall details, the student tries to get the flow and direction of the passage. Then it is easier to locate specific information.

The best way I have found to teach locating skills is through the strategy presented concerning interpretive comprehension (see page 189). With this strategy, students will be locating information that has already been determined as important. They can locate information for topics of their interest in the library and in other types of resource materials.

Difficulty Reading Content Material

Many students seem to read satisfactorily in reading classes but are not able to read content materials. One problem may have to do with the content and readability of the materials since we know the student can read. Another may be that students find success when working under teacher direction and difficulty when working alone.

The first consideration in such instances must be the readability of the material upon which students cannot perform. Often, there are extreme differences in readability between the books used in reading class and the books used in content areas. Content area books often are written at a level much higher than the graded reading books. On an informal basis, the teacher should note the differences in the size of the print, the length of sentences, the vocabulary load in terms of difficult words, and the difficulty of the concepts. If any of these factors varies noticeably from the reading class materials, the problem is probably one of material difficulty. Yoakham,[6] Gunning,[7] Spache,[8] and Fry[9] present readability formulas which may be used to obtain a grade level of readability, although they do not evaluate the concept load of the material. The "cloze procedure" also has been developed to enable teachers to determine the ability of the student to handle materials; it will also indicate the ability to handle concepts as well as word and sentence structures. Taylor claims it is of value in determining readability.[10] This technique has been used at the University of Maryland clinic with the materials students are expected to read and has been found to be most helpful. It involves:

1. Selecting at random several passages containing samplings of about 100 words each.

2. Retyping this passage, leaving out every fifth word. (Authorities differ on which word to omit, but I have found the fifth to be effective.) As a rule, neither the first word in a sentence nor proper nouns should be omitted. An example of a clozure test on easy material would appear as follows:

> Nancy was anxious to ＿＿＿＿＿ her birthday party this
> ＿＿＿＿＿. She had invited some ＿＿＿＿＿ to her room at

---

[6]Gerald A. Yoakham, *Basal Reading Instruction* (New York: Prentice Hall, 1955), Appendix I.

[7]William A. Jenkins, ed., "The Educational Scene," *Elementary English* 37, no. 6 (October 1960): 411.

[8]George Spache, *Good Reading for Poor Readers* (Champaign, Ill.: Garrard Press, 1968), Chapter 4.

[9]Edward B. Fry, *Reading Instruction for Classroom and Clinic* (New York: McGraw-Hill, 1972), pp. 230-33.

[10]W. L. Taylor, "Cloze Procedure—A New Tool for Measuring Readability," *Journalism Quarterly* 30 (Fall 1953): 415-33.

school. She _____ that they would all _____ able
to attend.

3. Have the reader read the incomplete sentences, filling in the missing
   words. To "cloze" properly, the student must know the words and understand the concepts, thereby anticipating the author's ideas.

As teachers gain familiarity with the clozure technique, they will find it
a valuable aid in determining whether the book is appropriate for a given
student.

Bormuth has found that a *clozure* test score of 38 percent right is
approximately equal to a *regular* test score of 75 percent right.[11] Therefore, as
a rule of thumb, clozure scores below 40 percent right should be regarded as
danger signs for that student with that material. Either instructional adjustments are needed or easier material must be used for instruction. (For limitations of the 40 percent criteria, see Chapter 4.)

Reading problems in understanding content materials usually do not
become pronounced until the student has reached the fourth grade. It is at this
point that content reading becomes a regular part of the school program and the
student with study skill problems is clearly handicapped.

Strategies to Assist Students in Reading Content Material.   The teacher should
use the D-R-T-A with materials in content areas. Students who fail to see the
need for attacking unfamiliar materials must be directed in the same manner
that was used in reading class. Each step of the D-R-T-A must be used
carefully in the development of skill in reading content materials, gradually
permitting students to guide themselves through the steps.

Older students may find it beneficial to follow a specific study technique
in their reading of content materials. Several of these are available, the most
prominent being SQ3R (survey, question, read, recite, review).[12] The effect
of this type of technique is the same as a D-R-T-A except that students are to
apply it to their studies without supervision. Independence in reading content
material is the desired objective of this system.

Activities in which the students organize and classify ideas are useful in
remediation. Students who cannot read in the content areas usually have
difficulty with outlining skills. Beginning with completed outlines of material
recently read, the teacher illustrates the method of following the author's train
of thought. An outline format then is presented for students to complete,
followed by simple outlining of clearly organized material with little or no
direction from the teacher. The *Reading For Meaning*** workbooks, de-

---

[11]John R. Bormuth, "Comparable Cloze and Multiple-Choice Test Comprehension
Scores," *Journal of Reading,* February 1967, p. 295.
[12]Francis P. Robinson, *Effective Study* (New York: Harper & Row, 1961), Chap. ii.

signed for the intermediate and secondary grades, have practice exercises to develop students' abilities to organize material through a gradual exposure to outlining techniques. The *SRA Organizing and Reporting Skills Kit*** has individualized exercises which gradually introduce the concepts of note taking, reporting, and outlining.

The ability to follow directions has a direct relationship to the ability to perform in study situations. Composite in nature, this skill depends upon students' abilities to follow the sequence and organization of the author's thoughts, as well as their abilities to obtain the main idea. The *Specific Skills Series* (e.g., *Using the Context, ** Locating the Answer***) includes sets of intensive exercises in following directions at the various grade levels. Once the ability to follow directions is mastered, remedial sessions should provide further experiences with this concept at regular intervals.

These examples of activities for following directions have been useful in helping students develop mastery of that skill. As has been suggested, the use of model cars, ships, and airplanes helps a reader to realize the importance of following directions carefully. Reading the directions on the box and following them step by step to completion can be a highly useful reading and learning experience. If students cannot read all of the instructions, they should work in pairs, helping each other. Learning centers can be developed to help students follow directions. Using pages from telephone books or newspapers, students can be instructed to follow directions ranging from the simple to the complex (e.g., find a given phone number, find a given phone number and address, find the phone numbers of three dentists—give their names, get their addresses, and determine which lives closest to your home).

Another SRA study aid is the *Graph and Picture Study Skills Kit.*** Designed to be adapted to any subject area, these materials are useful in developing a type of reading often overlooked in remedial programs. The *Be a Better Reader*** books provide specific suggestions for study in the major content areas, particularly for older students. The *Study Skills Library,*** which provides specialized instruction in developing the same type of concepts, is useful with younger students. Individualized for clinical use, these materials can serve a highly useful function with students who are deficient in this skills.

Adaptation of the language-experience approach to content subjects has been very effective.[13] Four teachers agreed to work with students in the seventh grade who had serious reading problems. They taught mathematics, science, social studies, and English through the language-experience approach and were pleased to find that these students could learn the content when the materials were presented in a personalized, readable manner. Reading

[13]Robert M. Wilson and Nancy Parkey, "A Modified Reading Program in a Middle School," *Journal of Reading,* March 1970, pp. 447-52.

specialists can work with classroom teachers to develop skill in presenting material and information to the students without using texts (e.g., lecture, discussion, tapes, films, pictures, demonstrations, experiments), in drawing students' verbal expressions of what they have learned, in writing language-experience stories based on the students' contributions, and in developing reading and content skills from the written stories.

Reading specialists also can help content teachers rewrite materials which are too difficult. Basically, the rewriting involves cutting sentence length, eliminating complicated sentence structures, and reducing word difficulty through the use of synonyms.

Failure to Comprehend Most Reading

For the student who does not respond to any type of comprehension check, even at relatively easy levels of performance, remedial techniques are difficult to apply because starting places are difficult to determine. The continued use of materials previously used with the students is difficult to defend. For these students, the level of the material must be easy, the interest of the material must be high, and the quantity of the material must be small.

Intensified use of experience stories permits a start with relatively easy, interesting material of as small a quantity as desired. Again, students are directed to demonstrate an understanding of the experience stories which, because they contain their concepts, can usually be done without difficulty. Once a feeling for this type of activity is developed, the student is exposed through the D-R-T-A to easy, interesting printed material.

Placing the student in reading situations which call for action and reaction is often successful too. Signs, posters, and flash cards calling for reaction are developed from the opportunities which appear daily in and out of the class-room. One type of action material (involving a reaction from students at each step) has been produced under the name of *Programmed Reading*.** As students read through the programmed books, they are expected to react to every sentence. Their reactions are immediately reinforced by the correct response (see Chapter 8). These materials place students in situations which demand thought about what they are reading.

Vocabulary exercises which involve the students in nonverbal responses to printed symbols have considerable usefulness here. The *Nichols Slides*,** or their equivalent can be used by starting with very simple, direct commands and progressing as students develop the skill (e.g., start with words such as *sit, stand,* and *jump,* and go to more complicated combinations of words such as *stand and sing now* or *jump three times.*) With these students, drill activities without contextual emphasis certainly should be discontinued until the desired awareness of meaning were developed.

Several techniques have been developed to encourage students to respond to reading in rather nontraditional ways. One involves the use of creative movement to display understanding of a story which has been read to the students or read by them. Materials entitled, *Teaching Reading Through Creative Movement*** have been successful with seriously handicapped readers.

Another approach is through popular music. With a phonograph, some records, and lyrics the stage is set. Students listen to the music and sing along. When the music is over, the meaning of the lyrics is discussed. Rereading is done to verify opinions. Older students seem to respond well to remediation involving music as the motivator.

Reading, which involves essential information for getting along in our society, has also been used effectively. For example, students use driver's manuals and job applications. There can be no doubt that these items are worth reading and that it is important to read them accurately.

EXTENDED REMEDIATION

The problems students encounter relating to speed of reading and distractability can become instructional concerns.

Reading Speed

It is not unusual to find that the responses of students are due to a slow speed. In these cases, students have been asked to read a selection (ample time must be allotted) and to answer several questions. Not having completed the material, their comprehension responses appear to be unsatisfactory. Upon careful examination, it is often found that they have responded properly to those questions related to the material which was read and have missed those concerned with material not read. Teachers must question why the students are reading slowly. If they are having difficulty with breaking the written code, then activities designed to increase speed of reading are useless. The same is true if they are struggling with unfamiliar concepts. However, some students read slowly because they have applied oral reading speeds to silent reading, lack concentration, or do not know how to read faster. In these cases, some remedial instruction may be helpful.

Using the first step in the D-R-T-A, students develop specific purposes and are instructed to be flexible in their approach. Practice is accomplished on easy, interesting materials in order to be certain that slow reading is not due basically to poor sight vocabulary or to word attack problems. The time permitted for reading small passages can be controlled. Time control can be gradually increased or reduced as the reading situation demands, and the students gain a sense of what is meant by "flexibility of reading rate."

Prepared materials are available for students to use for practice exercises in reading within certain time limits. The *SRA Laboratories*** have rate-building exercises in which the student must read and answer the question in three minutes. The student should be started with rate-building exercises at very easy levels. The emphasis here is on efficiency in relatively easy material of high interest. The *Standard Test Lessons in Reading*** also have the three-minute time limitation. In the remedial session, the three-minute time limit will often need to be adjusted. Since there is no magic formula warranting the three-minute limit, teachers should allow more time for those students who need it. Time should be controlled, however and the students should be encouraged to complete the work accurately as swiftly as possible.

Other available exercises are designed to motivate improved time performance by emphasizing such measures of reading rate as number of words read per minute. In remediation, none of this emphasis should be stressed without equal or greater emphasis on the quality of comprehension which accompanies the rate. The *Better Reading Books*** are an example of this type of material to be used with older students, providing personalized charts for easy motivation to better speed and better comprehension. I have found the best speed practice for slow-reading students is to time them while reading in materials of their choosing. In three- or five-minute timed sessions, students read for specific purpose. For example, if they are reading the sports page of the morning paper their objective might be to see how their team did last night as well as the other teams in their league. Or, if reading a novel, they will want to find out how the main character gets out of that difficult situation. Students will record their time and estimate how satisfactorily they met their objectives. In this way, students will see that they read very rapidly for some purposes and very slowly for others. And they become flexible in adjusting their reading rate to their purposes for reading.

Charts and graphs which illustrate the students' progress are always helpful. These should be constructed so that each student can note small gains in improved rate, so that the aspect of comprehension is charted as well as the reading rate, and so that the goals are realistically within reach. If students reach the graph's goal quickly, the teacher simply makes a new graph, again with easily reached goals. Again, all such charts are maintained as private information.

Distractability

Again, one must question why the student is distracted. One reason might be that the material is boring—everything else is of more interest than the material. In these cases, the purposes for reading might be adjusted, or different materials can be used. However, some students are distracted by the attractiveness of the classroom. Everything is asking for their attention —learning centers, bulletin boards, art work, and sometimes the teacher. In these cases, several suggestions are offered:

1. Distractable students should be placed so that the actions of the others are no more distracting than necessary. In the classroom, this would normally involve a front corner seat.

2. Teachers should dress plainly, wearing clothes which do not call unnecessary attention to themselves.

3. Remediation should not be conducted in physical surroundings in which pictures and other distracting objects are prominent. In clinical situations, a plain room where a student's total efforts can be directed to the book should be used initially. In the classroom, distractable students should take their reading instruction in an area of the room which lacks extensive decoration.

4. When distractability is recognized as a serious limitation, it is often helpful to use books which contain a minimum of pictures, thus permitting students to focus attention upon the print and the skills necessary to read it.

5. Distractable students will need to have skill exercises in periods of shorter duration. They should understand that their entire attention will be expected for a short period of time, after which they may move to another activity and return to reading skill activities later. In the clinic, we have found it helpful to vary activity as much as possible. Unfortunately, such adjustments are difficult and at times impossible in the classroom, for they disrupt the activities of the other students. The classroom teacher, however, should provide a variety of activities and at least refrain from punishing students for distractability over which they have no obvious control. In the more extreme cases, students should run, jump, and play actively in other ways between their periods of skill activities in reading. Opportunities should be used to get them to be active in class as well as out. For example, the teacher could have them come to the board for some of their work and let them pass out materials to others, thus providing them with opportunities to release some of their energy. In this way, their tensions are released, and they become more receptive to the required silent work at their seats.

6. Students who are easily distracted generally enjoy a program which has as much consistency as possible. When they can anticipate an interesting routine, they are more likely to be able to concentrate on it to its completion. In rare instances, continued distractable behavior, even after adjustments have been made, calls for medical referral. These students may be demonstrating symptoms of behavior which need medical attention.

MOTIVATION

In each of the comprehension areas, motivation was discussed as an inherent part of the remedial program. In the general area of comprehension, motivation is the most appropriately intrinsic element, for students readily sense their accomplishments. Comprehension, the goal in reading for both teachers and students, is a rewarding experience in itself. Specifically, motivation in comprehension includes:

1. improved performance in the content area in school.
2. free reading of enjoyable material.
3. enjoyment of reading for interpretation and reading for problem solving.
4. charts and graphs of progress.
5. creation of successful comprehension situations.
6. experience stories which permit students to assume the role of the author.
7. use of games requiring team work.
8. genuine appreciation of discovering the unknown.

The Reluctant Reader

Most handicapped readers are reluctant to engage in reading activities. However, the term *reluctant reader* as used in this section has to do with those students who have the necessary skills for reading but are reluctant to use them. The need exists for these students to see reading as a rewarding experience. In every lesson, they should be reading for purposes that they feel are important. Drill-type activities should be held to a minimum, and purposeful reading should be increased.

First of all, it is important for these students to develop the attitude that free reading is an activity which the teacher feels is worthwhile. Therefore, free-reading opportunities should occur periodically in all classrooms. *Free reading* in this case implies reading which is not followed by question-and-answer periods and reading in which the students choose the desired materials. As students develop the understanding that free reading can be fun and is important enough to take school time, gradual changes of attitude are likely to be noted.

The development of an attitude of willingness to read obviously involves the availability of books. The problem reader must have books available for free reading in the classroom library, in the school library, and at home. There is little chance to develop attitudes and habits toward reading when books are difficult or impossible to obtain. School administrators should note that attempts to be thrifty by cutting appropriations for classroom and school libraries place teachers in the position of being unable to encourage the reading habit.

Learning centers which provide students with opportunities for selecting the materials they are going to use, for pacing themselves, and for correcting their own work have been used with considerable success.

Every opportunity should be utilized to promote free reading through the use of peer group recommendations. Students who have read interesting books and want to share them with others can often create more interest than can the teacher. Sharing may be done through brief, voluntary, oral reports; through a classroom card file including the name of the book and the reasons that the student enjoyed it; or through a school book fair where interesting books are displayed.

The teacher can develop interest by reading to the students from books which would be too difficult for them to read themselves but which contain stories and ideas of interest. Teachers who read children's books are able to provide book summaries to develop interest in new books as they appear in the library. They also subtly develop attitude by showing enthusiastic interest in their own personal reading.

Teachers may find it useful to consult book lists prepared by authorities to facilitate the guidance of students and the recommendations they are expected to make. *A Teacher's Guide to Children's Books,*[14] *Children and Books,*[15] *Your Children Want to Read,*[16] *Good Reading for Poor Readers,*[17] and *Creative Growth through Literature for Children and Adolescents*[18] are five examples. Through the use of such resources, the teacher also can recommend to parents books which would be appropriate gifts. Teachers should encourage parents to consider a book a valued, highly desired gift.

Often reluctant readers are hesitant to select a book which is a threat in terms of volume alone. Perhaps due to pressure from adults, the readers have developed an attitude that taking a book from the library commits them to read the book from cover to cover. The teacher, of course, must discourage this attitude, for we all have been in situations where, after starting a book, we feel no desire to finish it. Nevertheless, too many false starts tend to discourage students from sampling brief portions of books prior to selecting the books from the library. Two materials which let students sample books are *The*

[14]Nancy Larrick, *A Teacher's Guide to Children's Books* (Columbus, O.: Charles E. Merrill, 1969).

[15]May Hill Arbuthnot and Zena Sutherland, *Children and Books* (Chicago: Scott, Foresman & Co., 1972).

[16]Ruth Tooze, *Your Children Want to Read* (Englewood Cliffs, N.J.: Prentice Hall, 1957).

[17]George D. Spache, *Good Reading for Poor Readers* (Champaign, Ill.: The Garrard Press, 1968).

[18]Margaret Gillespie and John Conner, *Creative Growth through Literature for Children and Adolescents* (Columbus, O.: Charles E. Merrill, 1975).

Literature Sampler** and the *Pilot Library*.** Both of these materials provide the teacher with a guide to the readability of the book and the interest factors involved.

Extensive use is made of book series which, while maintaining high interest, have low vocabulary levels and facilitate interesting reading for problem readers. Without books to reinforce the skills that are being developed in remediation, the chance for transfer of these skills is seriously limited. The following high-interest, low-vocabulary books have been used effectively in classroom and clinics:

Series	Vocabulary level	Publisher
About Books	2–4	Children's Press
All About Books	3–6	Random House
American Adventure Series	2–6	Wheeler
Bucky Buttons	1–3	Benefic Press
Cowboy Sam	1–3	Benefic Press
Dan Frontier	1–3	Benefic Press
Deep Sea Adventure Stories	1–3	Harr Wagner
Dolch First Readers	1–2	Garrand
Interesting Reading Series	2–3	Follett
I Want to be Books	1–3	Children's Press
Sailor Jack	1–3	Benefic Press
The Monster Books	2–4	Bowmar

Books such as these are inexpensive and readily available.

Free reading may be permitted in materials such as the *SRA Reading Laboratories*** and *The Reading Skill Builders*.** When used for free reading, these materials should be used without requiring students to answer questions or to do the vocabulary exercises and, of course, should be selections at the recreational reading level.

Survival and Functional Reading

Throughout the discussions on remediation, attention has been called to the types of materials which students need to read in order to function and survive in our society. These materials have strong appeal, are relevant, and are essential.

Survival materials include such items as medicine labels, danger signs, road signs, and warning notices. Students who cannot read these types of materials are in danger. Their chances of survival in our society are enhanced when remedial instruction includes these types of materials and the skills needed to read them. Functional reading materials include such items as newspapers, menus, employment forms, and phone books. Again, if students are unable to read such materials, their ability to function in our society is seriously limited.

Originally, survival and functional reading programs were being recommended for only the seriously handicapped reader. Today, however, these programs are recommended for all readers as an important part of the reading program. In many schools, these materials are developed in learning-center format, and students use them throughout the year.

In remedial programs, survival and functional reading materials are especially important. For seriously handicapped readers, the entire remedial program is developed around such materials. Older students with serious reading problems especially profit from survival and functional reading programs. Sight vocabulary, word attack, and comprehension activities are drawn from the materials. Experience stories supplement the materials. Lists of words such as The Essential Driver's List and The Essential Vocabulary List are utilized.[19] Such programs tend to encourage the readers, and they often ask for instruction beyond the survival and functional programs.

Students' interests and reading needs are surveyed. For example, a group of students might be about to obtain learners' permits for driving a car. All types of materials related to driving can be collected. The students can bring their driver's manuals and car maintenance manuals to the lessons, and instruction can be directed toward the understanding of such materials. Actual auto trips can be planned during which students utilize their learned skills.

One elementary school developed boxes of actual materials needed to function or survive in society. One box included medicine bottles; another contained boxes, cans, and bottles from the grocery shelf; another contained all types of maps. Students picked the area of concentration they wished to pursue and immersed themselves into the activities. A source of ideas about survival and functional reading activities can be found in the suggested readings at the end of this chapter.

REMEDIATION FOR THE CULTURALLY DIFFERENT

From diagnosis, the reader will recall that certain groups of students, due to experiential backgrounds which are quite different from those of the average student, do not make normal progress in reading. Remediation for these students must be designed to permit development of experiential background, success in decoding activities, and personal success in the total reading act.

---

[19]Corlett T. Wilson, "An Essential Vocabulary," *The Reading Teacher* 17 (November 1963): 94-96.

Teachers must take every opportunity to develop language experiences throughout all remedial sessions. For example, if the student who is reading about the zoo has never been to the zoo, either a trip to the zoo, a film, or pictures must precede a reading lesson that has to do with those types of animals that one finds in a zoo. It can be assumed that students have experienced considerable frustration by being placed in reading situations for which they have not had sufficient experiential background. For those who desire a systematic program of language experiences, the *Peabody Language Development Kit,*** the *Visual-Lingual Reading Program,*** and *Building Prereading Skills Kit-A-Language*** mentioned previously can serve as guides.

Decoding activities for these students should always be in terms of language involving concepts which they possess. The use of such auditory reinforcement aids as the *Language Master*** are particularly useful in developing sight vocabulary.

Although motivation is an important part in all remediation, for these students it is extremely important. Remedial sessions should have an aura of excitement about them, and the values of reading should be subtly stressed.

Selection of books for students from different cultures also should be of prime importance. Attempts to match books used in remediation with the culture of the students proves to be most worthwhile. Spache's book, *Good Reading for the Disadvantaged Reader* can serve as a useful reference.[20]

PITFALLS OF REMEDIATION

In concluding the discussion of remedial techniques, the classroom teacher and the reading specialist should consider the following pitfalls which, when not avoided, disrupt the efficiency of many remedial programs.

Fragmented Programs

Remedial programs which focus on the development of skills without the elements of practice and utilization of the skills are generally ineffective. Students in such programs often develop faulty concepts about the purposes for reading. Similarly, programs which fail to provide balance between materials at the independent and instructional levels of the students and materials involving reading content materials are limited in their effectiveness. Many packaged remedial programs are seriously fragmented and should only be used if supplements for balance can be provided.

---

[20]George D. Spache, *Good Reading for the Disadvantaged Reader* (Champaign, Ill.: Garrard Publishing Co., 1970).

Compulsion to Teach

Many well-designed programs are ineffective due to the teacher's compulsion to teach. Involving students in planning, materials selection, purpose setting, and follow-up activities really works. By using contracting, the D-R-T-A, survival reading, and other strategies that involve students, remedial programs have excellent opportunities for being successful.

Teaching to Needs

Constant attention to needs or weaknesses tends to overwhelm students. Every remedial program should be designed to focus on strengths of students a large portion of the time.

Oral Reading

Many programs stress oral reading and often oral reading at sight. While students should develop fluency in oral reading and while oral reading gives teachers useful diagnostic information, there is no justification for oral reading being the major emphasis of the program. Oral reading stresses word pronunciation, an important part of the reading process, but not the ultimate objective. In this chapter, silent reading comprehension has been stressed. Teachers should be certain that silent reading is a part of every lesson.

Oral reading at sight has no place in a remedial program. Students should always be permitted to prepare for oral reading by (1) practicing silently or (2) practicing orally by themselves. By such preparation, students will be able to produce their best, most fluent oral reading.

Illustrating Progress

While often delighted with the progress of their students, many teachers fail to relate this to the students. Through contracting, students can understand their progress as each contract is evaluated. Personal charts of progress in sight vocabulary development, books read, and skills mastered are effective. Without recognition of success, the students often become discouraged and quit trying.

Sharing Information

When more than one educator is working with a student, a communication system needs to be developed. Each person should know what the other is doing. Without communication, the student is likely to be exposed to conflicting strategies which serve to confuse rather than enlighten. This pitfall becomes very complicated when the student is being tutored outside of the school. In such cases, communication from one educator to another after each lesson is necessary.

SUMMARY

Comprehension instruction can be extremely rewarding to both students and teachers. By focusing on meaning in relevant materials, students can develop positive attitudes toward themselves as readers. Using the language of the seriously handicapped reader is always an appropriate starting point for remediation. In addition, utilizing materials from the real world as well as materials from the content areas makes reading meaningful. Keeping interest high and successes coming in large quantities assures positive student attitudes.

SUGGESTED READINGS

Carin, Arthur A., and Sund, Robert B. *Developing Questioning Techniques: A Self-Concept Approach.* Columbus, O.: Charles E. Merrill, 1971. The treatment that Carin and Sund give questioning is important. They illustrate how our questions help and hinder learning and learners. This is a book for all teachers.

———. *Functional Reading.* Vol. 1 and Vol. 2. Baltimore, Md.: Maryland State Department of Education, 1975.

Robinson, Francis P. *Effective Study.* New York: Harper & Row, 1961. The teacher of older students who desires to stress study skills in remedial sessions will find the SQ3R technique well defined and explained in this book.

Rowe, Mary Budd. *Teaching Science as Continuous Inquiry,* New York: McGraw-Hill, 1973. Wait time is presented in detail. Every teacher working with handicapped readers should be familiar with the research and recommendation of Rowe in relation to wait time.

Stauffer, Russell G. *Teaching Reading as a Thinking Process,* New York: Harper & Row, 1969. Stauffer provides rationale and procedures for use of the D-R-T-A. Any student not familiar with the D-R-T-A is referred to this source.

Wilson, Robert M., and Barnes, Marcia M. *Survival Learning Materials.* York, Pa.: College Reading Association, 1974. This book presents a rationale and many ideas for developing survival and functional learning materials.

Wilson, Robert M., and Gambrell, Linda B. *Programmed Comprehension for Teachers.* Columbus, O.: Charles E. Merrill, 1976. For those in need of foundations information in the area of reading comprehension this book will provide a quick overview of the process.

10

Evaluation of Remedial Reading

EFFECTIVE EVALUATION

Instruction that has been determined by effective diagnosis to meet the strengths and needs of students stands a good chance of succeeding. Upon completion of the remedial program students are likely to show signs of being improved readers. The problem for the educator is to determine what changes have taken place and how strong those changes are.

Many questions need answers if a remedial program is to be effectively evaluated. A few of those questions might be:

1. Has performance in reading improved?
2. Has attitude toward reading changed?
3. Has reading become a free-time activity of choice?
4. Could more have been accomplished with better diagnosis—or less diagnosis?
5. Was noted progress attributable to the remedial program?
6. Do parents notice behavior changes?

7. Were noted changes in areas stressed in the remedial program?
8. If the program was conducted outside of the classroom, has the classroom teacher been able to build upon progress noted?

These and other questions are to be answered. Naturally, not all of them apply to every situation. And some are more difficult to answer than others. For example, if a student made great gains during a remedial program which was designed to supplement what the teacher was doing in the classroom, to what does one attribute the progress? Maybe the teacher made important adjustments in instruction and is responsible for the student's improvement. Or maybe it was the remedial program. Probably it was some combination of the two.

Guidelines for Evaluation

The following guidelines, applicable to all of education, have particular application when evaluating the effectiveness of remedial reading programs.

Evaluation Should Be Broad in Base. Ample allowance must be made for factors such as improved medical attention, relaxation of home pressures, and reaction to both negative and positive diagnosis. If a student has been provided with glasses as a result of physical secreening, a proper evaluation of the tutoring program must give consideration to the effect of the glasses as well as to the instruction. In an examination of clinic cases at the University of Maryland, for example, it was found that students referred for inadequate visual screening performance made better progress (as a group) if the parents followed the referral advice than did students whose parents did not follow referral advice. Apparently, attention to the visual needs of these students had an effect upon the progress they made. The appropriate importance to be applied to each factor in evaluation is extremely difficult and, at times, impossible to determine.

Evaluation Should Be Continuous. Actually, evaluation is the final act of continual diagnosis. It involves many of the same processes as diagnosis (i.e., an evaluation of the student's skill development and reading effectiveness). Evaluation of past performance should be considered diagnosis for future instruction; therefore, evaluation is continuous.

Evaluation Should Be Objective. Objective measures of performance should be used as an effort to control bias. One often reads evaluation reports which state that the teachers and students were enthusiastic about the progress which had been made. Although enthusiasm is a highly desirable factor, it cannot be the sole basis for evaluation of program effectiveness. However, nonobjective evaluation techniques are certainly valuable and are not to be precluded by this guideline.

Evaluation Should Be in Terms of Established Goals. It is sometimes desirable and natural for considerable progress to be noticed in areas for which instruction had not been planned. Such progress, however desirable, must be considered secondary to the goals of the program. We cannot talk about attitude change, for example, unless the program included attitude change in its objectives.

Student Self-evaluation

Student evaluation of remedial progress and of remedial programs should not be overlooked. Students often render insights toward remediation which elude educators. Teachers should seek student self-evaluation and program evaluation, and they should use it in their evaluation of remedial programs.

Pupil-teacher conferences can be used for self-evaluation. If they feel that they will not be penalized for their honesty, many students can provide accurate, useful statements concerning their feelings about how they have done, about their remedial sessions, or about their reactions to specific materials and techniques. Questionnaires also can be used in student evaluation. Questions concerning how they feel they have performed in terms of specific objectives, the portions of the program they enjoyed most and least, and the changes they would recommend might be included. Finally, contract evaluation can be used for self-evaluation. Such evaluation occurs immediately after the contract is completed when students can evaluate their own work honestly.

CHANGE IN STUDENT BEHAVIOR

Of first concern is the effect of the program on student behavior. Basically, four avenues are open for observation of change in student behavior.

Attitude Changes

Selected first because of importance, attitude changes can be observed. If students enter remedial programs with poor attitudes toward reading, school, and themselves, then a major goal of the remedial program would be to improve those attitudes. Data for justification of attitude change is readily available. Behavior in class, willingness to attend to reading tasks, choice of reading for free-time activities, willingness to discuss ideas obtained from reading, and willingness to be helpful to others—perhaps as a tutor—are all examples of useful indicators of attitude changes.

Following remedial sessions at the University of Maryland clinic, parents are petitioned for information on changes they have noticed. The most frequent change noted is that the student is now reading. "He picks up the newspaper and actually reads it." "She reads road signs and bill boards now as we drive down the road." Such comments show that the students are happy to display their reading skills and see themselves as readers. Information can be obtained from students as well as the parents to assure the reliability of the responses. The inherent danger of interviews and questionnaires is the tendency for respondents to maintain a "halo" effect. Therefore, it is important that the interview or questionnaire be structured to avoid pointing to obviously expected responses.

Mager suggests that attitude behaviors can be objectively observed.[1] He classifies attitude responses as either *approach* or *avoidance*. Approach responses might include such behaviors as coming to remedial sessions on time or early, being ready and eager to work, bringing books to class to share, and asking for help with certain skills. Avoidance responses might include such behaviors as skipping remedial sessions, refusing to work unless directed, forgetting to bring books to class, and disrupting the learning of others. If teachers were to record both types of responses at the beginning, during, and at the conclusion of a remedial program, objectivity could be added to the measurement and evaluation of attitude changes. Attitude changes easily might be observed by parents and by teachers.

Reading Behavior Changes

During remedial activities teachers should keep records of reading behavior changes. What skills in reading can the students display that they could not display when the program started? This data will be available if teachers collect it as instruction proceeds. Evaluated contracts can be a source of such data. Informal, teacher-made check tests can be administered when the teacher feels that some students have developed a new skill. Teachers are more receptive to a discussion of reading behavior changes of their students than to a discussion of test score improvement. The changes in reading behaviors can be readily utilized in the daily classroom reading program.

Test Results

Using entry diagnosis as a starting point, post-testing can provide some information about student progress in a remedial program. But the problems are almost great enough to discourage much reliance upon prepost-test results.

First, the results which report gains in reading levels are impossible to interpret in terms of reading behavior. For example, a report indicating that a student gained four years in reading comprehension tells nothing about the student's reading behavior.

---

[1]Robert F. Mager, *Developing Attitude toward Learning* (Belmont, Calif.: Fearon Publishers, 1968).

Secondly, gain scores are notoriously unreliable. On many tests, a difference of one or two items can make a large gain score.

Thirdly, it is difficult to obtain two forms of any test which are truly equivalent. When different forms are used, it is difficult to say whether noticed gains are the result of the remedial program or the test form which was used.

When educators need test results for evaluation of remedial programs, teacher-made criterion-referenced tests (CRT) containing numerous items for each objective to assure maximum reliability should be used. For example:

1. Word lists taken from reading materials at various levels can be used to measure gains in word recognition.

2. Paragraphs followed by carefully constructed questions taken from materials of varying reading levels can assist in measuring gains in reading accuracy (when reading orally) and in comprehension (when reading silently).

3. Skill quizzes constructed by teachers to assess students' abilities to perform in the areas upon which instruction is given can be used to measure skill development. Such information is useful for those who will work with the students next. The information is reported in terms of reading behaviors and can be interpreted further if desirable. For example, with which vowel sounds does Sharon need more instruction?

TABLE 10

Use of CRT for Pre-Post Evaluation
Phonics

	Consonant Knowledge		Con. Blend Knowledge		Vowel Knowledge	
	Pre	Post	Pre	Post	Pre	Post
Brook	40%	100%	20%	80%	10%	50%
Sharon	80%	100%	60%	90%	50%	90%
Sara	0%	50%	0%	30%	10%	50%

Performance in School

For those students who have been removed from the classroom for remedial assistance, the ultimate evaluation of the success of the program is in terms of how well those students do when they return to the classrooms. Feedback from the classroom teacher is one source of information; grades earned are another.

Teachers can be interviewed or polled through a questionnaire to discuss observed changes in classroom behaviors. If the students improve behaviors in small groups out of the classroom, we must be certain that those changes carry over into the classroom setting. If not, then the program should be adjusted either in the classroom or for more extended remediation out of the classroom.

Grades are another way of looking at classroom performance; however, there are so many variables that it would not be justified to rely very heavily upon their meaning. Over a long period of time, the grades in Table 11 seem to tell us that Nancy was doing poorly prior to remediation and has done much better since remediation.

TABLE 11

Nancy

	Grade 2	Grade 3	*Remediation in Grade 4*	Grade 5	Grade 6
Reading	D	D	C	B	B
Language	C	C	C	B	B
Spelling	D	F	D	C	C

These changes cannot necessarily be attributed to the remedial program. Maybe Nancy got turned on to learning in fourth grade. However, if most students showed these kinds of improvements after remediation, a bit more confidence could be placed on the remedial program as having some effect.

WAYS TO MANIPULATE GAIN SCORES

The work of Bleismer is included for those who are interested in using gain scores regardless of the severe limitations they have for interpretation.[2] These manipulations of gain scores create some interesting problems when one is attempting to evaluate a remedial program through gain scores.

Grade-Level Improvement

Bleismer, in sighting three basic postremediation evaluation techniques, calls this a simple pre- and post-test comparison. If a student enters a remedial program reading at 4.5 grade level and leaves the reading program at 5.5 grade level, it can be concluded that he has gained 1.0 years in grade level. Obviously, the adequacy of the test instrument used to determine grade-level performance limits this aspect of evaluation. It does not account for the

---

[2]Emery P. Bleismer, "Evaluating Progress in Remedial Reading Programs," *The Reading Teacher*, March 1962, pp. 344-50.

student's chronological or mental age increase or for changes which would have occurred without remediation.

Reading skill performance as compared to grade level is of particular interest to both the classroom teacher and the principal, for it has much to do with the placement of the student in a particular room and within a class.

Reading Potential

Evaluation in this area attempts to determine whether students are working up to their potentials. Bleismer calls attention to the fact that potential will change with age and that estimates must be adjusted for effective evaluation.[3] Regardless of a student's grade-level performance and her ability to perform in an assigned classroom, growth up to potential is generally considered a desirable goal of remediation. If a student has an estimated potential of 5.0 and a reading level of 3.0, her working development is lagging behind her mental development by 2.0 years. If, after a semester of work, her reading level rises to 4.2, her potential will have to be reestimated before growth can be measured.

TABLE 12

Bob	January			May		
	Potential	Reading	Difference	Potential	Reading	Difference
Jim	5.0	3.0	2.0	5.8	4.2	1.6

Note that in Table 12, Bob's reading potential increased as he grew older, thereby lessening the apparent effect of the difference in reading grade-level changes. Remedial sessions accelerated his growth over his potential by .4 years (found by subtracting the differences). Reading potential techniques will be of more interest to the reading specialist than to the classroom teacher or the parent. One major problem with using potential as a standard occurs when remedial efforts are being made to improve potential. In those cases, potential is not a standard. For example, if a remedial program includes opportunities for language development, opportunities of potential improvement are also included. Such programs actually have resulted in considerable improvement on tests of intelligence.

Past Performance

Evaluation of skill improvement in terms of students' previous performance rates is of some advantage with older students. Again, Bleismer is asking that

---

[3]Bleismer, "Evaluating Progress . . . ," pp. 344-50.

the identifiable variables be controlled.[4] Suppose that Walter has completed six years of school and has scored at grade level 4.6 before remediation was begun. This indicates an average growth of .6 years of reading skill for each year in school $(4.6 - 1.0 \div 6)$. Note that 1.0 must be subtracted as all children start with a reading level of 1.0 (the zero month of first grade). If he obtained a reading level of 5.5 by the end of one year in remediation, he would have gained .9 years of skill in one year $(5.5 - 4.6 = .9)$. Yet he is not reading up to grade level and may not be reading up to expectancy. He has not progressed even one full year under intensive remediation. *But* his improvement is greater than it has been in the past, thus indicating that he is profiting from the remedial program.

TABLE 13

	Walter Years in School	Average Yearly Gain Before Tutoring	Gain During Yr. of Tutoring	Growth Attributed to Tutoring
Tom	5	.6	.9	.3

Note that the gain of .9 years is greater by .3 years than could have been expected from the average of previous efforts. While of interest to the reading specialist and the classroom teacher, the rate of improvement during remediation is of little interest to the student or the parent, especially if the student remains limited in ability to perform in the classroom.

Evaluation of past performance is limited by the unlikely assumption that the past performance was evenly distributed. However, older students who are seriously handicapped in reading are less likely to score effectively in the other aspects of evaluation even though they are making significant progress.

Limitations

All of the evaluation techniques suggested above are limited by the instruments being used to make comparisons. Standardized tests are inherently unreliable and cause notable gains to be suspect due to the error on the measuring instrument. Grade-level scores on these tests are not equal units for measuring gains. If such tests are used at all, standard scores should be used. In addition, the test selected may not measure the skills which were the objectives of the remediation, and the standardization population may be mismatched with the remedial group. It is recommended that standardized tests be used to

---

[4]Bleismer, "Evaluating Progress in Remedial Reading," pp. 344-50.

indicate gains with groups of students and that informal tests be used to measure the gains of individual students.

Two other problems occur when evaluating in terms of standardized tests. First, all standardized tests contain error in their measurement; the amount of error makes score changes possible by chance. Therefore, small gains over short periods of time cannot be measured by standardized tests. Second is the problem of the phenomenon referred to as *regression*. Stated simply, if a group of students were given a standardized test today and then the same test were readministered a week later, low-scoring students would tend to improve their scores (scores would move toward the mean), while high-scoring students would decrease their scores (scores would move toward the mean).

EDUCATOR EFFICIENCY

The efficiency of an educator is more difficult to evaluate and is, therefore, less likely to receive the evaluative efforts that student growth receives. Educator efficiency in programs should be evaluated in the following areas.

Adequacy of Diagnosis

Due to emphasis placed upon the proper use of diagnosis and the time spent in accomplishing it, there is valid reason for its inclusion in evaluation. Educators must determine whether diagnosis has uncovered the remedial strengths and needs of the student effectively and precisely. Furthermore, they must decide that the diagnosis, while not overextended, is complete enough to cover the areas of the students' skill development. When there is a failure to evaluate in all areas, there is a likelihood that inefficiency will develop in remedial sessions. At times, teachers use tests which, for them, appear to supply essential information for a diagnosis; however, upon closer examination, these tests do not provide any information that could not be determined more easily by other diagnostic techniques.

Adequacy of Remedial Approach

As educators become accustomed to working in remediation, specific approaches often develop into standard procedures with all students. The error resulting here, unless there are constant attempts at evaluation, is that diagnosis is disregarded since a given remedial approach is used with all students. For example, if all students were to be tutored through the use of the language-experience approach, the diagnostic conclusions would not be used to determine the remedial approach. It is through evaluation of remedial approaches that the educator is led to develop the variety of effective approaches prescribed by the diagnostic strengths and needs of the students.

Adequacy of Remedial Techniques

Similar to the difficulty of adequate remedial approaches, a prescribed technique used with all students regardless of the remedial approach is equally limiting and should be avoided through careful evaluation of remedial techniques. For example, a graph to illustrate progress will not motivate all students in all remedial techniques. The evaluation of techniques will save time in remediation and lead the educator to those techniques best suited to the strengths and needs of students.

Adequacy of Remedial Materials

As educators become familiar with the manuals and contents of the variety of materials available in remediation, they are likely to select and use those that appeal most to them. This action is proper when these materials are selected after an evaluation of their effectiveness; however, if they are selected on the basis of familiarity alone, their adequacy should be evaluated. As the flood of materials continues, the educator will need to be involved with more material evaluation.

A variety of techniques are available to assist the educator in the various aspects of evaluation discussed above. The teacher can and should consult with other teachers; ask for help from a reading resource person in the school or district; read evaluations of materials in the professional literature; talk with students about books they like and dislike; conduct studies using certain materials with one group of students and other materials with another group; examine the activities required by the materials and compare them to objectives for the remedial program; and give students choices of materials to use, observing their consistent selection of one over another.

If requested, the reading specialist should be able to conduct an evaluation of the total school efforts in the area of diagnostic and remedial reading. Assuming that the reading specialist is acquainted with research design and controlled experimentation techniques and has the ability to interpret research data, there is little reason for not using such techniques. Austin, Bush, and Heubner discuss the school survey in detail with specific suggestions for its implementation.[5] If many teachers are unprepared for this type of evaluation, it will be necessary to call upon others, for example, school or university personnel, to assist. Such a course of action has an added advantage in many

---

[5]Mary Austin, Clifford L. Bush, and Mildred Huebner, *Reading Evaluation* (New York: The Ronald Press, 1961).

cases, because evaluation conducted by persons not directly involved in the program lessens the role of bias.

SUMMARY

Evaluation should be carefully planned for all remedial sessions. To make valid comparisons, pretesting and noting of behaviors prior to remediation are essential. To evaluate the successes of students in a remedial program, teachers should be expected to use assessments of attitudes, reading skills demonstrated, test performance, and classroom performance. To assure this professional growth, teachers should continuously evaluate their own effectiveness in both diagnosis and remediation.

SUGGESTED READINGS

Ahmann, J. Stanley, and Glock, Marvin D. *Evaluating Pupil Growth*. Boston: Allyn & Bacon, 1959. In Chapter XIV, the authors discuss the aspects of evaluating personal-social adjustment. Chapter XVI is devoted to diagnosis and remediation. The entire book will provide the reader with an effective basis for evaluation.

Austin, Mary C.; Bush, Clifford L.; and Huebner, Mildred H. *Reading Evaluation*. New York: The Ronald Press, 1961. This entire book is devoted to the subject of evaluation in reading. Without restricting themselves to remedial evaluation, the authors have provided specific evaluation techniques and tests. The reading specialist will find this book to have particular value when he is considering an all-school survey.

Bleismer, Emery P. "Evaluating Progress in Remedial Reading Programs." *The Reading Teacher*, March 1962, pp. 344-50. A detailed explanation of three basic techniques for evaluating remedial programs is provided in this article. Reviewed in this chapter, these techniques can be studied more thoroughly by a quick review of this excellent article.

Farr, Roger. *Reading: What Can Be Measured?* Newark, Del.: International Reading Association, 1969. Farr takes an objective but critical look at evaluation instruments used by reading personnel in the schools and clinics. He provides guidelines for the application of research to work in reading. Farr has made a significant contribution which should be considered required reading.

Mager, Robert F. *Developing Attitude Toward Learning*. Palo Alto, Calif.: Fearon Publishers, 1968. This is a highly valuable book which stresses the need for teachers to observe objectively children's attitudinal responses to their instruction.

Mager, Robert F. *Preparing Instructional Objectives*. Palo Alto, Calif.: Fearon Publishers, 1962. This is an extremely well-written, short paperback designed to help
teachers gain skills in developing behavioral objectives. For those unfamiliar with
behavioral objectives, Mager's book is required reading.

Maginnis, George. "Evaluating Remedial Reading Gains." *Journal of Reading,*
April 1970, pp. 523-28. This article discusses several of the inherent problems involved in evaluation of remedial reading. Maginnis leaves the reader with several
positive suggestions for avoiding those problems.

Strang, Ruth, and Linguist, Donald M. *The Administrator and the Improvement of
Reading*. New York: Appleton-Century-Crofts, 1960. This booklet, designed for
the administrator, has evaluation clues built into each chapter. Chapter 4 addresses
itself to the evaluation of suitable reading programs. Appendix B is a guide for
teacher self-appraisal. These two references will be of interest to the reader who
desires more information on teacher effectiveness evaluation.

Wilhelms, Fred T. *Evaluation as Feedback and Guide*. Washington, D.C.: ASCD,
1967. This important book concerns the uses of evaluation for decision making—a
"must" reading for those planning evaluation programs.

11

Parental Roles in Diagnosis, Remediation, and Prevention

"Let your child alone!" or "Don't worry, we'll handle it." are quite often the only suggestions that some teachers have to offer parents who are seeking ways to help their children with reading difficulties. Today, such advice is inappropriate and will likely fall upon deaf ears, for parents *want* to help their children, *can* help their child, and *will* help their children! As the educational level of our adult population rises, as the emphasis upon education for success in life continues, as education continues to be examined in the public press, and as commercial exploitations of parental concerns expand, it is no longer defensible to keep parents from assisting their children with reading. It is imperative that educators realize this fact and seek ways for parents to be most helpful in terms of the educational goals which have been established.

On the other hand, left without guidance, parents may do things to "help" their children which may be inappropriate and often harmful. For example, it is not uncommon for uninformed parents, to attempt to motivate their child through comparison with brothers and sisters or playmates. More often than not, undirected parental activity merely compounds the child's aversion to reading and actually interferes with progress in a remedial pro-

223

gram. So, again, it behooves us to direct parents to that role which will fulfill most effectively the educational goals which have been established.

Although not a hard and fast rule, parental anxiety is likely to mount as a child's progress in reading declines.[1] There comes a point where parental anxiety is felt by the child to such a degree that it complicates the reading problem. These parents, too, must have their concern and anxiety channeled into useful, helpful educational activities. It *does not* help to tell the parents not to worry. The answer is to establish for them a role through which they can be most helpful.

Clinical and classroom diagnostic and remedial situations inherently demand that the parental role vary. The difference in roles is generally one of degree since, by the very nature of clinical situations, the parents are more actively engaged in what their child is doing. In this chapter, as the role of the parent is discussed in diagnosis, remediation, and prevention of reading problems, suggestions are termed in reference to the classroom teacher and the reading specialist so that they might direct the parent toward useful activities. It certainly is not to be assumed that all parents can perform all of the roles to be discussed. Final determination of the precise role of the parent is reserved for the educator who is working directly with the child.

PARENTS CAN HELP!

Parents teach their children to walk, to talk, and to do numerous other useful activities required in our society. Educators rely heavily upon the ability of the parents to do these jobs well. When they do not fulfill this responsibility, parents leave their children ill-equipped for progress in school. As the children develop difficulties in reading, it is logical to call upon their *first teachers,* their parents, to assist the educator in any way that will be useful. The suggestions that follow, then, are based upon the following beliefs:

1. Parents can help.
2. Parents often know what makes their children react most effectively.
3. Children want parental support and assistance and strive to please their parents through school success.
4. Without parent-teacher teamwork, success with severely handicapped readers will be unnecessarily limited.
5. When directed toward useful roles, parents are usually willing to follow the advice of educators.

---

[1]Robert M. Wilson and Donald W. Pfau, "Parents Can Help!" *Reading Teacher* 21 (May 1968): 758-61.

Parental Role in Diagnosis

Except for the classroom teacher, parents most likely will be the first to recognize that their children are not making satisfactory progress in the development of reading skills. When the classroom teacher fails to observe the signs of frustration in a given child, one can be certain that such awareness will not escape the parents for long. The responsibility for the initial identification of the problem reader often in such cases falls to the parents. Parents properly may be directed to observe their children in reading and to call any of the following symptoms of frustrated reading to the attention of the classroom teacher or the reading specialist. These symptoms are:

1. avoidance of reading.
2. inability to complete classroom assignments or homework.
3. inability to discuss with parents material which the child has just read.
4. habitual difficulty in attacking unknown words, especially if the problem is noticed after two or three years of schooling.
5. word-by-word, nonfluent oral reading, especially when the child has practiced this reading silently before reading it orally.
6. complaints from the child of visual discomfort in reading periods of fifteen minutes or more.

By directing the educator's attention to specific symptoms such as these, parents may identify reading problems before they become serious enough to necessitate the more formal types of reading diagnosis and remediation. Upon receiving observations such as these from parents, the educator should conduct as much diagnosis as is necessary to find the nature of the problem.

That many parents will become overly anxious while observing their children for these symptoms must also be considered. It is just as important for anxious parents to know that their children do *not* have reading problems, when this is the case, as it is for other parents to know the nature of their children's reading problems. In this way, needless anxieties can be relaxed, thus creating better learning situations.

Another important role of parents in diagnosis is the supplying of information in support of or in conflict with the tentative hypotheses which have been established in classroom diagnosis or initial screening techniques. The parents' role in clinical diagnosis, then, is to supply supporting observations concerning their children's work in school, attitudes toward reading, and physical well being. Without this information, which is frequently obtainable through either questionnaires or interviews, the reading specialist is likely to err in making judgements based on relatively short exposure to the children. It is generally more effective to obtain information from parents after tentative hypotheses have been reached, lest the feelings of the parents tend to bias the examiner.

Parents have complete responsibility for the follow-up in areas in which referral has been made. It is the right and the responsibility of parents to attend to the physical and emotional needs of their children, and it is the parents to whom we most often look for assistance in taking children to vision specialists, neurologists, psychiatrists, and other specialists.

As parents become involved in the diagnosis, it is important that they also be consulted concerning the findings. Perhaps nothing is more frustrating to parents than to know that their child has undergone extensive study, yet they have not been consulted about the findings. However, making diagnostic conclusions available to parents is far more than a courtesy, for quite often it is the parents to whom the suggestions alleviating the problem most appropriately apply. At times parents are consulted concerning their child's problem, with the result that, from that point on, the child improves and no longer needs remedial help.

Anytime a diagnosis has been conducted on a student, the parents should be informed, in detail, of the results. In the past, it was suggested that parents should not receive a full report with test scores because it was thought they could not interpret those scores and might misuse them. Consequently, parents were making inferences from vague descriptions, inferences that were far more serious than the case called for. Today the position has changed. Educators now suggest that parents get a full report of any diagnosis, including test scores. In this way, parents are not left with vague descriptions of their child's performance. The policy today is to give the parents the same report sent to the schools, discussing every aspect of the report with the parents, including test scores, their interpretations, and the recommendations.

Parents appreciate this openness. They feel fully informed, and they know what information is going to the school. They can follow up the report through a conference with the teacher. Naturally, instances will occur when a parent might abuse such information and to to the school with an "I told you so" type of comment. In general, however, far less abuse occurs when parents are fully informed than when they are partially informed.

Parental Roles in Remediation

For parents to have any role at all in remediation, there must be a general understanding of the educational goals set by the person conducting the remediation. It is not only ethically appropriate for the educator to inform the parents of such goals, but reaching the goal is far more feasible when the parents are effectively involved. The first task, therefore, is to inform parents of realistic goals and of the general approaches to be used in attaining these goals. It is extremely helpful if these goals are short range and easily attainable so that the child, the parent, and the educator all can see clearly that progress is being made. Of course, this will necessitate contacting the parent as the goals are readjusted and as progress in reading skills is made. Again, contacts with parents are most effective when they occur in consultation sessions.

The most appropriate role for the parent, after an understanding of the program has been made available, is to provide situations in the home whereby the skills learned in remediation can be *reinforced*. Although reinforcement activities may be time-consuming, parents should recognize the necessity for providing reinforcement opportunities. Specifically, this work involves parents in the following:

1. Providing a quiet, comfortable, and relaxing place for reading in the home.

2. Providing a planned time during the day when the household becomes suitable for reading: the television is turned off; other members of the family pursue reading interests; and a pleasant attitude regarding this time is created.

3. Assisting the child with material that is difficult in either word pronunciation or sentences and paragraph meaning. This work, of course, involves the availability of one of the parents but should not be construed to imply that the parent must be "breathing down the child's neck." On the contrary, the parent (while reading something of interest to himself) simply may be in the same room and available to the child, if needed.

4. Assisting the child with follow-up exercises which are sent home after a remedial session. The parent must understand that the child is learning a skill and will probably not be letter-perfect in these attempts. Neither the classroom teacher nor the reading specialist will send material home for practice unless there is relative assurance that it can be completed with some satisfaction. However, there will be instances when, regardless of the care taken, the child will bring home materials which are too difficult to read without assistnace.

5. Being available when an audience is needed or when discussion is desirable following either oral or silent reading. Parents should display interest in what the child has read, thus permitting a sense of having done something which pleases the parents.

6. Providing the praise and reward for demonstrations of skill development. Since the materials sent home for practice should allow the child to demonstrate reading strengths, positive reactions from parents can do much to help the child feel good about being a reader.

These activities should be conducted in cooperation with the reading specialist or the classroom teacher; specific activities should be originated by these educators in terms of the goals which already have been explained to the parent. Furthermore, it is helpful to demonstrate these techniques to parents. Illustrating how effectively the recommended suggestions actually work with their child builds the parents' confidence in the recommendations.

On the negative side, parents should understand what *not to do* as well as what *to do*. Depending upon the educational goals, the educator should anticipate the types of problems likely to arise and direct the parents away from them. For example, it is far better to have the parents in the role of reinforcing skills learned in remedial sessions than it is to have them attempt to teach these skills themselves. If the parents feel that there is a great deficiency in phonics skills, for example, the educator should be informed and the parents provided with an explanation of when that skill will become a part of the program. Furthermore, it should be made clear that no matter how great the temptation to have the child "sound out the word," it is the parents' job to tell the child unknown words until the sounding skill is approached remedially. Note that these examples relate to phonics. Although it is in this area that most parents feel most anxious, it is the area in which they do the poorest job of assisting the educators. As a general rule, therefore, parental attention should be directed away from instruction in phonics, while opportunities are provided for the parents to notice their child's development in reading through carefully prepared home assignments. Once again, children demonstrate their strengths to parents through such activities as reading orally an experience story which they have mastered, drilling for five minutes on the word cards they have mastered, and discussing exciting problem-solving activities which they worked on in school.

Another parental role in remediation is obtaining books for the children to read. Normally, the educator will supply the first books from materials available in the remedial program; however, since the supply of books is often limited, parents can be encouraged to assume responsibility for obtaining books. The educator, in this case, will supply the parent with a list of appropriate books for the child to read at home, asking the parents to obtain these books from libraries, friends, book stores, and the like. Consideration for the level and the interest factors of available books should be evaluated in the recommendations made to parents. It is particularly worthwhile to recommend books to parents near the child's birthday or at Christmas so that books can be included on gift lists. More than simply supplying the child with a book, such activity develops the attitude that a book is something of considerable worth, for it is given as a special gift.

Parents commonly desire to supplement the efforts of the remedial program with commercially available materials. Unless these materials are in accordance with the educational goals which have been established and unless the educator knows of the materials and can recommend their appropriateness for this child, *they should be avoided*. By placing parents in the teacher's role, unsuitable commercial materials involve the parents to a degree which is unprofitable for them, the child, and the educational goals for which they are all striving.

Parental Roles in Prevention

It is well to discuss the role of parents once children have developed reading problems, but it is far more important to reach parents before children develop such problems. Next to the classroom teacher, parents can do more to prevent the development of difficulties than anyone else. But part of the problem here is to communicate effectively with parents who are *not* anxious about their children's lack of success in reading. When unconcerned, parents are less likely to seek assistance even if it becomes necessary, thus implying to the children that their parents do not care. Each school and each teacher should take every opportunity to present preventive information to parents. Programs during Education Week, PTA meetings, individual conferences with parents, and notes sent to the home may be used to help parents prevent the occurrence of reading problems.

The following suggestions are designed to inform parents of activities which diminish the possibility of reading problems developing. They should be recommended by educators with discretion and for application when appropriate. No attempt is made here to supply a formula which will work with equal effectiveness with all parents.

Physical Care. Parents who desire to avoid the complications involved with failure in school (in reading, particularly) should reflect upon their children's physical needs. A visual examination prior to school entrance and at least every other year thereafter is excellent insurance. An annual physical examination with follow-ups which are recommended by the family doctor eliminates the necessity of waiting until symptoms of physical disability become so apparent that they interfere with success in school. Many physical difficulties go unnoticed until failure in school is so acute that remedial programs are inadequate to handle the particular problem. For example, if children have refused to read for years because of visual discomfort, they have a void of reading experiences for which, at times, it is impossible to compensate.

From the number of children who come to school too tired to accomplish the expected assignments during a given day, it seems that parents might well require ample amounts of sleep for their children. Since most teachers consider the first period of the morning the most effective instructional time, it is imperative that children be awake and alert. Parents who need suggestions concerning the amount of sleep their children require should consult the family doctor.

Hand in hand with alertness is the need for a substantial breakfast to replace an inadequate breakfast or none at all. Children who go without breakfast, fighting hunger long before the noon hour, are incapable of efficient use of school time. Recommendations for minimum breakfast requirements are readily available; however, when in doubt, parents should consult the family doctor. If parents send children who are physically sound to school, the educational program has a greater chance for success.

Emotional Climate. When the school receives children who are secure, loved at home, and understood, interferences with success in school are further reduced. Parents can implant an attitude that learning will be fun and, though difficult at times, always worthwhile. They can develop an attitude by incorporating (1) no threats for failures in school (e.g., withdrawing television privileges), (2) no promises for success in school (e.g., paying for good grades), (3) respect and confidence in the teachers, and (4) interest and enthusiasm for what is being accomplished in school. Parents should avoid criticism of the school and the teachers in front of their children. As parents, they have a right to voice their objections, but they should do so to the school authorities and the teachers rather than to the children. When children have the attitude that the school is weak and the teachers are incompetent, learning difficulties are compounded. Furthermore, parents can be directed to avoid as much as possible the direct and/or subtle comparison of their children to peers and siblings. The reaction of a child who is striving to do as well as a sister is seldom positive or desirable. More concern should be demonstrated over each child's ability to perform as well as possible; performance which matches a sibling's should not be the goal needed to satisfy parents.

Setting an Example. Probably all parents have heard that it is good for them to set an example for their children. In reading, parental example can be one of reading for enjoyment. Children who from their earliest years notice that both parents seem to enjoy spending portions of their leisure time reading can develop a favorable attitude toward reading before entering school. Some leisure reading may be done orally for the children or for the family. Note that all oral reading should be accomplished with as much skill as possible; therefore, parents should first read silently all materials which they plan to read orally. Often parents are inclined to discontinue oral reading as soon as their children develop skills in reading; however, oral reading by parents should continue. Parents should take every opportunity to read to children the books which are of interest to the children but which are too difficult for their developed reading skills. Children who come to school with family leisure reading experiences have definite advantages in learning to read, for they realize the wonders that reading can unlock for them.

Providing Language Experiences. Parents are to be encouraged to use every opportunity to widen their children's language experiences. Through such activities as reading to children, taking them on trips, and discussing events with them, situations are created in which language can be developed through experiences. Parents should be encouraged to lead children into discussions which will add listening and speaking vocabulary words to the experiences. It is, of course, the listening and speaking vocabularies upon which the reading vocabularies hinge. Parents miss opportunities to help their children by failing to discuss trips and experiences with them. Trips about which little is said are not necessarily useless, but all parents should be encouraged to reinforce experiences with language experiences relating to them. For example, during a trip, parents can let children help read maps, menus, and road signs; they can take photographs and discuss them later; they can help children write captions for photographs to be placed on the backs of pictures. Alerted to the potential of structuring language experiences, parents can learn to use them more effectively.

Regulation of Out-of-School Activities. Parents who permit their children to do as they wish with all out-of-school time indicate their lack of concern about what the children do. First, parents must understand that a full school day takes a good bit of concentration and is mentally fatiguing. Therefore, children should be exposed to opportunities after school for active, expressive free play. Outdoor play, which physically releases children, is desirable when possible. Secondly, the school program relies upon the interest and excitement which can be developed by the teacher and the materials from which the children are learning. Therefore, unusually large amounts of television viewing may interfere with the school program. After five hours of murder, passionate love, dancing girls, and the funniest of comedies, it is difficult to imagine that children are going to fully appreciate a program which features the elementary school band or a story in the first-grade reader which must be geared to a limited reading vocabulary. Although no formula is prescribed, limiting children to an hour of television viewing an evening is not unreasonable. Of course, parents cannot expect children to sit in the living room and *not* watch the shows that the parents are watching. This suggestion, then, implies that television viewing for the family should be restricted, especially during school days. Consideration can also be given by parents to the need for children to accomplish home assignments and have some quiet time. Again, quiet time, of necessity, involves the entire family.

Following Advice. Parents must be encouraged to follow the suggestions of school personnel in matters concerning the education of their children. The most difficulty in this respect is experienced concerning the age at which children should enter first grade and the decision to retain children in a given year. Each school system has its own method for determining whether or not children are ready to profit from first-grade instruction. When, after careful consideration, the school advises parents to withhold a child from first grade for one year, the parents must understand that it is foolhardy to insist upon entrance. Scenes creates needless anxiety for children, antagonize everyone, and generally result in the entrance of children into programs in which they will not be successful. Scores of children with reading difficulties are victims of early entrance against school advice.

School advice in connection with the retention of children generally receives parental concern which is passed directly to the children. Educators not only want the parents to comply with this advice but to embrace it with enthusiasm so that children feel they have not let their parents down. Unfortunately, in our pass or fail system, other children pick up the connotation of *failure* which will, unwittingly, create some disturbance within the children. Failure need not be compounded in the home by parental anxiety. To start with, parents can refer to repeating a year instead of failing a year. Hopefully, the time is near when retention in school will not be marked by failure to be promoted at the end of the year. All children should be on a program of continuous progress making it realistically impossible for such failure to occur. In the final analysis, it is our present system, not the children, that creates the failures. Many schools have instituted continuous progress programs, much to the satisfaction of parents, children, and teachers.

Reinforcement of Learned Skills. As discussed under "Parental Roles in Remediation," skills learned in school can be reinforced by understanding parents in the home. The suggestions made in the previous discussion apply equally well here but with special emphasis on the fact that home reading situations should *always* end pleasantly with children having feelings of satisfaction. Parents who cannot control their anxieties and tempers should avoid working with their children at home. When children read orally to anxious parents, difficulty frequently arises regardless of the care teachers have taken to make sure that the children can read the books which have been sent home.

In practical terms, when children come to unknown words, what should the parents do? In order to make the reading pleasant and meaningful, parents should tell the children the words. If they miss them again, they should be told again and again. Words missed with regularity should be noted and sent to the teacher for analysis of the type of error and the necessary instruction. However, parents are seldom satisfied with this limited role; thus, the following course of action is suggested. When children miss words again and again, it is helpful if the parent print the words carefully on cards. When the reading is finished and the story has been discussed, a *few* minutes can be spent glancing over these cards. As the words are pronounced, the children should be asked to use them in sentences which should be written on the back of the cards with the unknown words underlined. Preceding the next reading session at home, a little game-like drill can take place in which the children read the sentences and the unknown words. Casey makes further suggestions concerning the parental role in these cases.[2] Her booklet is available for distribution to parents and can be effective when her suggestions match the philosophy of the teacher.

Pitfalls in Parental Cooperation

Obviously, there are numerous opportunities for parental cooperation to go astray, creating more harm than good. Educators must be alert to these pitfalls and, when signs of their appearance occur, use alternate approaches to parental participation.

Lack of Contact. Perhaps the worst pitfall is to make no contact with parents. Since parental roles will be assumed, it is best that they be taken in terms of the school's program. Parental contacts should be periodic, calling for follow-up sessions to reinforce parental behavior. All too often, one parental conference is seen as meeting the need for parental involvement. On the contrary, in a six-week summer program, for example, three formal parental conferences and numerous informal conferences are needed to help parents become effective helpers.

Underestimating Parental Love. Parents, even those parents who appear to be unconcerned, love their children. However, parental love easily can be misdirected. For example, some parents criticize the school in attempts to make their children feel more comfortable. When parental love is ignored by schools, the result can be a lack of cooperation between parents and educators. As has been suggested, sending the children home with activities which will permit them to demonstrate their strengths to the parents gives parents opportunities to demonstrate their love for their children with positive reinforcement.

Needless Anxiety. Many parents confront educators with demonstrations of considerable anxiety. They are afraid, frustrated, and upset. For such parents to become useful partners, educators need to work with them to overcome their feelings of anxiety, for overanxious parents find it extremely difficult to work with their own children in any activity. When conversing with parents, the educator should listen to what they have to say. Really listen. Postpone judgments. Extra care should be taken to make activities for such parents as positive in nature as possible. As parents start to relax and gain confidence in the school's program, they can become more helpful partners.

---

[2]Sally L. Casey, *Ways You Can Help Your Child With Reading* (Evanston, Ill.: Row Peterson & Co., 1950).

One Parent. Educators often are forced to settle for the reactions and opinions of only one of the child's parents. One must avoid this pitfall, for children act to please *both* parents. Therefore, every opportunity should be made to involve both parents, even if a home visit is required to attain this end. Upon talking with the other parent, teachers have often reversed their opinions of the home and the learning climate.

Failure to Follow Up. When a remedial program is finished, the parents deserve to be given a summary of the results. Without this follow-up, parental activities may continue as the educator has directed following diagnosis, thus creating feelings of discomfort and needless anxiety within the children. The summary, therefore, should include specific recommendations for future parental roles concerning the changing needs of the children.

Assuming the Teacher's Role. Sending workbooks home so that parents are placed in a teacher's role is seldom useful and often harmful. Educators must clearly see the difference between the parents' role as reinforcer of learned skills and the educator's job of developing new skills. Workbook activities provide too many teaching situations for most parents to handle well. However, if children have worked in a skill activity successfully in school, allowing them to demonstrate that success to their parents is exactly what is desired.

Training for Parents. Today's parents are likely to have training sessions available to them. These sessions are usually designed to inform parents about reading and offer suggestions as to how they can help their children at home.

Many administrators are inviting parents to teacher in-service sessions. Those administrators feel that parents should know what training teachers are getting and what innovations are being suggested. By being informed in this manner, misinterpretations are avoided.

Some clinics offer classes for parents of children who are attending the clinic. They inform the parents about their objectives, their procedures, and the anticipated outcomes of the clinic experience. They talk about how reading problems get started and how they can be corrected. They offer strategies for parents to use when they need to contact school personnel about their children. And they offer ideas which parents can use at home. Attendance at such classes is excellent, and responses are enthusiastic.

Parents are serving as aides and volunteers in many schools. As such, they get two types of training. They attend workshops and seminars designed to instruct them concerning their role in the school, and they get on-the-job training from the teacher with whom they are working. Frequently, parents are enrolled in graduate classes, not working for a degree, but simply wanting to be better informed.

As educational opportunities for them increase, parents will become better informed and better able to provide useful support services to educators.

SUMMARY

Parents can help! Educators must evaluate the home situation and make specific recommendations to the parents of problem readers as to which roles are most appropriate to enable parents and educators to work as a team. All parental roles should be in keeping with the educational goals which the remedial program is attempting to accomplish. When parents are not actively involved, needless limitations are placed upon the educator's effectiveness. Based on the premise that most parents are going to help their children with reading, educators must direct their efforts toward the most useful purposes.

SUGGESTED READINGS

Artley, A. Sterl. *Your Child Learns to Read.* Chicago: Scott Foresman and Co., 1953. This book is a guide for parents to use with the Scott Foresman Series. However, it includes many practical suggestions for parents whose children do not happen to use this series in school. Of particular interest might be the graded booklist under the title "Guide for Building a Home Library."

Casey, Sally L. *Ways You Can Help Your Child With Reading.* Evanston, Ill.: Row Peterson and Co., 1950. This excellent little booklet provides specific, practical suggestions to aid parents in helping children with their reading. Since it is inexpensive, educators may find this a valuable book for parents to have available.

Landau, Elliott D. *Creative Parent-Teacher Conferences.* Salt Lake City, Ut.: E. D. Landau, 1968. This work presents guidelines for various types of conferences with which educators are confronted. It offers specific suggestions to make conferences effective.

Reading Teacher, May 1970. Through twelve articles featuring the role of parents in reading activities, this entire issue of the *Reading Teacher* focuses on the topic of this chapter.

Smith, Nila B. *Reading Instruction for Today's Children.* Englewood Cliffs, N.J.: Prentice-Hall, 1963, Chapters 19 and 20. This book provides two thorough chapters with specific suggestions on how to advise and work with parents. Included are sections on materials, selections, and some critical *do's* and *don'ts.*.

Wilson, Robert M., and Pfau, Donald W. "Parents Can Help!" *Reading Teacher,* May 1968, pp. 758-61. This article summarizes a study in which parents of children were asked how they helped their children at home. Children were grouped as below-average readers and above-average readers. Those children receiving most parental assistance at home were the below-average readers.

12

Professional Responsibilities and Roles

Public concern over school reading programs continues to grow. Newspapers, magazines, radio, and television focus public attention on the strengths and weaknesses of reading programs. Professional concern about reading is reflected in the large number of reading journals being published and the extensive amount of reading research as well as the volumes of books published each year. Public and professional concern combined have resulted in pressures on school systems to produce better readers and to supply more programs of reading support. Unfortunately, such pressures occasionally create more problems than they solve. Hastily developed programs may emerge; inappropriate materials may be incorporated; personnel with questionable qualifications may be hired; too many duties may be placed on personnel already employed. Therefore, consideration of professional responsibilities and roles may help both the teachers and the administrators who are planning reading programs.

PROFESSIONAL RESPONSIBILITIES

"Am I qualified to help problem readers?" "How will I be able to start a program in my classroom, in my school?" "To whom should I look for help?"

237

These are questions educators ask when they realize that many students with reading problems could be helped by establishing special reading services. Preceding a discussion of programs however, must be a clear understanding of the professional responsibilities of the educators attempting to establish programs for problem readers.

The Student

Regardless of the type of program or the competency of the person conducting it, consideration first must be given to the student who is to benefit from the program. Educators are professionally responsible for the direction of students toward those programs that seem to be best designed for their needs. Referral need not reflect negatively upon educators if they decide that they cannot assist the student as well as another can; rather, this action is to their credit. Clearly, many educators feel threatened when they become aware that they cannot help certain students. To call for outside help seems to indicate a lack of competency. However, the diagnosis and correction of many reading problems cannot possibly be handled by any one person. Consequently, to call for assistance when it is needed is a sign of professional maturity.

Cooperation

As mentioned in previous chapters, diagnosis and remediation are programs that cannot be conducted without full cooperation from all persons involved with the student. Programs which are conducted in isolation are limited in their ability to offer the student a complete program. Therefore, programs should not be instituted without thorough communication with the parents and with the student's classroom teacher.

Referral

When possible, all referrals—medical, psychological, and psychiatric —should be made prior to remediation and the final formation of diagnostic conclusions. It is inefficient to start a remedial program without consultation when a student demonstrates enough symptoms of difficulties in these areas. All conclusions should be considered tentative until final reports are available. The educator does not refrain from working with these students; however, the full efficiency of remedial programs normally will not be realized without referral reports.

When considering the role of the reading specialist, the school screening committee becomes important. As discussed previously, the screening committee consists of teachers, administrators, specialists, and sometimes parents or students. The committee works to bring the most appropriate resources of the school to assist the teacher with students who are experiencing difficulty with their learning activities.

Qualification

Since the terms *reading specialist, reading consultant, reading supervisor, reading teacher,* and *reading tutor* appear to be defined differently within various states and school districts, educators clearly are obligated to represent themselves as honestly as possible. The International Reading Association has established suggested requirements for reading specialists, and these requirements may serve as a guide to educators.[1] Many states now have certification in reading. By using the titles connected with the certification, educators can most properly represent themselves.

School Rapport

When remediation is conducted outside the classroom, the educator is professionally responsible for the avoidance of casting unwarranted reflections of inadequacies upon the school program, particularly to parents. However, if the school program is suspect, the educator is professionally obligated to consult appropriate school personnel in an effort to remedy the deficiency.

Here, the reader's attention is called to the Code of Ethics approved by the International Reading Association as it appears in Appendix D of this book.

Guarantees

Seldom can an educator guarantee specific outcomes as a result of specialized reading services. Many variables may influence a given student's performance in reading. To offer guarantees to parents or school officials is clearly unethical. What can be offered, however, are the best services of the personnel who willingly will submit their efforts to carefully conducted evaluations.

THE READING SPECIALIST IN THE SCHOOL PROGRAM

Program Suggestions

The following suggestions are designed to assist reading specialists in assuming the role which will best suit the needs of the schools for which they are responsible and the students within those schools. A reading specialist may

---

[1] *Roles, Responsibilities, and Qualifications of Reading Specialists* (Newark, Del.: International Reading Association).

assume responsibility for more than one of these program suggestions, for they are frequently related.

Diagnosis. As discussed in Chapters 2, 3, 4, and 5, clinical diagnosis is a major responsibility of most reading specialists. The reading specialist conducts the diagnosis and prepares the recommendations with directions for remediation. Many reading specialists feel that they can be very useful to the classroom teacher through diagnostic services, because it may be difficult for the classroom teacher to find the time that clinical diagnosis requires.

Remediation. Much of the job responsibility for reading specialists usually involves working instructionally with students. Three different strategies have been used effectively:

1. Some specialists find working with students in their classroom to be advantageous. The teacher works with some students and the specialist with others. Communication problems are diminished as both the teacher and the reading specialist have opportunities to learn from one another. By working in the classroom, the specialist has the opportunity to work with all types of readers. Such a strategy can also be a means for training a teacher to use a new technique. For example, one principal places the reading specialist in first grade for an hour every morning. The specialist works with students referred by the teacher, using the V-A-K-T technique with students having difficulty developing sight vocabulary. Working one to one, the specialist reinforces the words the students select to learn from their language-experience stories.

2. Other specialists prefer to work with the students outside of their regular classrooms. They establish a learning environment which is different from what the students are used to. Distractions are lessened, and students feel honored by such attention. This strategy usually calls for the specialist to work with small groups of students who have similar strengths and needs. One specialist has set up a rich learning environment and accepts students referred by teachers on a contract basis. The students might come one day for a little reinforcement, or they might come on a regular basis.

3. In order to service as many students as possible, some reading specialists establish mini clinics. A small group of students comes for a short time period to develop a specific skill. For example, a teacher might have seven third graders who are having difficulty locating information. A mini clinic can be set up for two weeks, one hour a day, for these third graders. At the end of the clinic, the students are evaluated; the evaluations are shared with the teacher; and a new mini clinic can be developed for others.

Most specialists will probably find it useful to use some combination of these three strategies with students in remedial situations.

Planning. Planning with teachers so that the educational programs of students is coordinated can be an important part of the reading specialist's responsibilities. In schools where teachers work and plan in teams, the reading specialist should make efforts to be a part of every planning session. If a unit on space is being planned, then that unit can be incorporated into the instruction being conducted by the reading specialist. The specialist might also have input to team planning in regards to sound reading instruction.

Clinic Director. In larger school districts, the reading specialist may direct a reading clinic in an attempt to serve severely handicapped readers. Clinics usually are established in buildings to which the students can be brought for help. As director of the clinic, the reading specialist may assume all of the above roles as well as the administrative functions of the clinic, supervision of staff, and the communication between clinic and classroom.

Inservice Education. Occasionally, the reading specialist will find it worthwhile to conduct inservice programs with teachers. Through demonstration, discussion, and consultation with authorities, teachers gain insights into effective methods of working with problem readers. In these situations, the specialist's responsibility is supervisory in order to inform teachers who have a common lack of understanding in certain areas. Reading specialists do not need to view inservice programs as formal, day-long types of training sessions. In addition, while having released time for inservice programs is desirable, it is not always necessary. Examples of two successful strategies involving small amounts of time follow:

1. Reading specialists prepare informational notes on recent developments in reading and pass them on to teachers. Any teachers interested in more details can contact the reading specialist. For example: (1) the specialist has just read an article on wait time and shares the idea in a note to the staff, or (2) the specialist has just received some new information about oral reading diagnosis and shares it with the staff.

   At times, one little idea has a better chance of being implemented than do ideas that require major changes and considerable training of the teachers.

2. Some specialists have developed modules for inservice programs, which can be conducted in fifteen minutes. These modules are single concept in nature and include handouts, transparencies, and materials for implementation. The specialist announces which modules are available, and interested teachers sign up for the modules of their choice. At a designated time, the teachers meet and the module is presented. Discussion follows, and the teachers decide whether they want to try the new idea. They also might decide they would like to try it but would need some help from the specialist during the initiation of the idea.

Resources for Classroom Teachers. Many reading specialists find their training best utilized when they can serve as resource persons to the classroom teacher. Instead of working with students outside the classroom in diagnosis and remedial activities, resource teachers can aid the classroom teachers in various ways:

1. by helping with diagnosis. Test administration, scoring, and interpretation can be conducted as a team, thus permitting the classroom teacher to learn diagnostic skills.
2. by helping in the classroom with students who are experiencing difficulty. Planning and team teaching special lessons as well as offering continued support to help the teacher better handle students with reading problems allows for teacher development as well as provides service to students.
3. by obtaining materials for the teacher. Instead of keeping reading materials in a reading room, the reading specialists can bring needed materials to classroom teachers and help them use them effectively. The resource teacher may obtain materials which the teacher requests and may recommend new materials for certain situations. Resource teachers can also suggest professional materials such as books, pamphlets, and articles.
4. by planning with the teacher to develop effective instructional goals. The teacher, using the knowledge and skills of the reading specialist, can develop better plans for instruction.
5. by evaluating program effectiveness. By applying research and evaluation skills, the resource teacher can assist classroom teachers in looking objectively at their reading programs, modifying portions of the programs which appear to be weak, and assisting them to emphasize portions of the programs which appear to be strong.
6. by interpreting for teachers the reading research which might have application for the classroom. As a result of their own reading, attendance at conferences, formal course work, and discussions with their colleagues, resource teachers should be alert to the most recent trends, research, methods, and materials.

Generally, reading resource personnel should be assigned duties which will allow them freedom to work effectively with teachers. They should not be assigned to evaluate teachers. They should not *set* policies which teachers must follow, nor should they force themselves into situations where teachers do not want them. In effect, resource persons should be assigned duties in which they can practice the philosophy of acceptance and challenge with teachers.

Summer School. An increasingly large number of schools are establishing summer programs for students who have not made adequate progress during the school year. Reading specialists probably will be responsible for such programs, with particular emphasis being placed upon the screening and selection of the students who are to be assisted. In addition, they might be responsible for the selection of the teachers who will be involved. The financing of these programs, normally assumed by the school, may to a small extent be supplemented by a nominal fee paid by the parents. Such a fee stimulates a more serious attitude toward the work required in the program. Through summer programs, it may be possible for students to remain in the classroom during the year, thereby providing them the fullest opportunity to benefit from the classroom program. Of course, students with serious reading problems cannot always profit from summer programs alone. To avoid the stigma of failure which is often attached to such programs, summer facilities can be developed for good readers as well. All types of readers can then be involved, making it no disgrace to attend a summer reading program.

Public Relations. Public relations duties, which include PTA meetings, conferences with parents, and home visits might fall to the reading specialist. At such meetings, the school's reading program can be explained, questions answered, and misinterpretations corrected. The reading specialist can take advantage of the suggestions mentioned in Chapter 10, "Parental Roles in Diagnosis, Remediation, and Prevention," when provided with opportunities to meet the public. Public relations opportunities such as conferences with parents and home visits as well as public-speaking engagements may be available to reading specialists.

Supervision of Tutoring. Some schools ask qualified teachers to tutor problem readers after school hours and on weekends under the direction of the reading specialist. It is the reading specialist's responsibility to help select the students, make available appropriate diagnostic and remedial materials, and, again, keep communication open between the tutor, the classroom teacher, the parent, and others.

Training of Paraprofessionals. As paraprofessionals become more available for reading assistance, the job of training those persons will fall upon reading specialists. The better the training, the more useful will be the paraprofessional. A model program for such training has been developed in Prince Georges County, Maryland. Hundreds of paraprofessionals are trained and supervised by reading specialists as they work with classroom teachers to reach individual students.

All schools are being encouraged to consider the maximum use of such personnel to assist overburdened teachers. Reading specialists will need to consider the many duties which paraprofessionals can perform and develop training programs to make their work as effective as possible.

Pitfalls for Reading Specialists

Programs developed by reading specialists are not without potential difficulties. Especially for those with little experience, there are certain pitfalls involved in establishing reading programs. Anticipation of several possible pitfalls before beginning such a program may relieve reading specialists of frustrating situations which ultimately can cause considerable difficulty.

Overloading. It is common to find reading specialists assuming responsibilities which overload them to a point of ineffectiveness. First, they should not be expected to assume all the roles which have been suggested in this chapter; rather, they should start where they can be most effective and slowly expand as they see opportunities. Secondly, in the diagnostic and remedial role, they cannot be expected to carry the student load that a classroom teacher does. The very nature of the clinical situation precludes large groups. When overloaded, the reading specialist's effectiveness will be limited unnecessarily.

Inadequate Housing. Teachers' rooms, damp basements, and even worse locations have been relegated to the reading specialist to conduct diagnostic and remedial programs. Assuming that a program is worth having, the school administrator must make provisions for a well-lighted, comfortable, nondistracting environment for the students and the teacher. To be most effective, housing considerations should be built into the basic plans for the program's development.

Screening. Final responsibility for determining which students can be helped most effectively must be left to the reading specialist. Without diagnosis, a given classroom teacher is likely to select the dullest student for remedial attention, when dullness alone is not a sufficient criterion for program enrollment. Reading specialists should provide for the screening of all referred students yet retain the right to reject any student they feel cannot profit effectively from the established program. They will have to reject temporarily those students who add to the tutoring load, creating class sizes which cannot be taught effectively. Interschool relations may be strained unless clear-cut systems are established concerning the final responsibilities for the identification of students to be accepted in the reading specialist's programs.

The Image. Specific efforts should be made to avoid the image that the reading specialist is the educator who works with failures. As previously suggested, reading specialists should work in the classroom, participating in all types of programs for readers. Such adjustment will help the students assigned to them by relaxing their anxiety about their failures. It will also prevent their getting a distorted opinion of the school's reading program. (This easily occurs when one works hour after hour, day after day with only the problems which a given system has produced.) Working with teachers in the classroom also aids reading specialists in maintaining perspective, especially concerning the difficulties teachers might have working with specific students in large groups.

Another aspect of image has to do with how teachers view reading specialists. Reading specialists should be treated as part of the teaching staff, assuming their share of teacher special duties such as bus duty or playground duty. They should attend all teacher's meetings and, in general, do what teachers do. If the image is developed that the reading specialists get special treatment, rapport with the teaching staff will suffer.

Demonstrations. Normally, demonstrations are requested when teachers are uncertain of how to use a new technique or material. Traditionally, the demonstrator replaces the teacher and thereby falls into a trap of ineffectiveness. It is suggested that demonstrations be conducted in cooperation with the classroom teacher as a participant. Specifically, the classroom teacher plans the lesson with the reading specialist; the classroom teacher teaches portions of the lesson; the classroom teacher remains in charge of the class; and the reading specialist assists with the planning and execution of the lesson. Immediately upon completion of such lessons, the classroom teacher and the reading specialist discuss what happened and how it can be applied to an everyday situation.

Using techniques such as those described above removes teachers from the passive, observing role and places them in an active, participating role. Teacher behavior is more likely to be modified with such an approach.

THE CLASSROOM TEACHER IN THE SCHOOL PROGRAM

Program Participation

With various degrees of competency, classroom teachers participate in school programs with problem readers in several ways. An understanding of the possibilities may assist each teacher to serve most effectively.

Classroom Diagnosis. As teachers develop skill in the techniques of classroom diagnosis, they are likely to find themselves assigned to students who are in need of this service. The best teachers will perform this type of function as an ongoing part of their teaching program. The administrator is cautioned that overloading excellent teachers is unwise, since excessive numbers of weak students obviously will hamper their efforts with all students assigned to them.

Classroom Remediation. Using their remediation skills, teachers should work to develop successful readers. The following strategies are useful for teachers working with handicapped readers in the classroom setting:

1. Flexible skills grouping calls for teachers to establish skills groups for specific purposes. When the purpose is accomplished, the group is disbanded and a new group is formed. If ten students need instruction on the use of initial consonant substitution, then a skill group is formed. As student's gain the skill they leave the group.

2. Utilizing small bits of time when all other students are occupied, teachers can provide the reinforcement necessary for practice sessions to be on target. For example, such time can be used to review a lesson taught the day before or to go over the student's sight words.

3. Some administrators arrange for released time for teachers with skill in remediation. This time is set aside so that small group instruction can take place without the distraction of the entire class. The benefit of such arrangements on student progress have been well worth the administrative inconvenience.

4. Some teachers find a few moments before and after school useful for that little bit of extra instruction and attention that makes so much difference to students.

5. Most of what has been discussed under remediation can be incorporated into the regular reading lessons being taught. For example, the regular lessons can focus on locating if students need practice locating information.

Classroom teachers will find combinations of these strategies effective ways of conducting classroom remediation.

Tutoring. Having developed skills in diagnosis and remediation through either inservice or formal course work, many teachers serve as tutors in school-established programs. The teachers' activities in these programs are usually supervised by the reading specialist and are directed toward the instruction of individuals and/or small groups.

Demonstration. When teachers are particularly skillful in either classroom diagnosis or remediation, other teachers should observe them. Observations may be made during after-school inservice programs or through released time. To create strong feelings about their teaching competencies, teachers should be permitted to evaluate their own strengths and to offer their rooms for observations. Reading specialists can assist teachers in the identification of strengths and urge them to offer their classrooms for the benefit of their colleagues.

Public Relations. All teachers have the responsiblitity of interpreting the school's program to parents. Those who have studied the program more thoroughly may assist in events such as the PTA in order to clearly illustrate the program's features to parents. Parents may accept the classroom teacher in this role better than they do the reading specialist, for they know that the classroom teacher works with their children each day.

Pitfalls for the Classroom Teacher

Similar to the reading specialists, the classroom teachers also must be alert to several pitfalls in their roles.

Overloading. Teachers who are skilled in diagnosis and remediation may become overloaded with poor readers. Ultimately, overloading is a detriment to effectiveness with these children. Even when using free periods, short sessions before and after school, Saturdays, and summers, many good teachers need more time to do an efficient job. In addition, teachers must regulate their time so that relaxation and recreation are also part of their daily schedule. Their major responsibility continues to lie with the whole class and the education of all students assigned to them; so overloading should be avoided.

Shortcutting. Attempting to diagnose without using the suggestions in Chapters 2, 3, 4, and 5 leads to inadequate classroom diagnosis. However, after limited experience, classroom teachers can start to modify and refine these suggestions to their classrooms and the needs of their students. After several diagnostic efforts, teachers will realize that their students are all proficient in some area(s) and that study in those areas is not essential in classroom diagnosis. However, this does not justify excluding major portions of classroom diagnosis.

Cooperation. Regardless of the feelings teachers may have toward the total school reading programs, they should work as team members. Gross distortions of the school program in an effort to satisfy personal philosophies of reading must be avoided when they interfere with the overall school objectives. By cooperating and attempting to convince the school of the need for basic changes, teachers will better serve their students. Needless to say, displeasures within the school should remain there and not be topics for community gossip.

Continued Study. As changes occur in the field of reading, teachers must have a system for continued study. Some find that the study of educational periodicals serves this purpose. Specific reference is made to the journals of the

International Reading Association,[2] the National Council of Teachers of English,[3] and the College Reading Association.[4] These organizations are striving to keep teachers informed of developments in the field of reading. Other teachers prefer inservice workshops and institutes; still others prefer formal course work in the colleges and universities. Of course, most teachers seek a suitable combination of methods.

OUT-OF-SCHOOL PROGRAMS

Many educators take part in "out-of-school" programs designed to assist problem readers. Some find themselves teaching in these programs; others have parents asking them for their opinions of the programs; and still others find these programs to be interfering with the educational objectives of the school. A brief look at the nature of some of these programs may assist the educator to make decisions concerning them.

Examples of Programs

Teacher-Education Clinics. Many teacher-education institutions operate reading clinics to educate teachers. Students who are brought into these clinics for assistance are generally diagnosed and tutored by teachers doing advanced work in the field of reading. Normally the costs for services in teacher-education clinics are small since the programs are not expected to pay for themselves. The effectiveness of these programs is generally related to the effectiveness of the clinical supervision which the teachers receive and the prerequisites for entrance of college students into clinical courses.

Some teacher-education clinics limit themselves to diagnosis, while others include remediation as well. Although the thoroughness of each program varies. they generally follow the lines of clinical diagnosis and remediation as presented in this book and are reliable.

Privately Operated Clinics. A variety of privately operated clinics are usually available in large population centers. Designed for financial profit, these clinics generally charge fees much higher than do teacher-education clinics. The effectiveness of these clinics is clearly limited by the personnel and materials available for diagnosis and remediation. Referrals to this type of clinic should be made only after acquaintance with the personnel and the

---

[2]*The Reading Teacher* and *Journal of Reading* (Newark, Del.: International Reading Association).

[3]*Language Arts* and *The English Journal* (Champaign, Ill.: National Council of Teachers of English).

[4]*Reading World* (Shippensburg, Pa.: Shippensburg State College, College Reading Association).

attitude of the clinic. Private clinics can accept this as a challenge: Work with the schools! Unless cooperation is achieved, the effects of privately operated clinics are limited indeed.

Private Tutoring. Ranging from excellent to horrible, programs designed by private tutors are generally restricted by the proficiency of the tutor and by the materials available for precise diagnosis and remediation. These private tutoring programs are most effective with mildly retarded readers. Students with severe problems seldom benefit; however, it should be noted that there are many excellent, well-qualified private tutors performing highly satisfactory services. Unfortunately, there are others who cause more harm than good. Private tutors are obligated to work closely with the school, which has the student in an instructional program every day. There is no justification for programs which do less. Referral should be based only on a personal evaluation of effectiveness.

Commercial Programs for Parents. Often advertised as panaceas, programs which place parents in teachers' roles assume that all teachers have a common deficiency and that instruction with a given technique can be done without diagnosis. Unless the educator is familiar with the contents of the program and unless a diagnosis has been conducted to pinpoint the remedial area, these programs are not recommended. These programs were mentioned in Chapter 11. Not all such programs are inherently bad; on the contrary, some of them are well designed and have been used with considerable success. The educator simply is advised to study them closely. An assessment must also be made in each case of the parent's suitability as a teacher.

Temporary Programs. Several private companies have organized crash programs designed to send materials and instructors into schools and industry to improve general reading skills. As crash programs, many of these are well designed and taught excellently; others are not. The long-term gains of such programs properly may be questioned, and these companies should be willing to answer questions and submit to research concerning these claims. The educator will have to evaluate the relative worth of any such program.

Outpatient, Parental Instruction. Several clinics have been established to diagnose children and then train parents to conduct remediation. Amazing results have been reported with this technique; however, the long-term gains are again in need of evaluation. Outpatient clinics usually handle large numbers of children and usually request periodic return for reevaluation and retraining for the parents. Since the programs are outpatient in nature, their overall costs are not great, although the per hour cost may be high. Note that these programs are generally designed for children with specific disabilities and usually should follow referral from medical personnel, psychologists, psychiatrists, or reading specialists.

Pitfalls of Out-of-School Programs

The basic limitations of each of these have already been mentioned. Specifically, however, the pitfalls of such programs include the points discussed below.

Goals. Do these programs assist us toward the most desirable educational goals or do they, in reality, interfere? Once this question is answered, referral may be made more specifically. When it is established that the programs are not in agreement with the school's goals, attempts should be made to reconcile the differences. When reconciliation is not possible, educators should strongly recommend nonparticipation by the parents of the students assigned to them.

Personnel. The effectiveness of all of these programs is dependent upon the supervisory as well as the instructional personnel. Weakness in personnel means weakness in the program. No compromise can be made by educators in demanding that out-of-school programs meet certain standards of quality.

Intention. Since each of these programs has other aims beyond simply assisting students, it must be determined if assisting students is even included in their aims. Naturally, they will claim to help problem readers, but do dollar signs or teacher education become so important that the student does not matter? When alternate aims prevail, the worth of the program is suspect.

ACCOUNTABILITY

That educators and commercial companies should be held accountable for their efforts with students is an issue of great interest, for this is, of course, the whole purpose of diagnostic teaching. Teachers should be accountable for providing efficient instruction based upon diagnostic techniques. Lockstepping students through one commercial program and indifference to individual learning styles are not to be tolerated. The teacher who knows the strengths and needs of children and who provides the best possible instruction is truly teaching with accountability.

Accountability has nothing to do with obtaining the same results with all students. It has nothing to do with helping each student to read on some type of mythical grade level. It refers to helping each student to successful learning—a task which can only be done with a diagnostic teaching approach.

SUMMARY

Once the professional roles of the classroom teacher and the reading specialist are understood, programs can be developed to incorporate them appropriately.

An awareness of the types of programs available within the realms of the school permits educators to strive to develop those which the needs of their community demand. All facilities—local school, county, state, college, and university—should be incorporated when it is felt that they can be helpful.

Out-of-school programs for children must be evaluated, and cooperation should be encouraged, when possible. In areas where out-of-school programs proliferate, more concentrated efforts will be needed to assure educational programs of the most effectiveness for students.

Accepting and challenging by teaching to strengths can make learning to read enjoyable and successful.

SUGGESTED READINGS

Cohn, Stella M., and Cohn, Jack. *Teaching the Retarded Reader*. New York: Odyssey Press, 1967. The Cohns discuss in detail the roles and responsibilities of reading personnel in establishing and administering reading programs. Based on experience in the city schools of New York, this book offers many practical suggestions.

Combs, Arthur et al. *Helping Relationships*. Boston: Allyn & Bacon, 1971. This book provides an interesting discussion of the ways people relate to one another. It also provides specific suggestions for developing successful strategies when working as a resource to others.

Gans, Roma. *Common Sense in Teaching Reading*, Chapter 20. Indianapolis: The Bobbs-Merrill Co. 1963. The reader will find this chapter a stimulating adjunct to the material covered in this book. Dr. Gans had added many practical considerations which will be helpful to those who are attempting to develop programs.

Kolson, Clifford J., and Kaluger, George. *Clinical Aspects of Remedial Reading,* Part III. Springfield, Ill.: Charles C Thomas, 1963. In this section of their book, Kolson and Kaluger provide excellent supplementary information to that presented in this chapter. On pages 101-103, they have included what they consider to be the hallmarks of a good clinic. The reader will find these suggestions very beneficial.

Robinson, H. Alan, and Rauch, Sidney J. *Guiding the Reading Program.* Chicago: SRA, 1965. The reader will find this entire book an excellent source of information. Subtitled *A Reading Consultant's Handbook,* the emphasis is on developing reader insights into all aspects of the reading program from the specialist's point of view. This, it would seem, is required reading for the reading specialist.

Spicknall, Stella, and Fischer, Drema, eds. *A Handbook for the Reading Resource Program in Prince George's County.* Upper Marlboro, Md.: Board of Education, 1969. This handbook describes the various duties of reading personnel in resource roles. The work, done in Prince George's County, Maryland, is one of leadership in seeing the reading specialist as a resource person.

Diagnostic
Instruments

Appendix A, provided for the reader's reference, is based upon the tests which have been cited in this book. No effort has been made to include all known reading tests, nor have evaluations of the tests' merits been included. For that type of information the reader is referred to Buros' *Reading Tests and Review*.

The age range of each test is approximated. We realize, of course, that in diagnosis the use of a test will depend upon the instructional level, not the age, of the child. The educator must determine this instructional level and then select the appropriate test.

Administration time for tests often varies with the age of the child. The reader should accept these times as approximate—a factor which may determine the use of a test in a particular situation.

Publishers are coded. The key to the code is in Appendix C. The reader is referred to the publisher for the cost of the tests, the specific directions, and other desired information.

Designed to Assist in Evaluation of:

Name of Test	No. of Forms	Type	Age Range	Approximate Administration Time, Reading Section	Speed	Comprehension	Vocabulary	Word Attack	Spelling	Auding	Other	Publisher's Code
ACHIEVEMENT												
Botel Reading Inventory	2	Individual and Group	6-18									FOL
Phonics Mastery				15-25 min.				X				
Word Recognition				4-12 min.			X					
Word Opposite (Reading)				20-30 min.		X	X					
California Achievement Test	4	Group	L. Prim. 6-7, U. Prim. 7-9, Elem. 8-12, Jr. Hi. 12-14, Adv. 15-20	1 hr.		X	X		X		Arithmetic, Language	CAL
Dolch Basic Sight Words	1	Individual	6-8	15 min.			X					GP

Test	No.	Type	Levels	Time	X	X	X	Subjects / Notes	Publisher
Durrell Listening-Reading Series	1 1	Group	Prim. 6-8 Inter. 9-12	80 min.	X	X		X Compares Listening Ability with Reading Achievement	HBJ
Gates MacGinitie Reading Test Survey	3	Group	8-15	1 hr. •	X X X				TC
Gates MacGinitie Reading Tests	3	Group	Prim. 6-7 Adv. 7-8 Basic 9-12	40-60 min.	X	X			TC
Iowa Test of Basic Skills	2	Group	8-14	70 min.	X	X		Language Work-Study Arithmetic	HMC
Metropolitan Achievement Tests	4	Group	6-8 9-12 12-18	50 min.	X	X	X	Science Language Arithmetic Social Studies	HBJ
Stanford Achievement Tests	4	Group	6-8 8-9 10-12 12-15	45 min.	X	X		Arithmetic Study Science Social Studies	HBJ
Wide Range Achievement Tests	1	Individual	6-18	40 min.	X				CAL

Designed to Assist in Evaluation of:

Name of Test	No. of Forms	Type	Age Range	Approximate Administration Time, Reading Section	Speed	Comprehension	Vocabulary	Word Attack	Spelling	Auding	Other	Publisher's Code
DIAGNOSTIC												
California Phonics Survey	2	Group	13-20	40 min.				X				CAL
Diagnostic Reading Scales	1	Individual	6-14	1 hr.	X	X	X	X		X		CAL
Diagnostic Reading Tests	2-4	Group and Individual	5-13	Varies	X	X	X	X				CDRT
Diagnostic Reading Test (Bond-Balow-Hoyt)	1	Group	8-14	90 min.				X		X		LC
Doren Diagnostic Reading Test	1	Group	8-12	3 hrs.			X	X				ETB
Durrell Analysis of Reading Difficulties	1	Individual	6-12	40-60 min.	X	X	X	X	X			HBJ

Test		Type	Age	Time								
Gates-McKillop Reading Diagnostic Test	2	Individual	6-12	1 hr.	X	X	X	X				TC
Gilmore Oral Reading Test	2	Individual	6-14	15 min.	X	X	X	X				HBJ
Gray Oral Reading Test	4	Individual	6-18	15 min.	X	X	X	X				B&M
Mills Learning Methods Tests (Revised)												MC
Monroe-Sherman Group Diagnostic Reading Aptitude and Achievement Tests	1	Group	8-14	90 min.	X	X	X	X	X	X	Arithmetic	NEV
Reading Versatility Test	2	Group	11-15 16-Adult	25 min.	X	X						EDL
The Roswell-Chall Diagnostic Reading Test of Word Analysis Skills	2		7-12	5-10 min.			X					EP
Standard Reading Inventory	1	Individual	6-14	40-50 min.	X	X	X					PP

Name of Test	No. of Forms	Type	Age Range	Approximate Administration Time, Reading Section	Speed	Comprehension	Vocabulary	Word Attack	Spelling	Auding	Other	Publisher's Code
INTELLIGENCE												
California Test of Mental Maturity	1	Group	5-6 6-8 9-13 12-14 14-19 15-21	50 min.							Language and Non-language	CAL
Durrell Listening Series	1	Group	5-7 8-11 12-14	25 min.						X	Part of Durell Listening-Reading Series	HBJ
Full Range Picture Vocabulary	2	Individual	2-Adult	10-15 min.						X		PTS
Illinois Test of Psycholinguistic Abilities	1	Individual	2-10	1 hr.							Language Development	UIP
Peabody Picture Vocabulary Test	2	Individual	2½-18	15 min.						X		AGS

Designed to Assist in Evaluation of:

Slosson Intelligence Test	1	Individual	2-Adult	10-30 min.	General Mental Maturity	SEP
Stanford-Binet Intelligence Scale	1	Individual	2-Adult	1 hr.	General Mental Maturity	HMC
Wechsler Intelligence Scale for Children	1	Individual	5-15	1 hr.	Verbal Performance, Mental Maturity	PSY

SCREENING TESTS

Vision:

Keystone Visual Survey Telebinocular	1	Individual	5-Adult	15-min.	Far and Near Point, Visual Skills	KEY
Reading Eye Camera	1	Individual	6-20	10 min.	Photograph Eye Motion	EDL
Spache-Binocular Reading Tests	1	Individual	5-Adult	5 min.	Binocular Reading Efficiency	KEY

Auditory:

Audiometer	1	Individual or Group	3-Adult	15 min.	Auditory Acuity	MAI

Designed to Assist in Evaluation of:

Name of Test	No. of Forms	Type	Age Range	Approximate Administration Time, Reading Section	Speed	Comprehension	Vocabulary	Word Attack	Spelling	Auding	Other	Publisher's Code
Test of Auditory Discrimination	1	Individual	5-8	20 min.							Auditory Discrimination	AGS
Wepman Auditory Discrimination Test	2	Individual	5-10	10 min.							Auditory Discrimination	JMW
Personality: The California Test of Personality	2	Group	5-8, 9-13, 13-15, 14-21	50 min.							Personal and Social Adjustment	CAL
Incomplete Sentences	1	Group and Individual									Personal and Social Adjustment	Mch
Dominance: Harris Test of Lateral Dominance	1	Individual	5-Adult	5 min.							Hand, Eye and Foot Dominance	PSY
STUDY SKILLS												
California Study Method Survey	1	Group	12-18	40 min.							Study Habits	CAL

Survey of Study Habits and Attitudes-Brown Holtzman	1	Group	14-21	20 min.	Study Habits	PSY
PERCEPTION						
Frostig Developmental Test of Visual Perception	1	Group and Individual	3-8	30-45 min. (Ind.) 40-60 min. (Gr.)	5 Aspects of Visual Perception	CPP
Purdue Perceptual Motor Survey	1	Individual		1 hr.	Perceptual Motor Abilities	CEM

Remedial
Materials

Appendix B provides a reference for reading aids based upon the materials which have been cited in this book. Specific information concerning these materials may be found in publishers' catalogues and brochures. The publishers' key may be used by checking with Appendix C.

Many of the cited materials may be used in a variety of ways to help problem readers. The cited use is based upon experience but in no way is intended to suggest that a material be limited to these functions.

The suggested age level must be considered flexible and regarded as the difficult level. The educator will find many of these materials to be used with children of older age and interest levels.

Teacher-made materials are often more suitable to the need of children experiencing severe difficulty with reading. Teachers should take opportunities to continuously update their knowledge concerning materials for instruction. Most journals carry reviews of materials periodically. *Reading Teacher* carries a section on new materials each year [e.g., "New Materials," *Reading Teacher* 29, no. 5 (Feb. 1976): 474-85].

Primarily Designed To Assist In Instruction of:

READINESS

Name of Material	Approximate Level		Format	Publisher
	Age	Interest		
Adventures in Living	5–7	5–7	Books	WP
Beaded Alphabet Cards	5–6	5–6	Cards	Ideal
Building Pre-reading Skills, Kit-A-Language	6–7	6–7	Kit	Ginn
Concepts for Communication	5–8	5–8	Kit	DLM
Developing Pre-Reading Skills	5–6	5–7	Act. Cards	HRW
Follow the Path	5–7	5–7	Act. Cards	TE
Goal	5–7	5–7	Kit	MB
Invitations to Story Time	5–6	5–6	Books	SF
Kindergarten Evaluation of Learning Potential (KELP)	5–6	5–6	Kit	McH
Language Activity Cards	5–6	5–7	Kit	SAD
Learning Basic Skills Through Music	5–7	5–7	Record	EA
Palo Alto Sequential Steps in Reading	6–8	6–8	Basal	HBJ
Peabody Language Development Kit	5–7	5–10	Kit	AGS
Peg Board with Designs	5–7	5–7	Act. Cards	DLM
Pick Pairs	5–7	5–8	Game	MB
Picture Forms (Design for Reading)	5–6	5–8	Kit	HRW
Picture Readiness Game	5–6	5–6	Game	GP
Read and Tell (Level 3)	5–6	5–8	Pictures	MAC
Sound, Order, Sense	5–7	5–7	Kit	FOL
Teaching Reading Through Creative Movements	7–8	7–8	Record	KIMBO
Visual Discrimination	5–7	5–7	Dittoes	CPP
Visual Motor	5–7	5–7	Dittoes	CPP

Visual Perception	5-7	5-7	Kit	DLM
WORD ATTACK				
Consonant Lotto	6-7	6-9	Game	GP
Durrell-Murphy Phonics Practice Program	5-7	5-7	Kit	HBJ
Phonics Rummy (Level A-E)	6-10	6-12	Game	KEN
Phonics Skilltexts	6-10	6-12	Workbook	CEM
Phonics We Use	6-9	6-9	Workbook	MCP
Phonics We Use	6-10	6-12	Game Kit	LC
Prescription Games			Game	INN
Reading Lab I—Word Games	6-9	6-9	Game Kit	SRA
Sea of Vowels	6-9	6-9	Game	Ideal
Sound Hunt	6-8	6-8	Game	APA
Sounds Floor Games	6-7	6-8	Game	SIN
Speech to Print Phonics	5-7	5-9	Kit	HBJ
Spelling Learning Games Kits	6-12	6-12	Game Kit	LC
Syllabication	6-11	6-11	Workbook	DW
The Syllable Game	8-9	8-11	Game	GP
Take	6-8	6-8	Game	GP
Vowel Lotto	7-8	7-10	Game	GP
What the Letters Say	5-6	5-7	Game	GP
Working with Sounds	6-11	6-11	Workbook	BL
COMPREHENSION				
Better Reading Books	10-15	10-18		SRA
Bill Martin Instant Readers	6-8	6-8	Books	HRW
Break Through	12-16	12-18	Kit	AB
Camera Patterns	7-8	7-8	Books	SAD
Following Directions	6-4	6-11	Workbook	BL
Getting the Facts	6-11	6-11	Workbook	BL

Primarily Designed To Assist In Instruction of:

Name of Material	Approximate Level		Format	Publisher
	Age	Interest		
Incentive Language Program	10–14	10–16	Kit	BOW
Invitations to Personal Reading	6–12	6–12	Kit	SF
Listen and Think Series	9–12	9–14	Kit	EDL
The Literature Sampler	12–18	12–18	Kit	LM
Locating the Answer	6–11	6–11	Workbook	BL
The Monster Books	6–12	6–12	Books	BOW
Nichols Slides	7–15	7–18	Designed for use with Tachistoscope	KEY
The Owl Books	5–7	5–7	Books	HRW
Pilot Library	9	7–12	Kit	SRA
	11	9–14		
	13–14	10–18		
Reading For Understanding	8–13	6–13	Kit	SRA
	13–18	6–18		
	10–21	6–21		
Reading Incentive Program	10–17	10–17	Kit	BOW
Reading Skilltexts	6–14	6–16		CEM
Rochester Occupational Reading Series	13–18	13–Adult		SRA
Scholastic Literature Kits	12–15	12–15	Kit	SBS
Scholastic Pleasure Reading Library	5–14	5–14	Kit	SBS
Standard Test Lessons in Reading	7–18	7–18		TC
Understanding Questions			Workbook	DW
Using the Context	6–11	6–11	Workbook	BL
Visual-Lingual Reading Program (Tweedy Transparencies)	6–7	6–7		TT

Willy the Wisher and Other Thinking Stories

VOCABULARY		6-10	6-10	Book	OC
	Basic Sight Cards	6-8	6-9	Cards	GP
	Compound Words	7-8	7-8	Game	DLM
	David Discovers the Dictionary	9-11	9-15		COR
	Developing Your Vocabulary	9-12	9-12	Workbook	SRA
	Elementary Crossword Puzzles	10-12	10-12	Workbook	SRA
	Gillingham	1-3	1-3		ES
	Gold Cup Games	9-12	9-12	Game	BOW
	Homonym Cards	7-8	7-8	Game	DLM
	Homonyms	6-11	6-11	Workbook	DW
	Homophone Cards	7-8	7-8	Game	DLM
	In Other Words	8-12	8-12	Book	SF
	Lessons for Self-Instruction	9-11	9-15		CAL
	Linguistic Block Series	6-7	6-7		SF
	Match	5-6	5-8	Game	GP
	Non-Oral Reading Series	6-8	6-8		PES
	Pictocabulary Series	7-12	7-12	Workbook	BL
	Picture Word Cards	6-7	6-8	Cards	GP
	Sight Phrase Cards	7-9	7-9	Game	GP
	Spello Word Game	8-12	8-12	Game	Ideal
	Storybooks	6-7	6-7		WMcH
	Understanding Word Groups	6-11	6-11	Workbook	DW
	Vocabulary Builder Series	9-12	9-12	Game	CA
	Words to Use	7-9	7-9	Book	SAD

Primarily Designed To Assist In Instruction of:	Name of Material	Approximate Level		Format	Publisher
		Age	Interest		
STUDY SKILLS	Dictionary Skills	10–12	10–14	Workbook	CA
	EDL Study Skills Library	9–14	9–14		EDL
	Graph and Picture Study Skills Kit	9–12	9–15	Kit	SRA
	Map and Globe Skills Kit	9–14	9–16	Kit	SRA
	Organizational Skills	10–12	10–14	Workbook	CA
	Organizing and Reporting Skills Kit	9–12	9–12	Kit	SRA
	Reading for Meaning	10–18	10–18		JBL
	Reading Without Words: How to Interpret Graphic Material	10–14	10–14	Workbook	SBS
ALL SKILLS	Basic Reading Skills	9–11	12–14		SF
	Be a Better Reader	12–14	15–18	Workbook	PH
	Careers	12–18	12–18	Kit	HBJ
	Controlled Reader	10–14	10–Adult	Machine	EDL
	GO	6–Adult	6–Adult	Workbook	SBS
	Language Master	7–12	7–14	Machine	BHC
	Leavell Language Development Service	6–Adult	6–Adult	Machine	KEY
	Let's Read	6–9	6–9	Basal	CLB
	The Macmillan Reading Spectrum	6–7	6–7	Workbook	MAC
	Merrill Linguistic Readers	9–12	9–13	Basal	CEM
	New Reading Skill Builder	5–7	5–7	Kit	RDS
	Newslab	10–12	10–14	Kit	SRA
	Phonetic Keys to Reading	11–17	11–17	Basal	EC
	Programmed Reading	5–12	5–12		WMcH

Read Better Learn More	10–14	10–16	Workbook	Ginn
Reading Accelerator				SRA
Reading Attainment System	11–16	11–11		AAP
The Reading Box	10–14	10–14	Act. Cards	EI
Reading Lab IA	6	6–8	Kit	SRA
IB	7	6–9		
IC	8	6–10		
IIA	9	7–12		
IIB	10	8–13		
IIC	11	9–14		
IIIA	12–13	13–16		
IIIB	13–14	10–17		
IVA	14–17	13–19		
Reading Response Cards	7–12	7–14	Act. Cards	CTP
The Reading Skill Builders	6–14	6–Adult		RDS
Scope	10–14	10–16	Workbook	SBS
SRA Reading Series	5–12	5–12	Basal	SRA
Tachistoscope	6–Adult	6–Adult	Machine	KEY
Tactics in Reading	12–18	12–18		SF
Target	7–12	7–12	Kit/Tape	Field Ed. Pub.
Teaching Reading Through Creative Movements	6–8	6–8	Kit	KIMBO
The Thinking Box	10–14	10–14	Act. Cards	BP

Key to Publisher's Code

AB	Allyn and Bacon 470 Atlantic Avenue Boston, Massachusetts 02210	BL	Barnell Loft, Ltd. 111 S. Centre Avenue Rockville Centre, New York 11571
AGS	American Guidance Service 720 Washington Avenue, S.E. Minneapolis, Minnesota 55414	BHC	Bell & Howell Company 7100 McCormick Road Chicago, Illinois
AAP	Ann Arbor Publishers 611 Church Street Ann Arbor, Michigan 48104	BP	Benefic Press 10300 W. Roosevelt Road Westchester, Illinois 60153
APA	American Publishing Aids Covina, California 91722	B&M	Bobbs Merrill Company 4300 West 62nd Street Indianapolis, Indiana 46206
AVR	Audio-Visual Research 1509 Eighth Street, S.E. Waseca, Minnesota 56093	BOW	Bowmar P.O. Box 5225 Glendale, California 91201

CAL   California Test Bureau
      5916 Hollywood Boulevard
      Los Angeles, California
      90029

CEM   Charles E. Merrill
      Publishing Company
      1300 Alum Creek Drive
      Columbus, Ohio 43216

CLB   Clarence L. Barnhart
      Reference Books
      Box 359
      Bronxville, New York

CDRT The Committee on
      Diagnostic Reading Tests
      Mountain Home,
      North Carolina 28758

CPP   Consulting Psychologists
      Press
      Palo Alto, California 94306

COR   Cornet Learning Programs
      Coronet Building
      Chicago, Illinois 60601

CTP   Creative Teaching Press
      514 Hermosa Vistas Avenue
      Monterey Park, California
      91754

CA   Curriculum Associates
      94 Bridge Street
      Chapel Bridge Park
      Newton, Massachusetts
      12158

DLM   Developmental Learning
      Materials
      7440 Natchey Avenue
      Niles, Illinois 60648

DW   Dexter Westbrook, Ltd.
      958 Church Street
      Baldwin, New York 11510

EC   The Economy Company
      529 N. Capital Avenue
      Indianapolis, Indiana
      46204

EA   Educational Activities

(EA continued)
      P.O. Box 392
      Freeport, New York 11520

EDL   Educational Development
      Laboratories
      Huntington, New York
      11746

EI   Educational Insights
      211 South Hindly Ave.
      Inglewood, California 90301

ETB   Educational Test Bureau
      720 Washington
      Avenue, S.E.
      Minneapolis, Minnesota
      55414

EnC   Encyclopedia Brittanica
      Educational Corporation
      425 N. Michigan Avenue
      Chicago, Illinois 60611

EP   Essay Press
      P.O. Box 5
      New York, New York 10024

FOL   Follett Publishing Company
      1010 W. Washington
      Boulevard
      Chicago, Illinois 60607

GP   The Garrard Press
      Champaign, Illinois 61820

Ginn Ginn & Company
      72 Fifth Avenue
      New York, New York 10011

HBJ   Harcourt Brace Jovanovich
      757 Third Avenue
      New York, New York 10017

HMC   Houghton Mifflin Company
      53 West 43rd Street
      New York, New York 10036

HRW   Holt, Rinehart and Winston
      383 Madison Avenue
      New York, New York 10017

Ideal Ideal
      Oak Lawn, Illinois 60453

INN Innovations for
Individualizing Instruction
P.O. Box 4361
Washington, D.C. 20012

Inst Instructo Corp.
A Division of McGraw-Hill
Paoli, Pennsylvania 19301

IOWA The State University of Iowa
Bureau of Audio-Visual
Instruction
Iowa City, Iowa 52240

JBL J. B. Lippincott Company
East Washington Square
Philadelphia, Pennsylvania
19103

JMW Joseph W. Wepman, PhD
950 E. 59th Street
Chicago, Illinois

KEN Kenworthy Education Service
P.O. Box 3031
Buffalo, New York 14205

KEY Keystone View Company
Meadville, Pennsylvania
16335

KIMBO Kimbo Educational Records
Box 55
Deal, New Jersey 07723

LM Learning Materials
100 East Ohio Street
Chicago, Illinois

LC Lyons E. Carnahan
Educational Publishers
Affiliate of Meredith
Publishing Co.
407 E. 25th Street
Chicago, Illinois 60616

MAC The Macmillan Company
Front and Brown Streets
Riverside, New Jersey
08075

MAI MAICO Electronics
21 N. 3rd Street
Minneapolis, Minnesota

MC Mills Center
1512 E. Broward Blvd.
Fort Lauderdale, Fla.

MB Milton Bradley Co.
Springfield, Massachusetts
01101

MCP Modern Curriculum Press
14900 Prospect Road
Cleveland, Ohio 44136

NEV Nevins Publishing Company
Pittsburgh, Pennsylvania

PP Pioneer Printing Co.
Bellingham, Washington
98225

PSP Popular Science
Publishing Co.
McGraw-Hill Text Film
Dept.
330 W. 32nd Street
New York, New York 10036

PH Prentice-Hall
Englewood Cliffs,
New Jersey 07632

PES Primary Educational Service
1243 W. 79th Street
Chicago, Illinois

PAR Programs for Achievement
in Reading
Abbott Park Place
Providence, Rhode Island
02903

PSY Psychological Corporation
304 East 45th Street
New York, New York 10017

PTS Psychological Test Specialist
Box 1441
Missoula, Montana 59801

RH Random House
457 Madison Avenue
New York, New York 10022

RE Reading Education
10008 Kinross Avenue

(RE continued)

Silver Spring, Maryland
20901

RDS   Reader's Digest Services
Pleasantville, New York
10570

SAD   W. H. Sadlier
11 Park Place
New York, New York 10007

SBS   Scholastic Book Service
Sylvan Avenue
Englewood Cliffs,
New Jersey
07018

SRA   Science Research Associates
259 E. Erie Street
Chicago, Illinois 60611

SF   Scott Foresman & Company
433 E. Erie Street
Chicago, Illinois 60611

SIN   Singer Education Division
1345 Diversey Parkway
Chicago, Illinois 60614

SEP   Slosson Educational
Publications Press
140 Pine Street
New York, New York 14052

TC   Bureau of Publications
Teachers College
Columbia University
New York, New York 10027

TE   Trend Enterprises
P.O. Box 8623
White Bear Lake, Minnesota
55110

TT   Tweedy Transparencies
207 Hollywood Avenue
East Orange, New Jersey
17018

UIP   University of Illinois Press
Urbana, Illinois 61601

WMcH   Webster Division
McGraw-Hill Book Company
1154 Roco Avenue
St. Louis, Missouri 63126

WP   Western Publishing Co.
1220 Mound Avenue
Racine, Wisconsin 53404

WWS   Weston Woods Studios
Weston, Connecticut 06880

IRA Code
of Ethics*

INTRODUCTION

The members of the International Reading Association who are concerned with the teaching of reading form a group of professional persons obligated to society and devoted to the service and welfare of individuals through teaching, clinical services, research, and publication. The members of this group are committed to values which are the foundation of a democratic society —freedom to teach, write, and study in an atmosphere conducive to the best interests of the profession. The welfare of the public, the profession, and the individuals concerned should be of primary consideration in recommending candidates for degrees, positions, advancements, the recognition of professional activity, and for certification in those areas where certification exists.

Ethical Standards in Professional Relationships

1. It is the obligation of all members of the International Reading Association to observe the Code of Ethics of the organization and to act accordingly so as to

Code of Ethics, International Reading Association, Newark, Delaware.

advance the status and prestige of the association and of the profession as a whole. Members should assist in establishing the highest professional standards for reading programs and services, and should enlist support for these through dissemination of pertinent information to the public.

2. It is the obligation of all members to maintain relationships with other professional persons, striving for harmony, avoiding personal controversy, encouraging co-operative effort, and making known the obligations and services rendered by the reading specialist.

3. It is the obligation of members to report results of research and other developments in reading.

4. Members should not claim nor advertise affiliation with the International Reading Association as evidence of their competence in reading.

Ethical Standards in Reading Services

1. Reading specialists must possess suitable qualifications . . . for engaging in con-sulting, clinical, or remedial work. Unqualified persons should not engage in such activities except under the direct supervision of one who is properly qualified. Professional intent and the welfare of the person seeking the services of the reading specialist should govern counseling, all consulting or clinical activities such as administering diagnostic tests, or providing remediation. It is the duty of the reading specialist to keep relationships with clients and interested persons on a professional level.

2. Information derived from consulting and/or clinical services should be regarded as confidential. Expressed consent of persons involved should be secured before releasing information to outside agencies.

3. Reading specialists should recognize the boundaries of their competence and should not offer services which fail to meet professional standards established by other disciplines. They should be free, however, to give assistance in other areas in which they are qualified.

4. Referral should be made to specialists in allied fields as needed. When such referral is made, pertinent information should be made available to consulting specialists.

5. Reading clinics and/or reading specialists offering professional services should refrain from guaranteeing easy solutions or favorable outcomes as a result of their work, and their advertising should be consistent with that of allied professions. They should not accept for remediation any persons who are unlikely to benefit from their instruction, and they should work to accomplish the greatest possible im-provement in the shortest time. Fees, if charged, should be agreed on in advance and should be charged in accordance with an established set of rates commensurate with that of other professions.